291546

THE TWELFTH MAN

THE
TWELFTH MAN

A BOOK OF ORIGINAL CONTRIBUTIONS
BROUGHT TOGETHER BY

THE LORD'S TAVERNERS

in honour of their patron

H.R.H.
PRINCE PHILIP
DUKE OF EDINBURGH

K.G., K.T.

WITH A FOREWORD BY
H.R.H.
THE PRINCE OF WALES

EDITOR: MARTIN BODDEY

CASSELL · LONDON

CASSELL & COMPANY LTD
35 RED LION SQUARE, LONDON WC1
Sydney, Toronto
Johannesburg, Auckland

First published 1971

I.S.B.N. 0 304 93752 5

Printed by The Camelot Press Ltd,
London and Southampton
F.371

FOREWORD

BY HIS ROYAL HIGHNESS
THE PRINCE OF WALES

I hope that the Twelfth Man of The Lord's Taverners will forgive me for agreeing to write this Foreword. Apart from anything else, it is an ideal opportunity to present every kind of filial respect and wish on the anniversary of the Twelfth Man's semi-centenary. When he plunges into his full centennial year perhaps there will be a grandson to write the Foreword.

The idea to present my father with a birthday book was a very touching and spontaneous one. All the authors, and there is an impressive list of them, gave their contributions without expecting reward, and many have written appropriately humorous pieces. Since the person to whom the book is dedicated has interests in every sort of subject, there is a wide variety of essays, which I should think will give my father immense bedtime (or some other time) pleasure.

The aim of all the contributors to this book is to wish the Twelfth Man the happiest of fiftieth birthdays—and so do I.

Charles

Contents

CONTENTS

Ever since I was a small boy I have been fascinated by tales of Eastern princes celebrating birthdays and other occasions for rejoicing by being popped onto a pair of scales and weighed against precious stones, which are then distributed to those in need of such things. I would give much to witness one of these ceremonies but, alas, their practice seems to have fallen into disuse. I find this a cause for much regret, for although it would be regarded as flamboyant by some of the more conservative of our citizens, it has a panache which is sadly lacking in most of our present-day social functions.

When the opportunity presented itself to The Lord's Taverners to make some gesture of gratitude and affection to their royal patron, wistful thoughts were cast along these lines; but romance had to give way to practicalities. It was not merely considerations of taste, or a natural diffidence, which prompted a more sober approach, but niggling little matters like the lack of some hundredweight and a half of diamonds.

However, the decision to publish this book has at least one distinct advantage over the precious stone routine. It will enable us to give His Royal Highness on his fiftieth birthday a personal present of a specially bound copy, autographed by all the contributors, whilst at the same time affording him the pleasure of making gifts to charities of his own choice out of the income from the world-wide sales of the book.

It is generally held that, in any well-run organization, new ventures should be considered first at committee level. Accordingly, early in 1969, I called together a small committee of fellow-Taverners to propose the project to them. They were Jack Broome, Michael Parker, Bruce Seton and John Snagge. Three main resolutions were made at that meeting: That it was a good idea; that you couldn't edit a book by committee; that I had better get on with it. The committee never met again. Michael Parker returned shortly afterwards to his native Australia and became not readily available for impromptu conversation. Bruce, my good friend and gay companion of many years, did not live long enough to help with more than a rough outline of our plans. How he would have loved the adventure!

And so it remained to Jack Broome and John Snagge to sustain me and give me counsel. This they have done with unfailing humour, and the book owes much to their guidance and practical assistance. It also owes much to Dennis Castle, a Lord's Taverner whose enthusiasm never wanes, and who will always make time to write a helpful letter and take the trouble to follow it up.

Messrs Cassell, from the beginning, entered wholeheartedly into the spirit of the enterprise and sparked off some splendid ideas. To them, and especially to Kenneth Parker who jogs a very patient elbow, I tender my thanks for their understanding and their tolerance of a tiro editor.

Finally, to the distinguished company of contributors I offer my heartfelt thanks. They responded to my requests with imagination and generosity which were oft times moving and at all times gratifying. They have made my self-appointed task one of complete enjoyment. Their terms of reference were necessarily as wide as the interests of the royal gentleman to whom they have dedicated their work, so that from none of them did I ever know what to expect until it arrived . . . which is the essence of all good presents. The Lord's Taverners will always be greatly in their debt for helping them to make this unique gift to our Twelfth Man.

MARTIN BODDEY

The Lord's Taverners,
1 St James's Street,
London, S.W.1
March 1971

THE
TWELFTH MAN

BERNHARD, THE PRINCE OF THE NETHERLANDS

Prince Philip

It gives me the greatest pleasure to contribute a few words to this book for Prince Philip.

Not only because we are very good friends, but also because we have so much in common in our position, our work and our interests. As he himself has stated, we are members of a very small, distinguished trade union, with only two members and some aspirants. This is of course true, but more than that, it is, I believe, very fortunate that many of our interests and the work we are doing are complementary and therefore more effective.

In the equestrian field he has succeeded me as President of the Fédération Equestre Internationale, after my holding the job for nine years, and we were both working in the Jury of Appeal at the Olympic Games in Mexico. Not an easy task on that occasion!

In the field of conservation of nature—flora, fauna and environment—we have the same desire to do everything we can to stop the daily growing pollution of air, water and land and to preserve for future generations what is left alive on earth today. Alas, how much has been lost even in the last hundred or even fifty years! We also share the attacks from those people who think that conservation and shooting are incompatible and do not know that usually people who shoot are better and more knowledgeable conservationists than those who do not—and we both have to try patiently to explain this matter to our mistaken, but mostly well-meaning critics.

We share the love to fly an aeroplane and I believe that I was at least partly responsible for his decision to learn to be a pilot. In fact some high-ranking people in the Air Ministry blamed me for it and to my surprise did not approve at all in the beginning. My reaction of course was: 'Is your training system not as good as it was when I learned to fly in the RAF?'

Wherever possible, we both try to do a great deal to further good causes, especially when the future of the next generation is concerned. The problems of the younger generation, which will soon take over from ours, interest us very much and we try to let them have the benefit of our experience and the experience of our generation whenever our advice is welcome.

Finally we share, I am sure, the same sense of frustration when some ideas of either or both of us, of which no one has been able to convince us that they are not feasible or wrong, are not put into practice or tried out or even considered, because the executive power lies in other hands.

However, we both carry on, because we believe in our work—because, I think, we both have the same dedication to the task we have chosen to take on.

The Horse from Thessaly

In the year 343 BC, or thereabouts, a Thessalian horse-coper called Philonicus rode north over the passes, on a business trip, to Pella in Macedon.

Thessaly with its well-watered uplands had been the horse-pasture of Greece time out of mind. Its autocratic tribal chiefs rode before they walked, and disdained to put foot to ground, except indoors. Every kind of horse had its breeders there: fast ponies for racing chariots; race-horses; high-steppers for processions; war-horses broke to noise, up to the weight of an armoured man, and trained to leave him a free hand for sword or spear. One of these last, Philonicus had with him.

Greek bloodstock owners practised random breeding, within carefully hand-picked herds. Such strains were distinguished by a brand-mark, often of wide renown. A horse-dealer who could make good in Thessaly was in business anywhere. This was true of Philonicus, since the buyer he had in mind for his charger was King Philip II.

History says no more of Philonicus. About the horse we know rather more.

'In stature he was tall,' Arrian records, 'and in spirit courageous. His mark was an oxhead branded on him, and hence his name Bucephalas. Others, however, say he had a white mark on his head—the rest of him being black—which was just like an oxhead.' Very likely he had both.

How tall his stature really was, it is hard to say, since Greek breeds were small by today's reckoning; give or take a little, perhaps fifteen hands. Philip's portrait-head shows a stocky, solid build; he would have needed a good weight-carrier, though in the event this virtue was never tested. Certainly the horse must have been highly trained in the disciplines of his calling, for he was expensive, though nearly twelve years old.

This is the more remarkable, in that the Greeks disliked buying horses once they had lost their milk teeth; the veteran Xenophon, in his treatise *On Equitation*, strongly advises against it. One would question the age, but for the consistency of the records, and the fact that Arrian's source Ptolemy, later to found the dynasty which ended with Cleopatra, was a close connection of the Macedonian royal

5

family—some say a bastard son of Philip's adolescence—and knew the horse's future owner from birth till death.

Accepting the age, however, one can hardly credit the asking price. Plutarch puts it at thirteen talents; which, allowing for purchasing power then and now, has been reckoned to equal about £25,000.

Life-expectation of Philip's war-horses was notoriously short. Still under forty, he was already seamed with war-scars. One eye had been blinded by an arrow, one leg lamed by a spear; he had had a badly broken collar-bone; we hear of one horse at least, probably two, having been killed under him. Evidently, he would value a steady, dependable mount; but this seems a pretty steep price to pay for it.

There may, however, be an explanation for the legend. Earlier in his reign, a racehorse of his had brought him the immense prestige of a win at the Olympic Games. Greek only by remote descent and regarded by southern Greeks as semi-barbarous, the kings of Macedon had barely scraped their way into the Olympic entry-list, which was open to Greeks alone. In spite of frequent snubs, Philip was almost touchingly philhellene; the victory had so elated him that he had had the horse put on his coinage. Then as now, a race-horse of this quality could well have changed hands at Plutarch's figure. This single remembered fact about it may have attached itself, over the generations, to a successor of more lasting fame.

News of the Olympic win had reached the King on a red-letter day. Before its sunset, two more couriers had come in. One announced that his general, Parmenio, had routed the troublesome Illyrians. The third message was from his Palace. His young Queen, Olympias, a beautiful Epirote princess whom he had courted on impulse after a chance meeting at a shrine, had been delivered of a healthy boy.

Some thirteen years had passed since these events. Philip had won no more Olympic races, but several more wars, and half a dozen more wives. Polygamy was a Macedonian royal prerogative. The wives were of minor rank; but Olympias, a proud and violent woman, found them an unforgivable affront, and a threat to the succession for her adored and only son. She had become the King's inveterate enemy. For years the boy had been torn between them, fought over and trampled in their wars like some disputed battle-standard. He had survived, on his own terms. If he carried deeper scars than his father's, they were out of sight. When Philonicus arrived, he was there to see the horses; quick-moving, restless, with grey eyes and red-gold hair; small for his age, though hardy; pre-cocious and temperamental, with looks that favoured his mother.

In due course, the dealer produced his show-piece, the black horse with the white blaze. Philip eyed his points approvingly, and asked to see him work.

What paces he had been meant to show the King, we shall never know. From Xenophon's treatise we can conjecture some of them. Nearly a millennium had still to pass before some ingenious Celt invented stirrups; meantime, even to mount, a man needed much co-operation from his horse. Xenophon recommends that, if tractable enough, it should be taught to kneel, but that a horseman should be able, at need, to mount in the normal way: that is, if armed with a spear, he should take it in his left hand, along with the lead-rope, which would not be dispensed with till he was up; his right hand should grasp the reins, and the mane above the withers; he should then use the spear to vault. If unarmed, with the left hand free, he should use it to grip the mane between the ears. And he must try to take off with a good spring so as to keep his right leg straight; thus he would not 'offer an unseemly sight from behind' (Greek riding-tunics were short). The good soldier, prepared for all emergencies, would practise mounting on the off side as well as the near. As a last resort, when wounded or very elderly, he could train a groom to give him a leg-up in what Xenophon slightingly describes as 'the Persian way'.

Saddles were as far ahead as stirrups. Men rode either bareback or on a soft saddlecloth, using seat-bones and thighs to direct the horse, the feet hanging free except when using the spur. When the rider is up, says Xenophon, the horse should stand quiet while he gets the edge of his tunic out from under him, and transfers his spear to his right hand; to balance it, the horse should be trained to lead with the near leg. It should be worked across rough country, and over the natural jumps there; when jumping, or on steep slopes, the rider should grasp the mane, to ease the bit. (Good reasons for this injunction, besides the fear of falling off, will soon appear.)

The cavalryman whose horse has been trained thus to jump and scramble, should then accustom it to warfare, first by taking it through crowds, then by mock-duelling with a friend, casting blunted javelins, closing and wrestling, each man trying to unseat the other. But an officer, Xenophon points out, must aim at possessing a 'brilliant horse' which will do him credit at parades, though not all will have the needed qualities: 'you must have one naturally endowed with greatheartedness of spirit and strength of body'. Only such a horse was likely to be offered to King Philip. 'A curvetting horse is a thing so admirable that it captures the eye of all beholders, both young and old.' The black horse called Oxhead had probably had schooling, then, in airs above the ground.

The King, his party, and the dealer waited expectantly to see him justify his price by executing some, or most, of these manœuvres. Philip, with a game leg, would certainly be interested in the kneeling trick. He was to be disappointed. 'They went down into the plain', says Plutarch, 'to try the horse; but he was found to be so very vicious and ungovernable, that he reared up against all who tried to mount him, and would not so much as endure the voice of any of Philip's attendants.'

This was a highly priced animal, brought some distance for an important sale. Either he was, after all, an unbroken colt, and all the histories are wrong by ten years, which is unlikely; or something had lately happened to him. What it was, again we shall never know. Perhaps a wolf or leopard had frightened him on the way. It seems, however, that the enemy he loathed was man.

'The one best precept and custom', says Xenophon with emphasis, 'in treating the horse is: Never lose your temper. For anger is without foresight, and often does things which later will cause regret.'

Xenophon, however, for his day, was an exceptionally humane and patient horseman. 'If you ever wish to treat a good war-horse so as to make him more splendid and showy to ride, you must avoid pulling at his mouth with the bit, and spurring and whipping him, by which behaviour most people think they make their horses brilliant. For these people get results the very reverse of what they aim at.'

Some teach the curvetting action, he says, 'either by striking the horse with a rod under the hocks, or by having someone run alongside with a stick and hit him on the quarters. But I consider, as I keep saying, that the best training is to give the horse some relaxation whenever he does as the rider wishes.' What sort of grace, he asks, would one expect from a human dancer, if he were taught by whipping and spurring? With the spirited horse, he goes on to warn, one must especially be careful, for 'spirit is to a horse what anger is to a man'.

Someone, perhaps Philonicus himself, perhaps one of his men, may have neglected Xenophon, or thought his methods soft. Someone, in drunkenness or aggression (the sort of person who now overtakes on a blind rise) may have roused rebellion in the black horse, and with the sale so near had been in a hurry to enforce submission. He had got, if so, the reverse result.

For a spirited horse, Xenophon advises, a smooth bit is better than a rough. He speaks advisedly. Not for nothing, among the easel-painters of the time, was blood and foam on a horse's mouth a regular artistic convention. The 'rough' bits have to be seen to be believed in. Spiked rollers; barbed cheek-pieces squeezing the lips;

projections of iron or bronze pulling up into the roof of the mouth; chain-bits with toggles in them; a collection of these things is an equine chamber of horrors. In the absence of the control which stirrups and saddle-tree give today, almost nothing human cruelty could devise had been left unused to curb a recalcitrant horse. This one, if he had been giving trouble before the sale, would certainly have a rough bit on, and probably a severe one.

The struggle to mount him continued vain. The royal party looked on; the King in growing impatience, the boy in growing distress. 'Spirit is to a horse what anger is to a man.' To the end of his short life, the intolerable tensions of his childhood, suppressed under a powerful self-control, would find release at long intervals in bursts of concentrated rage. Anger is without foresight, and does things which later will cause regret.

Meantime, Philip had had enough. He 'ordered the horse to be led away, thinking him entirely wild and unbroken'. It was at this point that the boy became difficult.

The King at first ignored his protests, which were impertinent; a boy of thirteen should not call out before his elders that a great horse is being lost for want of skill to handle him. However, 'he kept saying things like this, and seemed very much upset'. At length, in some exasperation, his father asked if he was finding fault with older people, in the belief that he could do better. 'I could with this horse,' he said.

Philip decided to take him up on it. It seems a risky challenge; but out of several successive Kings of Macedon, only one had died in bed; danger was a family way of life. The boy accepted with alacrity; if he won, the horse was to be his own. But, his father reminded him, this was a wager. What was *his* stake going to be? He answered, 'I'll pay the whole price of the horse.'

(This seems to dispose beyond doubt of the thirteen talents. He had been strictly brought up by a draconian tutor, who forbade not merely luxuries but even comforts. Any allowance he was getting at thirteen is most unlikely to have been of such an order.)

In any case, he had now ensured that he would own the horse, whether or not he mastered it. He was not one as a rule to cherish reminders of failure. It must have been love at first sight.

He may already have known his Xenophon, as he certainly did later, at any rate the *Persian Expedition*, and the *Life of Cyrus*, which seems to have been his bible next after Homer. But, whether or not he had read *On Equitation*, just now he probably did not need it.

He had noticed the horse shying at its own shadow, and turned it at once to face the sun. Then he eased the bit. Taking some reassurance from his touch, it let him stroke it. He allowed it to move forward a little; then, shedding his cloak, which apparently in his eagerness he had forgotten to do before, he gripped at the mane, and vaulted. Softly he took in the reins; the horse obeyed them. He kicked with his bare heel and gave the word to go. They dashed off at a gallop, but 'made the turn in the proper way'.

Thus Alexander the Great acquired Bucephalas.

One is struck by the detail, like that of an eye-witness, in Plutarch's account. Ptolemy may have supplied it; but my guess is that it came, in a manner of speaking, from the horse's mouth. Plutarch says later of Alexander that he would sit long over the wine, because he liked to talk; and that although in the general way no one had more charming conversation or delightful manners, when loosened by wine he would fall to bragging like a common trooper. Tiresome as it must have been for his entourage, it gives a moving glimpse into his boyhood's insecurities. He can be pictured in the royal tent, pitched somewhere in central Asia; the company of generals, satraps, visiting envoys and chroniclers sits at tables laden with gold vessels looted from Persepolis. Someone, who means shortly to ask a favour, brings up the subject of war-chargers. Alexander's eye lights up. 'You know my horse, Bucephalas? Of course you do. Now I'll tell you something. He'd have been hound-meat at the knacker's, but for me.' The guest, who has heard it from at least three other sources, expresses astonished curiosity. Tactless Cleitus gives an audible groan; wise Ptolemy hacks his shin under the table. The familiar tale proceeds.

At any rate, Bucephalas belonged already to Alexander when in his fourteenth year he went up to the hillside schoolhouse at Mieza, to finish his education with Aristotle. He rode him in his youthful wars under his father's standard: when, Regent of Macedon at sixteen in his father's absence, he crushed a border rising in wild country near today's Bulgarian frontier; when he reduced the rebel cities of the Chersonese and the tough mountain-bred Illyrians. Bucephalas, a still vigorous stallion of seventeen, carried the eighteen-year-old cavalry general in the great charge that broke the ranks of the Sacred Band at Chaeroneia. And when, at the last and most dangerous of Philip's weddings, Alexander threw a cup at the groomsman's head, just missed being spitted on his father's sword, and spent some months in bleak exile, Bucephalas cannot have been left behind.

In the critical time after Philip's murder by a cast-off favourite, when all the lands he had conquered rose at once in hopeful revolt, Bucephalas must have gone with Alexander through his lightning northern campaigns, and southward when he came down like a thunderbolt to wipe out Thebes. Indeed, it can be seen that the horse's greatest days were over, before the man's had begun.

For Bucephalas had reached the respectable age of twenty-one when, aged twenty-two, Alexander crossed to Asia. At the battle of Gaugamela, only three years later, we read already that 'as long as he was riding about to make his dispositions, addressing or briefing his men, or inspecting them, he spared Bucephalas, who was now getting old, and used another horse; but when he was going into action, he sent for him, and mounted him just before starting the attack.'

To be conspicuous in the field, for friend or foe, was part of the 'Alexander touch'. He wore white wings in a helmet polished like silver; his gorget and his belt were jewelled. Not all the adornments were for himself. 'Bucephalas when undressed would permit his groom to mount him; but when all caparisoned in his royal trappings and collars, he would let nobody near him but Alexander. If anyone else tried to come up, he would charge at them neighing loudly, rear, and trample them if they did not get away quickly.' For Alexander, he 'would even lower his body to help the mounting'. (Xenophon would have approved his pupil.) And if he could no longer endure the burden of a whole day's battle—it was another horse that was killed at Issus—we can guess that it was always he who appeared at the victory parade; curvetting, no doubt, to the delight of all beholders.

Gaugamela was the last of Alexander's great pitched battles till he reached India. After Gaugamela, Bucephalas kept him company, not as the fire-breathing warrior of romance, but as an indispensable old friend, nursed carefully over high passes and hot plains, as Alexander nursed along, sometimes with his own hands, elderly Lysimachus who had been the kindly pedagogue of his childhood. One probable reason why he had no tolerance for people who let him down, is that he himself was almost fanatically loyal.

In those gruelling marches, he must have changed horses several times a day (horseshoes were a Roman innovation). Bucephalas was being led by grooms through the densely wooded country of the Mardians, when raiding tribesmen swooped down, and carried him off.

'Because of this animal's superior qualities,' says Diodorus, 'the King was enraged, and ordered every tree in the country to be felled, while he gave out to the people through interpreters that if the horse was not brought back, they would see the land laid waste to its furthest end, and everyone in it massacred.' These measures were efficacious; before the hostages had done much tree-felling, Bucephalas was returned. 'He treated them all kindly', Plutarch contributes, 'and gave a ransom for his horse to those who had captured him'—no doubt in the reaction of relief. The fate of an old horse fallen among thieves must have been grimly predictable.

This was, as far as we know, Bucephalas' last adventure. Presently came the long pull up the Khyber. He was still alive at the time of the great battle at the Hydaspes against Porus and his elephants; but it is unlikely that the pensioned veteran took part, or that he sired on the local mares that host of foals, from which Afghan chieftains down to this day trace the lineage of their favourite steeds, as they claim to do their own from Alexander.

'In the plains where the battle was fought, and from which he set out to cross the Hydaspes, Alexander founded cities. The first he called Nicaea, from his victory over the Indians; the other, Bucephala, in memory of his horse Bucephalas, who died there, not wounded by anyone, but from exhaustion and age. For he was about thirty years old, and was the victim of fatigue.'

So too, after long labours, fevers neglected or ignored, and many wounds, was his master. He had only three more years to go.

'It is said too that when he lost a dog, named Peritas, which he had reared himself and loved, he founded a city and gave it the dog's name.' He might have done the same for the last of his three comrades, his friend Hephaestion, for whom he ordered the manes of all the horses to be shorn in mourning. But a month after Hephaestion's Homeric funeral rites in Babylon, Alexander was dead.

The site of Bucephala still eludes the archaeologists. But at Rawalpindi there is an ancient Buddhist *stupa*, in the shape of a low broad dome. For some reason lost in the mists of folk-tradition, the local peasants honour it as Bucephalas' tomb.

Bella Boule!

In the boatyard in the Old Port in Cannes, M'sieu Pairseel leans against the blue side of a large motor yacht. It's shored up with miscellaneous timbers on the hard.

The yacht towers above him. M'sieu Pairseel is grateful for its shade. No one else is allowed to take advantage of this shadow because M'sieu Pairseel is—more or less—in charge of the boat and is jealous of his rights. What he should be doing, to justify his authority, is painting the blue side of the boat white, to match the other one, but what M'sieu Pairseel is doing is playing boules. The contest probably began at about 7.30 this morning. Now, with the midday break of two or three hours approaching, it is only warming up, because in all probability it will go on far into the night.

M'sieu Pairseel has won his name because of the blinding whiteness of his overalls. It's an undeserved tribute to Persil, because he has never had to have the overalls washed.

It must be weeks since he held a paintbrush, so that his 'working' clothes have retained all their original purity.

This, if he knew about it, would certainly bring a spasm of pain to the man who pays M'sieu Pairseel's wages, and buys his overalls and all kinds of subsidiary necessities for M'sieu Pairseel that appear on other accounts.

The yacht is British registered. It's fair to guess that at this moment the owner may be battling with the London Stock Exchange, so that in addition to the outgoings on M'sieu Pairseel he can also meet the berthing fees, the fitting-out charges, the cost of new equipment, and so on, and on, and on.

Pairseel is bothered about none of this. He leans against the blue side of the yacht, watching the game with a single, malevolent eye. The other one is invisible, veiled by a drooping lid that never moves. It gives him a look of such villainy one can only suppose that the owner has never met him face to face, in that if he had he wouldn't have hired M'sieu Pairseel to look after half a rubber dinghy.

In the corner of his mouth is the stub of a Gauloise. Cradled along his left forearm, resting on a strip of shammy leather, are the three steel boules. They weigh about $1\frac{1}{2}$lb, and are something like three inches in diameter. He looks after them tenderly, giving them a light polish with the leather from time to time.

PATRICK CAMPBELL

A call comes from the other players: '*Pairseel—tirez!*'

He advances with frightening purpose from the shade of the yacht, which he ought to be painting, stations himself upon some invisible mark, surveys the other boules lying around upon the rough, uneven ground, and suddenly slings one of his own with appalling savagery. It's an underarm action, with the back of the hand towards the objective.

M'sieu Pairseel's boule strikes one of the other ones with a crack like a pistol shot. His stops dead beside the jack—a very small wooden ball—and the other one shoots away, to disappear under the cradle of another yacht. A great cry rings out from the many spectators: '*Bella boule! Bella boule!*'

M'sieu Pairseel, with a wolfish grin, retires to the shade of his boat, while a small man with pince-nez and a beret, wearing a blue suit with the red ribbon of the Légion d'Honneur, bends low to the ground and sends his boule rolling gently along the baked mud that constitutes the field of play.

I have absolutely no idea what they are trying to do, or how they score, or whether the little man with the pince-nez is allied or opposed to M'sieu Pairseel, but I am resolutely determined to find out. I love the look of the little cannon-balls. I love the feel of high strategy, the planning, the decision making, and most of all I love the pistol crack—for whatever purpose it was made—as M'sieu Pairseel played his *bella boule*.

We had had our own boules court for several weeks before I found out how the game was played.

Marcel, our part-time gardener, and I built it together. Marcel was an almost square young man, with a drooping yellow moustache and pointed teeth. He probably weighed about fifteen stone, stripped for summer gardening. Against the heat of the sun he wore a high-crowned hat, made from one complete copy of *Nice Matin*, a very small pair of shorts and heavy brown boots on his otherwise bare feet. Passers-by tended to look at Marcel twice.

Through the good offices of a friend of his we had a lorry-load of coarse gravel delivered. The gravel was the size of small rocks. I unloaded tons of it into a wheelbarrow while Marcel and his friend sat on the sunny side of the lorry, chatting and smoking cigarettes. I spread the rocks around so that they covered an area of about thirty feet by twelve.

The friend had also brought a roller which a horse might have pulled with difficulty. I was struggling to unload it when Marcel came to my rescue. He whipped it out of the lorry with one hand. It fell on the road with a tremendous crash, leaving a large hole which is there to this day. Marcel and I spent the afternoon dragging the roller up and down the rocks.

There followed a longish interval of some three weeks. The friend was supposed to be bringing another load of finer gravel, but Marcel explained that he was having trouble with his father-in-law, that his wife had fallen downstairs and one of the children had measles.

When the friend eventually appeared with the finer gravel I commiserated with him upon his domestic troubles. He seemed surprised, '*Moi*,' he said, '*j'étais en vacances, quoi.*' Marcel made no contribution.

Once again I unloaded the gravel while they chatted on the sunny side of the lorry, and once again Marcel and I rolled it in. The friend went to sleep by the side of the road, waiting for us to finish with the roller. He leant against the lorry while Marcel and I burst everything pushing the roller up a plank. He then presented me with a bill for £25, and drove away, not to be seen again.

My wife had given me a birthday present of eight boules, at £7 a pair. I tried rolling them up and down for a while, but the surface proved hopelessly uneven. The boules bounded from stone to stone in an entirely unpredictable way. Admittedly, M'sieu Pairseel and his friends appeared to be content with a much rougher pitch, but I felt we were entitled to something better.

I asked Marcel about it. He seemed surprised to find that I regarded the court as finished. What we now required was a load of red sand but, *malheureusement*, this was extremely difficult to obtain. Another friend brought a lorry-load of it a month later. This set me back another £25, but after I spread it, stamped it in and watered it it certainly did give the court a more professional look.

Shortly afterwards we had a night of thunder and torrential rain. When I went out in the morning I saw that nearly all the sand had been washed off the court on to the lawn below it. After endless negotiations another friend of Marcel's arrived, with three Algerian labourers. They built a low wall around the court, for which I paid £100, plus various gratuities to the Algerians. Then we had another £25 worth of red sand and I decided, positively, that the court was as good as it was ever going to be.

On the following Wednesday Marcel failed to arrive for his weekly stint. I thought he might have retired on his 10 per cent of the construction costs, but learnt later that he had taken a job in the old people's home on the other side of the valley. My informant told me that Marcel had said that he had found it too hard, working for me, and had now become 'un grand homme d'affaires', in a white nylon coat, looking after the old ones.

We no longer had a gardener, but we certainly had a boules court. I added up the cost.

Eight boules	£28
Two loads of gravel	£25
Two loads of red sand	£50
One low wall	£100
Gratuities	£3
GRAND TOTAL	£206

It was time I learnt the rules, and put this costly investment to some use.

A sports outfitter in Grasse provided them, in a small grey booklet entitled, *Règlements Officiels Petanque et Jeu Provençal*. The publication had been approved by *Le Ministère de L'Education Nationale*. A promising start.

The sports outfitter gave me the booklet free of charge, for the reason—as it turned out a moment later—that he believed I was about to buy a full set of eighteen boules. When I said that I had eight of them already he nearly took the booklet back, but contented himself with remarking that the ones I had were probably toys for the babies. 'You will return,' he said confidently.

I drove home very quickly, and opened up Page One. From it I learnt that before beginning play each team had to present their licence, furnished with a photograph stamped by the Departmental Committee. On the other side we had to have the stamp of the French Federation.

My attention wandered from Page One to Page Two. Here I found that each player had to throw his boule from inside a circle big enough to hold both feet. Tolerance, however, was accorded to those with mutilations of the lower limbs, or over sixty-five years of age.

Page Three revealed that the jack, having been thrown, is lost if it's *introuvable*, or unfindable.

I must confess that I began to skip at this point. There was an over-precise, almost pettifogging quality about the rules that made them hard reading.

I learnt that while play was going on the greatest silence had to reign both among the spectators and the players. The adversaries were not allowed to walk, gesticulate or do anything else to derange the opposition. Furthermore, all violence committed by a player against a judge, an arbitrator, a spectator or another player would be punished severely by the National Committee of Discipline.

The last line said that correct dress was obligatory. The nude torso was not permitted.

I still didn't know how to play boules, but I thought we ought to give it a try.

My wife and I went out to the new, infinitely costly boules court. I gave her the jack, or *cochonnet*. I said, 'You've got to throw it at least six metres.' She said, 'How much is that?' 'Just throw it,' I said, 'fairly far.' She did so, and with a circular action, as though stirring soup, discharged her first boule.

It tottered along across the smooth red sand and came to rest right up against the *cochonnet*. A voice cried, '*Bella boule!*'

With loathing I saw, peering over the cypress hedge, the dotard from the old people's home. He takes his promenade past our garden every day, probably to get a rest from the ministrations of Marcel. He trapped me one afternoon and said, 'They tell me you are a writer. Now, *I* have a story. What a story! It's unbelievable, but I was denounced to the Germans by my mother-in-law!'

It seemed to me to be a sensible course of action on the lady's part, but I said, '*Formidable!*'

'You can say it,' he replied. 'With my help, you will start to write it today.'

I've been dodging him ever since, but here he was now, peering over our hedge, crying '*Bella boule!*'

I ignored him, and played my own stroke. Nowhere near. My wife began stirring, preparatory to discharging her second one, when the old gentleman had a kind of seizure. He struck at the hedge with his stick, shouting, '*Non, non, Madame! Pas à vous! Vous avez pointé! C'est à lui!*'

In a lovely blinding flash I saw how the game of boules was played. I even knew what M'sieu Pairseel was at, and which side the small man in the blue suit, with the pince-nez and the Legion of Honour, was playing on.

Obviously, after Player A and Player B have done their bit, and Player A is nearer than Player B, *then* Player B goes again, and again, if Player A is still the nearest.

It was like watching the slow, welcoming opening of the Pearly Gates.

Pairseel, the *tireur*, or 'shooter', had shot out the other side's best boule, leaving his own beside the *cochonnet*. Then it had to be the Legion of Honour's turn, for the opposition. He, a mere *pointeur*, or point scorer, tried his little trickle, to get closer than M'sieu Pairseel.

I nudged my wife out of the way. 'Evidently,' I cried to the dotard, still leaning urgently over the hedge. 'Women are mad. *Sans doute, ça c'est à moi!*'

We've never looked back since.

The best game of all is four a side, with three boules each, so that at the end of each play there are twenty-four boules littering the court. Then comes the dramatic measuring, the dissension, the re-measuring, the grudging agreement, the re-charging of the glasses and then we're off again, this time down the hill instead of up.

The splendid thing about the game is that anyone can play it. There is no specific technique to be learnt, as there is in golf or tennis, or even polo. If you're physically equipped to throw a stone underhand you can play boules, often with astonishing success.

We've really got it going now, with a spotlight in each of the two olive trees beside the court, so that often, in the blissful heat of the Mediterranean night, we are at it until two and three o'clock in the morning.

Much of the play would be frowned upon by the National Commission of Discipline. Nothing like the greatest silence ever reigns, and some of the gesticulations, aimed at the derangement of the opposition, are of an extremely provocative nature.

Nor are we too finicky about dress. Mostly we wear bathing things, because we find it sharpens the eye and increases the thirst to nip into the swimming-pool in between games.

The ladies wear bikinis, for ease of action, a habit that puts temptation in one's way, as the game involves a good deal of bending.

One unusually hot afternoon, I slipped three cool boules into the back of the lower section of a lady's bikini, just as she was about to shoot me out.

On that occasion, the *torse nue*, so sternly frowned upon by the Departmental Committee, simply wasn't in it.

Sketches from a London Notebook,
Royal Zoological Gardens, April 1969

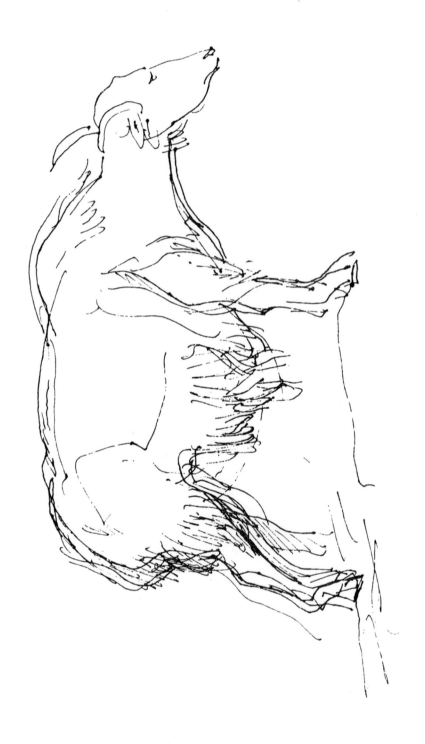

Royal Wines

'It all depends', as Professor Joad was prone to preamble, 'on the context in which you use the word "Royal". Royal Wines. . . . The favourite wines drunk by Monarchs and their Courts? Wine coming from vineyards owned by Royalty? Generic wines of regal quality or wine from a single vineyard or vigneron so glorious in texture, so delicious in taste, so easy on the eye and fragrant to the nose that it is Royal in its own right?'

Burgundy has long been known as the King of Wines and Bordeaux the Queen which a champenois, quick as a flash on a commercial, changed to 'If Burgundy is the King and Claret the Queen, Champagne is the gay old Millionaire'.

Let us look at each of the possibilities, not forgetting that the King of Kings who made the vine Himself blessed the wine that man made from it, and took it as the symbol of His blood; nor that in 'the guid book' Paul advised Timothy to 'drink no longer water but use a little wine for thy stomach's sake and thine often infirmities'. Note the word 'little' and this in the days before pre-prandial aperitifs or scotch-on-the-rocks and the American habit of blaming intoxication on the odd glass or two of wine whilst ignoring the hazards of an hour or two's previous indulgence in hard liquor.

Champagne may be a 'gay old Millionaire' of a wine but one way and another it has been the drink of sophisticated Kings for at least 1,200 years. Champagne was a still wine when most of the thirty-seven Kings and eleven Queens and Regents of France came to Rheims for their Coronations—a practice said, on somewhat flimsy evidence, to have started when the Pagan ruler, Clovis, turned Christian in 496, but more likely to have begun with Charlemagne's son Louis the Pious in 816. It is at least certain that from 987 onwards Rheims was the scene of all French Kings' Coronations—a fact, according to Patrick Forbes in his delightful book, *Champagne, the wine, the land and the peoples*, of great comfort to the episcopacy of Rheims as making it the most important ecclesiastical authority in France and of transcending importance to the commercial future of this regal wine. On the other hand the burghers of Rheims were a bit solemn about this honour as they had to foot the entire bill for wine, food and entertainment of all the guests.

On the debit side the winefield was fought over numerous times, though François I, who was devoted to his 'Champers', had the decency to fight his wars a considerable distance away; whereas Edward III of England took fighting to the very walls of the City and was responsible for a dirty piece of chicanery by allowing a French force to recapture a wagon-load of Champagne and then beating them up when they got drunk on it. One wonders if the wine was much stronger then than now, for some forty years later good King Wenceslas, King of Bohemia and Emperor of the Holy Roman Empire, got so regally drunk when he came to Rheims to discuss church matters that he was out for several days before signing a mass of documents Charles VI put before him when he was still under the influence.

England and France were still at war in Henry VII's time, and he, too, attacked Rheims; but one Henry later, the VIII, was so in with the French that he, like François I, Pope Leo X and Charles V of Spain, bought a vineyard in Ay—always one of the outstanding Champagne vineyards. It subsequently became a favourite of Henri IV of France, who installed presses and an administrator there.

By about 1700, and thanks largely to the Monk Cellarman, Dom Perignon, whose Abbey at Hautvillers has been largely restored by the famous Champagne house of Moët & Chandon, Champagne was becoming increasingly a sparkling wine, though the secret of how to stop the bottles bursting (some two million burst in 1840 alone) was not solved for over 150 years.

By the middle of the eighteenth century sparkling Champagne was being drunk at the English Court where Lord Chesterfield, the Steward of George II's household, made a memorable toast to it. 'Give me Champagne, and fill it to the brim, I'll toast in bumpers ev'ry lovely limb.' In 1762 it was on sale at 8s a bottle at the Pleasure Gardens in Vauxhall, and from then onwards has been the automatic choice for the great family and official occasions of all who can afford it. Thanks to the Veuve Cliquot it conquered the Russians in 1814, and whilst there was Royalty in France they and theirs were devoted to it. With all these Royal sponsors there is little wonder that Champagne sales soared in the relatively short period between 1783 and 1853 from 300,000 to 10 million bottles (today they stand at about 94 million and are drunk in nearly every country in the world), with an immense leap forward in England in Victoria's day thanks largely to the affection the Prince of Wales had for it.

Truly a Royal wine—but so is Claret.

In May 1152 the Plantagenet, Henry II, aged nineteen, married thirty-year-old Eleanor of Aquitaine and, as may be surmised, this uneven marriage brought immense possessions to the English Crown.

In France, a country which, like Germany, was a long way from becoming united under a single Crown, the English already claimed parts of Touraine and all Anjou, Maine and Normandy, and with Eleanor's dowry came the remainder of Touraine and most of western France and Gascony. And so for 300 years this vast tract of country and its valuable winefields became a British possession, and enjoyed many important tax exemptions and commercial privileges, coming gradually to be considered an English province rather than a Royal property. At this time of appalling roads it was, in fact, far easier to transport wine by ship to London from Bordeaux, Libourne or La Rochelle than it would have been to send it overland to Paris which, for much of the period, was even denied the wine of nearby Burgundy, which had its own autocratic Dukes who cared little for the hegemony of the so-called Kings of France. So Bordeaux wines, or Claret as the English called them, became the wines of the English court, much to the annoyance of English vignerons who, in an appreciably warmer climate than we suffer today, were making wine in large quantities, mostly in the area south of the Wash.

Those who want to argue it that way can certainly claim that Claret has been the Royal wine of England for over 800 years, and undoubtedly the tremendous commercial prosperity of the Bordeaux winefield was, until the relatively recent rise of the American market, largely due to English patronage, English-made laws and the comparative safety of seas policed by the English men-of-war. The Bordeaux wine fleet sailed regularly from England with mixed cargoes including even the cobblestones which still enhance the look of the streets of that most lovely wine town, St Emilion, where I once remember hearing a children's choir singing *Auld Lang Syne* and their conductor, the curé, assuring me that it was a traditional French song, and laughing unbelievingly when I assured him it was a Scottish song. On the return journey these wine ships used to carry up to 300 *tonneaux* of wine each—some 400,000 bottles, and there were many of them, as with Royal encouragement the English were mad about Claret—Edward II, according to Edmund Penning-Rowsell in his comprehensive book *Wines of Bordeaux* ordering the equivalent of 1,152,000 bottles for his wedding to Isabella of France. In those days old wines were almost undrunk as there was no known way of keeping them until corks were thought of.

Trade was not always good—pestilence, wars and taxation took their toll—but one could surely argue that Claret has always been the Royal wine of England. But what of Burgundy?

Until the last century or so roads were always so bad that even fastidious people like Madame de Sevigné hazarded travelling along the turbulent Rhône rather than risking the bumps and brigands of the highway. All the same Burgundy was so Royal a wine that it overran its natural boundaries, particularly after Louis XIV's physician dealt Champagne a nasty blow by prescribing Burgundy to his Royal master 'for health reasons'. This was indeed hard on Louis who adored Champagne and had brought both the province and the trade great prosperity, but it occurred towards the end of his life and, according to the Champenois, hastened it!

One of Burgundy's greatest Royal patrons was the Emperor Charlemagne who adored the red wine of Corton. The story goes that when he was ageing he found it embarrassing to drink in public because it stained his white beard. Regretfully he instructed the court cellarer to obtain a white wine from the same slopes so that his affection for wine would not become too obvious on ceremonial occasions. The white wine was duly produced by substituting the Chardonnay grape for the Pinot, and the Emperor approved it. Thenceforth he always drank it in public though returning to his favourite red in private. An iconoclastic friend of mine assures me that the Emperor had no beard!

Undoubtedly Burgundy is a Royal wine in every sense. . . .

There will be those who rate German wines highly in the Royal Stakes, and sophisticated cricketers would certainly accord the wines of Mosel, Saar and Ruwer the adjective so often associated with an innings by Tom Graveney. Yes, 'elegant' is the word! They would also refer to the many Royal owners of Germany's finest vine-yards and to Queen Victoria's alleged partiality for Hock. Yet, though thousands of German wines are delightful, and many out-standing, they will not, on a majority vote, oust the wines of France, nor will Portugal, despite the Old Alliance and the regular Royal feeling encouraged by a vintage Port, or a rare tawny.

Few but Cypriots will press the claims of that luscious, rich sweet wine, Commandaria, though it is palatable when young and delicious when old. Yet five Kings are said to have drunk it at the famous dinner given in honour of King Peter I of Cyprus at the Vintners Hall in 1362, the other four Kings being Edward III of England, David of Scotland, Jean of France and Waldemar of Denmark. Of the great wines, that leaves Sherry and Madeira, but splendid though each is in its time and place their claims cannot be serious.

So, which is the truly Royal wine? The light, happy wine of Champagne that laughs its way into your heart, captivating your senses? A smooth, elegant Claret of one of the great chateaux and vintages, lovingly entombed and quietly decanted some twenty to thirty years later, equally attractive to nose, eye and palate, feminine and curiously feline? Or is it a luscious Burgundy, bottled by one of the great vignerons, looking, as it lies in the thin crystal glass that should bring it to your lips, as if you could somehow chew the depth of its colour. Its fragrance enigmatic but compulsive, its texture . . . ?

Yes, to hell with it, I must admit to being a Burgundy man. Still, as the buskers say as they diddle you, 'Fair's fair'. All three are Royal wines and the choice is yours even if the Chancellor of the Exchequer mulcts you of the equivalent of three bottles for every one you drink.

JOHN ARLOTT

Cricket for Breakfast

Cricket is pre-eminently the breakfast-time sport, recognized and enjoyed all over the world, though nowhere quite so deeply nor so frequently as in England. In the life of the English county cricketer, breakfast is in many ways the symbol of his achievement. While other men are choking down a cup of tea and dashing out to be at work at eight or nine o'clock, the county cricketer is at his leisure. At away matches he strolls downstairs in the hotel without hurry—though not always with the entire approval of the dining-room staff—with the ease of a man who does not have to start work until half-past eleven. True, some captains call for a half-past ten report on the ground but even that leaves time for relaxation, a three-course meal, an extra cup of coffee at the end: and above all, the paper.

You may always identify a county cricket team at breakfast in an English hotel because they are all reading the morning newspapers; not simply one apiece but passing them round so that they all see them all. They are, of course, reading the cricket scores and reports so that, by the end of the meal, most of them know—without consciously committing it to memory but from sheer interest—just what every team and individual did in the previous day's play. Being a county cricketer is not simply playing for a county; it is following all the other counties. These are the ultimate 'shop' men.

The conversation stirred by this morning study has an established and traditional form. 'I see'—comment on anything read in the paper always begins with 'I see'—'I see old Fred got a hundred against Derbyshire: must have been a beautiful track for him to get runs against Alan Ward.' 'But perhaps Alan wasn't really fit—?' 'Must have been, they gave him eighteen overs.' Every game is weighed up. They have not missed a trick. 'I see old Eddie got another star [a not out] against Sussex; bet that made Snowball mad.'

They know who is fit, who is playing well; they notice tactical details a hundred miles away: 'Why did Brian only bowl a dozen overs yesterday if it's a turner at Weston, then?' 'Why did he keep Skinny on for forty overs when he only took one?'

The difference between the first-class cricketers and their followers is that the players have longer to go about this delightful morning pursuit. Other games, such as football, produce morning reading only once or twice a week—and anyway it is not quite the same on Sundays. England is the best breakfast-cricket country because every day in the season there is a match to be reported somewhere. Since my childhood the special flavour of summer has always been the cricket scores in the morning. There was one brief period when, living in North Hampshire where the local club is called Basingstoke and North Hants, I thought we had two county teams—Hampshire and Northants—and was only relieved of the anguish of not knowing which to support in a match between the two by my father's explanation.

Like millions of other small boys, I knew all the county cricketers from the morning papers before I ever saw any of them play. There was no television then; cricketers were to be seen only in the papers—photographs, and Tom Webster, then in the heyday of his economic, laughing line—on cigarette cards, or in the mind. There were not even any evening scores on the wireless so that the rumour someone had heard from a man who saw it in the Stop Press of an evening paper, that Mead had been 77 not out in the afternoon, left us in a state of agonized suspense until next morning's news confirmed that he had scored his century (he usually did, though several of us were rendered uneasy for years after he got out in the nineties twice during the same fortnight).

Test Matches in Australia were tantalizing; in the years before the relayed commentaries there was a terrible wait for the morning editions of the evening papers: they did not arrive until we had gone to school, there was no chance of a glimpse of one in the mid-morning break and it was horrid not to know even the worst until lunchtime.

It is never quite the same after one has grown up. Of course many breakfast-table cricketers follow their native counties faithfully all the summer through the morning reports. For them, though, the players themselves are not distant and unattainable: they simply do not bother to go to the matches when they might. For us, as boys, remote from the county grounds, the morning paper was the only link with those splendid creatures. The heavy tread of Armstrong's Australians echoed through England in that blazing summer and, all at once, though their game was not even a distant relation of our rough-ground skirmishes, they spellbound me. So each breakfast-time, when my father had gone out to work, leaving the paper for me, there was regular news of the great: Jack Hobbs—until he fell ill, Hendren, Hearne, Russell, Woolley, Sandham, Tyldesley, E., Freeman, White, Macaulay, Rhodes, Parker, the destroying Australian fast bowlers, Gregory and McDonald, the splendid Macartney—and, of course, *all* the Hampshire players, but especially Tennyson,

Mead and Brown, who almost alone defied the Australians. All of these I was to see and many of them I later came to know personally.

Many others, though, remain fresh in my mind, cricketers I followed through those distant summers, men I never set eyes upon, but whom I still remember (initials as well, if pressed) in the pictures my mind made of them all those years ago: Wells, Murdin and Buswell; Curgenven, Cadman and Bestwick; Coventry, Preece and Tarbox; Mounteney, Coe and Benskin; Gillingham, Perrin and Farnfield; and, from the 'new' county, Whittington, Hacker, Creber, O'Bree and Pinch. Do cricketers ever realize, I wonder—to how many millions of people they will never know—they are breakfast-table heroes?

How can They know that Joy to be Alive who have not Flown?

Greek mythology gave us the original aviators, Daedalus and Icarus. Father Daedalus—obviously a Founder Member of the Royal Aeronautical Society—fixed wings on himself and son Icarus and off they both took. Regrettably, Daedalus had done his sums wrong. As a result, so the story goes, the young and press-on Icarus flew too near the sun and suffered wax-fatigue of his shoulder harness. Off came his wings and down he fell into the sea. Thereafter this was named the Icarian Sea, and is to this day to witness if I lie. It was a pity Icarus did not last. He had the makings of a fighter pilot.

Down the ages in tale and fable, flying has always fascinated man. Yet the great moment did not arrive until 17 December 1903, at Kittyhawk, North Carolina, when Orville and Wilbur Wright achieved the first powered controlled flight. It is true that Montgolfier and others had gone aloft in hot-air balloons or similar devices, but this was the real thing. In the early morning of 17 December Orville actually left the ground and stayed airborne for a distance of 120 feet (40 yards), at a height of probably no more than six feet. What a tremendous thrill it must have been. Possibly a greater surge of elation for Wilbur as he stood and watched it happen than for Orville who might not even have been sure he was off the ground until his brother confirmed it. Kittyhawk has not changed. I was there some years ago. It is reminiscent of Rye in Kent. Flat grassland by the seashore with the sandhills of the golf links behind. In the shelter of a sand dune stands a black wooden hut with a single door in the middle of the front wall, flanked by square glass windows. The door is locked. Through the left window you can see the sleeping-room with its two wooden bunks, through the right the living-room with a table, chairs and some plates and dishes beside the stove in the back of the room. The hut and its contents have been kept as they were to add a touch of realism to surroundings which scarcely need it.

As always when one stands on ground hallowed by history, the years roll back and the very scene unfolds before you. The pale morning light, no wind, the sea like glass, the temperature cool. The door of the hut opens and there stands Orville, savouring the full beauty of the dawn with those fresh smells which only the early

33

morning brings. His gaze lingers on the biplane contraption of wood and fabric on which he and his brother have been working for so long.

He turns and speaks into the hut: 'Come on, Wilbur. It's perfect.' Out they go and line up the aeroplane in the most favourable direction. Orville climbs into the seat, the heavy, unreliable engine is started. Orville opens the throttle and the machine slowly trundles over the flat sage grass. At perhaps 30 mph it comes off the ground.

As you walk away from the hut and along by the sea you notice white marker posts like old English milestones; you look down at the first and read on it 'Orville Wright   December 17 1903   120 feet'. A little farther on the second post tells of 'Wilbur Wright', same date, a few more feet. You continue a few more yards to the third post which says 'Orville Wright', same date, yet more feet. You walk quite a distance to the fourth and final post and there it is: 'Wilbur Wright   December 17 1903   852 feet'—the last and longest of the four flights made by those brothers between dawn and midday. As you slowly turn away, you reflect: '284 yards—a long hitter can drive a golf ball farther.'

Orville Wright made the first flight of forty yards at a height of a few feet. Sixty-five years and two World Wars later another American stepped on the Moon. There are people alive today who can recall both historic events.

It is not my intention to write the history of aviation, nor to stray into the military sphere. I mention the two World Wars because of the tremendous impetus they gave to the development of aeronautics.

To my mind, one contribution of the Wrights to succeeding generations has been to provide them with the *fun* of flying. In this day and age most people fly; in fact they travel in comfort in a pressurized tube with upwards of a hundred others. That is not flying. In the same way that the sailing enthusiast enjoys measuring his skill against wind and tide in the small boat, the flying enthusiast likes the little aeroplane for the same reasons.

I learned to fly in 1928 when cockpits were open, undercarriages were fixed (as was the propeller pitch), wheels were tail not nose and were skids anyhow, and the instruments consisted of a rev. counter, airspeed indicator, altimeter, an oil pressure gauge and a spirit level set horizontally across the dashboard. When you did a correctly banked turn the bubble stayed in the middle. When you hurtled out of a cloud out of control but in a perfectly banked steep spiral the bubble was in the middle also. It was all good fun. The noise of the flying wires and the wind on your cheek told you if you were flying accurately. Hands mattered. It was always said that a good horseman would be a natural pilot, and this proved true in many cases. Sailing is akin to flying in this context as a number of good fliers have proved.

Radio and navigational aids were in the distant future. You found your way by reading a map which sometimes blew out of the open cockpit. Nearly all grass fields provided landing opportunities, and sometimes you landed and asked the first chap who turned up where you were. As when you stop in a motor-car to ask the way he was invariably 'a stranger in these parts'. That made two of you. Railway lines were the great navigational aid and you soon got to know them. Any old Imperial Airways pilot will tell you the bad weather route from Lympne to Croydon was to follow the Ashford–Tonbridge railway line. It was known as the Iron Dog. Take the second branch line to the right, through the valley, and there was Croydon.

Due to an error of judgement in December 1931, Isaac Newton's law of gravity caught up with me. I left the Royal Air Force in May and joined the great Shell Company in June 1933.

The 1930s were the pioneering era of long distance flying. In 1933 the American Charles Lindbergh flew the North Atlantic alone in his little single-engined monoplane *Spirit of St Louis* in 33 hours, landing at Le Bourget in the middle of the night to a tumultuous welcome. Girls scarcely out of their teens like Amy Johnson from Hull and Jean Batten of New Zealand were setting records to Australia and South Africa, while men like Bert Hinkler, James Mollison, Charles Scott, Campbell Black and others were breaking such records again and again. Amy Johnson flew the North Atlantic east to west in a Puss Moth with her husband Mollison; Jean Batten flew the South Atlantic solo in a Percival Gull from Dakar to Natal. That great Australian Charles Kingsford-Smith roamed the Pacific in his Tri-motor *Southern Cross* with Patrick Gordon Taylor; Francis Chichester flew the Tasman from Australia to New Zealand in one of the most remarkable navigational feats of all time, in a little Moth seaplane. Now 'Sir Francis' for his wonderful solo trip round the world in a sailing-boat, at the age of sixty-five, he will never be forgotten by my generation as a great aviator.

Some of the large oil companies, like Shell, used to sponsor these flights not only for their advertising value but also as a contribution to the development of aviation. In countries like Britain, Egypt, East Africa, South Africa, India, the Straits Settlements, and Australia, Shell's aviation representatives were ex-RAF short service officers. They flew company-owned Puss Moths or Percival Gulls around their areas. They used to send back to the London office airfield plans, route information for flying through the various countries, indicating easily identifiable check points, and meteorological data about monsoons, rains, and the best time of year for

35

flying in their part of the world. This type of stuff was invaluable to other pilots, many of whom had little actual flying experience, while most had no knowledge of conditions outside the British Isles. These pilots were mostly youngsters who flew for fun. The idea of going to Australia or South Africa in a little aeroplane intrigued them. What was it like outside their home territory? How did you clear Customs, or didn't you? What was the best route to take? Where did you get this information? The Shell Aviation Department or the A.A. who had good strip maps? Strip maps were no good, much better get complete ones from Stanford's. These were the young men and women who followed the trail-blazing example of the famous Alan Cobham in the 1920s. They were the pioneers of the air routes down Africa and to the Far East. Their aerodromes were not the hideous concrete monstrosities we know today. They were literally fields with a white circle in the middle with the name written across it, with usually a windsock in one corner which sometimes caught the attention and identified the landing place. In the sand and dust areas of Africa, the Middle East, the Persian Gulf, and India the white circles were the same colour as the surrounding country and difficult to find.

Memory holds the key and reminiscence crowds it as the years gather. In November 1939 I returned to the Royal Air Force, leaving it once more for Shell in July 1946. There was a tremendous upsurge of aviation business. Airlines and charter companies were sprouting mushroom-like all over the world. There were thousands of surplus aeroplanes and young American and British pilots ready to do anything so long as it meant flying. The world was littered with airfields. Rules of the air were simple and easily interpreted. Radio was not mandatory for small aircraft; there was no VMC, no IMC, no Controlled Airspace, no Airways, none of the jargon of the modern methods. You flew quadrantal heights odd and even thousands plus 500 feet. Air misses? We'd all had them so often in the crowded skies of war we never noticed. If you passed another aeroplane you waved. We were all friends now. My wife and I landed in Rome in a Proctor in 1948 on the way to the Far East. After thirty minutes of failing to get the Italian official to appreciate that the aeroplane was a private one and a passenger manifest was unnecessary we were all becoming hysterical, when the Italian said: 'I know, she is the hostess.' I always remember that splendid Italian in my prayers. He has saved me much form filling. During hundreds of hours in the succeeding twenty-two years, I have never carried any passengers, only crew.

On that trip we were sitting in the hut on Akyab airfield drinking coffee and flies with a young American pilot wearing the uniform of a small Bengali airline. My wife asked him, as women will, why he was flying for such a company. He replied, 'Waal, I had to get into this country somehow.' He reckoned he could make enough on the side, by smuggling, in two years to leave and buy that farm back home. We wished him luck as we left for Rangoon.

One of the most beautiful sights I have seen was the golden dome of the Shwedagon Pagoda at Rangoon, reflecting the setting sun behind us, as we approached it from twenty miles at 5,000 feet across the flat Irrawaddy delta.

In Rangoon we found a splendid Australian flying Doves for some local company. Under his shirt he was wearing a wide leather belt which he stuffed with gold on every return trip from Bangkok. He reckoned another year would satisfy him. He also got our good wishes as we left. Happy days!

While in Calcutta, I had sought an experienced pilot who had been flying up and down the coast between there and Rangoon since the late 1930s. We were due to meet the monsoon in Southern Burma and it would be new to me. He said: 'The monsoon is mainly heavy rain with a cloud base seldom lower than 500 feet. You can follow the coastline even in the heaviest rain. Its intensity will vary continually. There will be periods of no rain when you will be flying under a 1,200 feet base with good visibility. Thunderstorms you can see and are usually over land, so do not present a hazard. There are three sorts of monsoon raincloud: white, black and brown. White is heavy rain and presents no problem. Black is linesquall stuff and best avoided by flying along it and round it; they are usually ten to fifteen miles long and very bumpy underneath. *Never* go into the brown.' His advice was a great help when we found the monsoon between Mergui and Penang a few days later. We ran into the inter-tropical front between Djakarta and Singapore on our return. A rose by another name, the ITF is merely a low pressure system of monsoon-like intensity which covers no great area and is on the move. After years of flying small aeroplanes on the Far Eastern route and up and down Africa, I have remembered that wise pilot's advice, which has again and again been confirmed by my own experience. I have never encountered his brown cloud. On several occasions I have met the black linesquall round the West African coast. Returning from Capetown once in the Proctor, between Cameroon and Fernando Po, I found the long narrow black cloud with rain streaming from it. After flying along it for several miles I saw through the rain the sun shining on the sea the other side of it. I turned through it and in one minute I was in the sunshine. The most agreeable linesquall I ever met.

Once when I stayed in Lagos for some days, my driver was a tall

Hauser named Joseph. A Miles Gemini with VHF and a radio compass had replaced the Proctor. Out at Ikeja airfield one day, I asked Joseph if he would like a whizz round in the air. He was keen, so off we went. There was cloud at 1,000 feet from early stratus which was burning off gradually. At 2,000 feet we were in sunshine on top of cotton wool with Joseph looking around in obvious enjoyment. After ten minutes or so he turned and said, 'Master, how you find your way? There are no signposts in the sky.' I tuned in the radio compass and replied, 'Look, that needle points at Ikeja.' I turned so that he could see the needle move as we changed direction. His eyes remained glued to it. We came down through the thin cloud ten miles short of the airport. I said, 'See, Joseph, we follow the needle. In a minute you will see Ikeja.' He saw it and turned to me with a huge smile. I said, 'That's white man's ju-ju.' We both laughed. As Joseph drove me home to Lagos, he suddenly observed, 'Master, there is not much foot-palaver in aeroplane,' a splendid remark which I treasure. I last saw him in April 1969 during the civil war when I was in Port Harcourt and Lagos. We greeted each other as old friends do.

The Sahara has always fascinated me, probably from reading *Beau Geste* as a youngster. When I found myself there with the Gemini, I was not disappointed. The French had this desert well organized. It was open only from October to March to light aeroplanes and surface transport. There were no sandstorms, temperatures varied from zero at night to 70° at midday. Provided you stuck to the rules you were all right. Essential equipment comprised a standard medical box, some packets of ghastly French rusks, water, Very pistol and cartridges, a rifle and fifty rounds. My wife and I had the Gemini groaning with our baggage and flight spares on our first foray. I asked why the rifle? If you landed in the desert, you were to fire three shots every hour to help the searching Foreign Legion to locate you. We left Algiers secure in the knowledge that this great Regiment was on the alert. The unbreakable rule of the desert was *suivez la piste*. It was easy; the visibility was immense, and the *piste* was like a furrow in the brown sand and a white path across the black rock of the desert. At this time of the year the buses of Compagnie Generale Transsaharienne were carrying travellers across this vast desert to Tamanrasset in the Hoggar Mountains to the south. We stopped the night in El Golea, a little town some hundreds of miles south of Algiers. The French proprietor of the hotel used to shut it in April, go to France for a week or so and then always to Scotland which he loved because it was green and rained!

One year I was in El Golea with a Shell colleague. We were bound for a newly established exploration camp three hundred miles to the south. We decided that he, Roy, would go down to the camp that night by truck. I would bring the Gemini down in the morning by which time he would have chosen a suitable landing site. He would mark the up-wind end with smoke when I was overhead and the rest (about three hundred yards) as best he could. After supper, off he went.

That evening the Shell superintendent, a splendid ex-Foreign Legion NCO, was explaining to me how to get to the new camp. I have his map to this day, drawn with a ballpoint pen on the back of a menu card six inches by four. His instructions were simple: 'Follow the *piste* to Fort Miribel.' This grandiose title served to identify a small white bungalow (once a Foreign Legion *poste*) which was a sort of Joe's Café used by desert truck drivers. 'Past Miribel the *piste* forks left to In Salah; you go straight on for Aoulef.' I recalled Joseph's 'signposts in the sky' remark. This time I would be without 'white man's ju-ju'. 'Another 130 kilometres and you will see a large cairn of stones beside the *piste*. They are huge, you cannot mistake them. Turn right and you will find the camp.'

In the morning I took off on this three-hundred-mile flight, clutching the menu. All went well. Fort Miribel came up on ETA, so did the Aoulef fork. I was thinking I must do more flying by menu. Then ETA Stones—no Stones. Of course my menu was a truck driver's guide, not a flying map. I saw a little track running north from the main *piste* which was 250°. He'd said, turn right at the Stones. I was descending from 3,000 feet to *piste*-level to have a look when I sighted a dust plume approaching across the desert from the west, caused by a jeep. It turned north up the little track as I turned over it at 500 feet, thinking 'he knows the way'. After six minutes there was the camp with its few tents and caravans tucked behind the north side of a bluff which had screened it from me. Up came the smoke and I landed. I have seldom received so warm a welcome as I got from Roy, knowing that he had now finished with desert trucks.

My day was made, however, by the arrival of the jeep crew in the mess tent. They rushed across to thank me for flying above them and directing them to the camp, as they had been lost! Lunch became quite a party.

E. F. HAYLOCK

Today a yacht would, perhaps rightly, be described as a vessel built solely for the pursuit of pleasure, be it for the sport of racing or for the romance of cruising. Although present-day yachts may be driven by sail or power, their purpose is the same, but it has not always been thus. Early yachts were built mainly as a convenient means of personal transport for royalty, and were also used by wealthy merchants or by corporations, such as the Dutch East India Company. In countries where roads were few, and beset by footpads, but where water was plentiful, a small handy sailing ship provided a comfortable, convenient, and even a comparatively quick means of travel and communication.

Yachts have probably existed in all maritime nations from the earliest times. The Phoenicians and the Greek and Roman Emperors certainly had them. As we delve into the frail records of antiquity we find that it was customary to set sails of various colours to denote the purpose of the vessel. We know, for certain, that the sails of royal yachts were purple and that this continued for many centuries. Ezekiel, in 588 BC, in his lamentation for Tyrus, Chapter XXVII, describes, in considerable detail, ships with benches of ivory and sails of 'fine linen with broidered work from Egypt . . . blue and purple . . .'.

This indicates a degree of luxury not found in merchant vessels of any period. Although 'benches of ivory' may not match modern ideas of comfort, the added mention of purple sails leads us to the fairly safe conclusion that Ezekiel was describing a yacht probably used by royalty or by the royal entourage.

Perhaps the most renowned royal barge, galley, or yacht was that of Cleopatra, Queen of Egypt. Shakespeare described her:

> The barge she sat in, like a burnished throne
> Burned on the water; the poop was beaten gold,
> Purple the sails and so perfumed, that
> The winds were lovesick with them; the oars were silver,
> Which to the tune of flukes kept stroke
> And made the water which they beat to flow faster,
> As amorous of their strokes.

To rely upon 'The Bard' might seem unwise were it not that he, in turn, must have been indebted to the historian, Plutarch, who described Cleopatra's vessel in even greater detail. He does not give her a name, but naming ships was probably a later custom brought about by the need to distinguish one from another as numbers increased.

But note, the sails were of purple silk, indicating a royal yacht which carried a large number of servants and attendants, to say nothing of a couple of hundred slave oarsmen to propel her to windward or through calms. 'The beautiful boys, like Cupids, fanning her.' 'Her women, representing the Nerids and Graces, who leaned negligently on the sides and shrouds. . . .' 'The troops of Virgins, richly dresst . . .' who, on arrival at their destination, kept pace along the banks of the River Cydnus burning incense and scattering rich perfumes. Then there were the musicians, an essential part of seduction '. . . who kept time to the beat of the oars'.

With so many people on board sanitation must have been something of a problem; hence, perhaps, the emphasis on perfumes! 'Laden also with the most magnificent offerings and presents of all kinds', this vessel must have been of considerable size.

The square sail, or sails, of this vessel, as in all ships of that time, were only set with the wind abaft the beam. When headwinds were encountered, the silver-sheathed oars of the slaves flashed in the perpetual Egyptian sunlight.

Strangely, it was the Egyptians who first found out how to make a vessel go to windward. In Egypt, the prevailing wind has always been from the north so that, fortuitously, the passage up the Nile against the current was simply a matter of hoisting a square sail and sitting and steering. The return voyage, aided by the stream, so it was not too bad, was accomplished under oars. The slaves did the rowing, so what matter? But they, and their meagre rations, took up room in the ship which could more profitably be used for cargo or paying passengers.

Then some ingenious fellow discovered that by tacking down one corner of the square sail to the stem, a laden boat, although almost certainly flat bottomed, would go in a windward direction by virtue of the keel surface of her sides. Thus, instead of eternally rowing down stream, it was possible to zig zag (or tack), between the river banks by harnessing the wind and, aided by the current, to make progress.

The square sail was not ideal for the purpose, but presently it was discovered that by tilting the yard so that the 'peak' of the sail pointed above the masthead, while the 'tack' came to the deck, and by adding a boom, a more efficient rig was devised. The Egyptian 'nuggar' used this rig for nearly two thousand years, but the triangular lateen sail gradually replaced it, and the remarkable sailing ability of the Arab dhow demonstrates its efficiency.

In the early Middle Ages, the lateen rig enabled the Venetians, Genoese, Spaniards and Portuguese to become great European maritime nations. Not easily reefed or quickly furled, the lateen sail is admirably suited to the equable Mediterranean weather. In the great days of trade-wind sailing, the square sail returned, but the Mediterraneans retained lateen spankers, while the Northern Europeans developed the gaff sail. But so far did the old rig of the Nile cast its spell that the balanced lug, with part of the sail before the mast, was still carried by many a small boat in Britain and Northern Europe as late as the early part of the twentieth century.

The Egyptians progressed far beyond the slab-sided, flat-bottomed barge, and designed hull forms which kept pace with the development of sails. Their influence can be traced as far east as Java, as an illustration in a Dutch book of travels published in 1598 discloses.

Strangely, the obvious advantages of windward sailing do not appear to have occurred to the Vikings, magnificent seamen, who deemed it dishonour to die on land, and whose elegant longboats retained square sails and oars many centuries after the Mediterraneans had developed the lateen.

The yacht, as we know it today, by far excels in windward ability anything that has gone before. How did it come about?

The Dutch, whose shallow waters forced them to build shoal draft vessels, are credited with the invention of the leeboard, although they probably owed it to the Spaniards, during their occupation of the Netherlands. Nevertheless, it was the centreboard which seems first to have been evolved.

In 1531, the Spaniards sent an expedition of two ships to the Pacific commanded by Bartolomé Ruiz. While sailing south of Panama he was surprised to sight a 'vessel', carrying a large sail. As he overhauled this 'vessel' he found that she was a native raft of huge trees of balsa, a very light wood, lashed tightly together and covered with light reeds. The large square cotton sail, spread by a yard, was supported by a bipod mast of two sturdy poles lashed together at the top.

The raft was steered by a crude rudder, but directional stability was conferred by a broad movable plank inserted between the logs. Ruiz was fascinated to see that this forerunner of the centreboard, correctly adjusted, with the sail set at the proper angle, enabled the raft to hold her course in almost any desired direction without the need for correction by oars or paddles. The 'Balsa', surmounted by a thatched hut, still serves as a convenient means of transport for passengers or goods on the rivers and along the comparatively calm shores of the Pacific in this part of South America.

43

The discovery of the movable keel or leeboard made a profound impression upon the navigators of that era. It seems probable that it was introduced from the Pacific into Holland by the Spanish who also influenced the construction, rig and, particularly, the decoration of Dutch ships.

At the end of the sixteenth century the Dutch sent two expeditions to cruise the South Seas. Both were accompanied by 'yachts'. Both returned safely after voyages of two and a half and three years, having proceeded safely through the Strait of Magellan and then home via the Cape of Good Hope. These were probably the first *yachts* to circumnavigate the globe; but they were vessels of considerable size. One named *Merry Messenger* was 150 tons, while *Hope*, the biggest ship in the fleet, was only 500 tons.

We do not know exactly how tonnage was calculated in those days. A paper recently published by the Society for Nautical Research traced it back to the custom of ordering ships for the wine trade by the number of tuns, large casks of wine, they were to carry. During the course of time, by common usage, the word 'tunnage' became 'tonnage'. These wine casks were about ten times the size of today's hogshead and weighed about a ton. We have therefore a fair idea of the displacement of ships of that time.

Yachts of that period, although fast, were well armed. In 1614, off the South American coast, one English so-called yacht *Sea Mew* sank *St Francis*, the flagship of a Spanish fleet under the command of Admiral Roderigo de Mendoza.

Yachts acted as despatch vessels to battle fleets until the end of the Napoleonic wars. They were still armed, for even when not on official duty they risked capture. As late as 1827 yachts of the Royal Yacht Squadron mounted guns which were much used for saluting and for calling attention to signals. A description of *Scorpion*, a cutter of 110 tons, built for racing, describes her as 'carrying four brass guns 4- and 6-pounders, an armoury of fine rifles, pistols and cutlasses, all by an eminent maker . . .'. Larger yachts even carried 18-pounders.

From time immemorial, the River Thames was much used for personal transport and commerce because roads were little better than cart tracks and beset by footpads. Important personages were rowed in barges, but it was not until the accession of Charles II to the throne that sailing for pleasure on its waters began.

It is therefore understandable that in Holland, where windmills were commonplace, and where there was as much water as land, or thereabouts, that travel by water was accomplished under sail. The origin of the yacht, even in Holland, is obscure, probably because it had long been accepted as a part of normal life. The earliest mention is to be found in an account of a great water-festival at Amsterdam, on 17 March 1580, in honour of Prince William I of Orange. The occasion was his return home after the successful resistance by the eastern provinces of the Netherlands against the Spaniards. Taking part were three vessels disguised as Spanish galleys, six yachts, three boeiers (fishing vessels?), and other craft. There are records of other important water-festivities in which yachts took part, in 1638 for the reception of Maria de Medici and, in 1697, in honour of the Tzar Peter the Great, who went to Holland to learn shipbuilding in a shipyard in Zaandam where yachts are still built today. All these events took place before the then beautiful waterfront of Amsterdam, which was lost when the Central Railway Station was built.

In the early part of the seventeenth century there were three 'yacht harbours' in Amsterdam which were run like a Guild. At least once a year, 'Admiral Sailing' took place. Fleets were drawn up each under its 'Admiral' who gave orders for various manoeuvres, by flag signals, to the accompaniment of much firing of guns, the purpose of which was to draw attention to the flags. Sham fights were also part of the proceedings. They were either re-enactments of famous battles or just mock fights for the sheer joy of it. Afterwards there followed a great banquet with abundant drinking. These events take place in Holland to this day, banquet included.

The word 'yacht' is derived from the Dutch 'jaght' meaning something swift, to do with hunting or pursuing. The word is a corruption of the verb 'jachten' which means to hurry, which is still part of the Dutch language. It was applied to swift things such as 'jacht-Hond' (hunting dog), or 'jaght-Vogel', to do with falconry. A 'yacht' was originally a small, fast vessel which accompanied the fleets of cargo ships either to Portugal or to the Baltic. Yachts acted as messengers and ferried people either between ships or from ship to shore. They were particularly useful at intermediate ports where taking a big unhandy sailing ship into a strange harbour was a laborious and tedious business, quite apart from disorganizing the fleet. In those days merchant ships sailed in convoy for safety and therefore manoeuvred like a battle fleet because chaos and stragglers made them vulnerable to attack. Such yachts were known as 'Staten Jachten' and owned, not by individuals, but by the East India Company, by corporations and by townships.

The word yacht was unknown in the English language until Evelyn, in 1661 referring to the yacht *Mary*, recorded in his diary that yachts, or pleasure boats, 'Were not known among us . . . till the Dutch East India Company presented that "curious piece" to the King [Charles II].' Charles, during his exile, had lived in Holland, and because of his great love of sailing, the Dutch had placed their finest yacht at his disposal. She was one built for the Prince of Orange and the largest of a fleet of thirteen yachts used by the Prince, his entourage, and by persons of rank.

Charles was so delighted with the yacht that, on his return to England, he asked to have one built like her. The Burgomaster of Amsterdam at once offered, as a parting gift, a yacht of the same size recently built in Amsterdam. Charles did not accept her as a present but arranged that she should be bought by the Board of Admiralty. Even so, the kindly Dutch, with whom Britain was to be at war within four years, lavishly decorated the vessel with carvings and gildings. Their best artists were commissioned to make beautiful paintings and sculptures 'with which to embellish her within and without'. The yacht *Mary* duly arrived on the Thames and was also described by Pepys.

We have a fairly accurate picture of *Mary* from contemporary Dutch paintings. She set a cutter rig on her single mast. Her large gaff mainsail was loose-footed with two rows of reef points. She carried a staysail from the stemhead and a jib on a steeved-up bowsprit upon which the national flag was flown from a small jack-staff. On her *gilded* topmast she set a square topsail, and from her topmasthead she flew a huge royal standard, while, on her stern, she carried a large 'red ensign'. Her high poop was adorned with much painting and gilded carving and surmounted by three lanterns. Ornamented gun ports ran the length of her topsides, which were painted with a broad band of royal blue. The after-ports were probably windows, for she only carried six guns. The whole effect must have been incredibly picturesque.

This handy rig was used throughout the first half of the nineteenth century in small fast vessels such as revenue cutters. The square topsail served much the same service as today's auxiliary motor. With it, the vessel could be hove-to, turned in her own length, or even made to go astern.

Nothing like the yacht *Mary* had been seen in British waters, but similar vessels were soon being built by famous shipwrights on the Thames and Medway such as Commissioner Pett, Sir Pheneas Pett, W. Castle, and at Portsmouth by Sir Anthony Deane. Twenty-eight yachts were built for the King between 1661 and 1670, ranging from 25 to 180 tons, carrying crews of four to forty-five men. *Mary* was 52 feet and 100 tons burden. *Bezan*, also presented by the Dutch, was much smaller, being only 35 tons.

Catherine, 94 tons, was built at Deptford by Commissioner Pett for the King's brother, the Duke of York. According to Evelyn, it was with her that, on 1 October 1661, he challenged the King to a race from Greenwich to Gravesend and back for a stake of £100.

His Majesty in his new yacht *Anne*, 100 tons, built at Woolwich by Christopher Pett, won, 'sometimes having taken the helm himself'.

Evelyn records that the King's barge and kitchen boat were in attendance, and that he (Evelyn) was taken aboard '. . . where we all eate together with His Majesty'. The 'kitchen boat' was another heritage from the Dutch who went in for great feasts aboard their yachts.

Two hundred and sixty years were to pass before another English King took the helm of his own yacht in a race starting on the River Thames. On 16 July 1921, King George V raced his mighty 221-ton cutter *Britannia* from Southend to Harwich, beating *White Heather*, 179 tons, and *Nyria*, 169 tons.

Pepys has many references to yachts, never forgetting his 'vittels', in his inimitable day-to-day accounts of his life and times. Here is perhaps one of the first accounts of a cruise, a short one, but merry and in pleasant surroundings, in days when cattle grazed on the banks of the Thames outside the towns while the Swale and Medway were rural and the waters comparatively unpolluted.

> *2 March 1663*   We went down four or five miles [below Woolwich] with extraordinary pleasure, it being a fine day and a brave gale of wind, and had some oysters brought us aboard newly taken, which were excellent and ate with great pleasure. There also coming into the river two Dutchmen, we sent a couple of men on board, and bought three Holland's cheeses, cost 4d apiece, excellent cheeses.

His comments on the behaviour of Sir W. Batten's yacht are a delight.

> At my lady's desire with them by coach to Greenwich where I went aboard with them on the *Charlotte* yacht. The wind being fresh I believe they will all be sicke enough, besides that she is *mighty troublesome on the water.*

Samuel Pepys, MA, FRS, Clerk of the Acts and Secretary to the Admiralty (to give him his full title), seems to have had the run of the royal yachts when not in use by his Royal Master, and good use he made of them, to his, and now to our, pleasure. In two short paragraphs he paints a gay picture:

> *17 August 1665*   To the *Bezan* yacht [at Greenwich] where Sir W. Batten, Sir J. Minnes, My Lord Brouncker and myself with some servants on the yacht and down we went most pleasantly. Short of Gravesend, it grew calme, and so we came to an anchor, and to supper mighty merry, and after it, being moonshine we out of the cabbin to laugh and talk, and then as we grew sleepy, went in, and upon the velvet cushions of the King's that belong to the yacht fell to sleep.

18 August 1665 Up at five o'clock and dressed ourselves, and to sayle again down to the *Soveraigne* at the buoy at the Nore and thence to Sheernesse. Thence with great pleasure up the Meadeway, our yacht contending with Commissioner Petts, wherein he met us from Chatham, and he had the best of it.

Before 1700, most yachts, of which anything is known, were either Royal or State owned. There is little doubt, however, that both Dutch and Englishmen also used small craft for pleasure. Pepys (in 1683) says: 'Colonel Wyndham is the only gentleman of State ever known to addict himself to the sea for pleasure. . . .'

To Roger North, born 1651, a barrister and younger son of the fourth Baron North, we are indebted for a description of a cruise on the East Coast, so fresh and vivid that it might well have been written in the early part of this century when navigation of the East Coast rivers and shoals was under sail. It is significant that he did not appear to think it unusual.

The early yachts dating from King Charles II's *Mary* were little ships. This we know from contemporary pictures, but no pains were spared to make them as fast as possible. The importance of good sails was already appreciated and the best Holland duck was imported. Expense was no object. *Catherine*, for instance, had a new suit of sails within two months of launching.

The matter of ballast was also given much thought. At that time ships were normally ballasted with stones as they had been since the days when, *circa* AD 80, the Romans dumped their ballast on arrival at Fishbourne on Chichester Harbour before loading grain for the return voyage. On 19 September 1663 Christopher Pett, the famous shipbuilder, wrote:

> If stones are used instead of shot for ballast of the King's new yacht she will be damaged, for the quantity of stones required would make it needful to half fill the cabin, and would make her run to leeward.

The word 'shot' conjures up visions of iron cannon balls, but yachts were ballasted with *lead*, using scrap musket shot from the Tower of London.

This appreciation of the need to have heavy ballast as low as possible was, to some extent, also lost sight of during the next two hundred years. Yachts in Britain, and later in America, were ballasted internally with iron or iron ore. It was considered a great innovation when the iron ballast of the schooner *America* was specially cast to fit between her floors and frames in order to get it as low as possible to increase stability and the power of the vessel. External ballast was not thought of for another fifty years.

Seventeenth-century yachts used neither centreboards nor lee-boards to help them to windward. Although the latter were known in Holland at that time they were used only for small flat-bottomed boats. As already mentioned, credit for the centreboard certainly belongs to South America. Over two hundred years after Ruiz, in 1774, Admiral Schank is reported to have been the first to fit a centre-board to a boat. Subsequently many of the ships of the Royal Navy were designed with three or even four centreboards. Contemporary models of them can be seen in the National Maritime Museum at Greenwich. The Admiral's invention would not be the first to be forestalled, for William Bourne in his book *Inventions and Devices* (1578) had this to say:

> Wherefore if you would have a Shippe to draw but a little water, and to sail well by the winde, then doe this. She must have a flat bottome, like as the Binelanders and Plaites . . . in Flanders. . . . That place where as the Keele should stand must open into the Shippe, and made tight on both sides as high and deep as the Shippe doth goe into the water when she is loden, and in that there must be made a thing to be letten downe, and to be wound up again as neede shall require . . . and then that will not suffer the Shippe to go to Leewardes. . . .

Although the catamaran is comparatively new to yachting in this country it is common knowledge that it is probably of Polynesian origin—but what about this? Pepys reports:

> *22 December 1664* I went to the launching of a new ship of two bottoms invented by Sir William Petty . . . his Majesty being present gave her the name of the *Experiment*.

She was lost in a storm at sea in the Bay of Biscay, and although much was said to her detriment—which is usual when someone has the courage to do something different—fifteen other vessels 'mis-carried' (Pepys). That she was a success, there is little doubt. She made a record run on the Irish Mail service. Her high speed with shallow draft were among her advantages rightly claimed by her designer.

From the writings of Bourne, Sir W. Petty (who Pepys tells us was eminent in mathematics and mechanics) and other contem-poraries, we learn that the importance of light displacement was studied and appreciated in the late sixteenth and seventeenth centuries. The naval architects of that time were able to calculate displacement from the plans of a vessel. Little progress was made in yacht architecture until the latter half of the nineteenth century. Yachts of the Water Club of the Harbour of Cork (later the Royal Cork Yacht Club) established in 1720 appear from contemporary illustrations to differ but little from those of the days of Charles II, although they were shorn of much of their gilding and scrollwork.

The advantages of the centreboard did not penetrate the skulls of English yachtsmen until, in about 1800, Commodore Taylor of the Cumberland Fleet had built a yacht with no fewer than five centreboards. The pivoted centreboard was devised by Captain Shouldham in 1809 but thereafter forgotten.

Yachts were still heavily built, like miniature warships, despatch vessels and revenue cutters, and mounted guns until well on in the nineteenth century. The thoughts of Petty and others had been disregarded.

The arrival in British waters of the schooner *America* in 1851 set the cat among the pigeons. She was followed by the little American 3½ ton *Truant* (1852), a light displacement, centreboard boat, with a rig far in advance of her time. On the Thames she outsailed her English rivals by an 'immense distance'.

Organized yacht racing in England was not practised until the foundation of the Cumberland Fleet in about 1775. It was so called after the Duke of Cumberland, Admiral of the White and younger brother of King George III. The Royal Cork Yacht Club, already mentioned, did not race, but cruised 'in company' every spring tide between April and September. This exercise was similar to Admiral Sailing as practised by the Dutch, and was also followed by a dinner regulated by quaint rules which are well worth quoting, if only in part:

> RESOLVED: That no Admiral presume to bring more than two Dozens of Wine to his Treat . . . except when my Lords the Judges are invited.
>
> ORDERED: That no long-tail Wigs, large Sleeves or Ruffles be worn . . .
>
> RESOLVED: That all Business of the club be done before Dinner . . .
>
> ORDERED: That . . . no Man be allowed more than one bottle to his Share and a Peremptory.

There are also sailing rules:

> ORDERED: That when any of the Fleet join the Admiral, if they have no guns to salute, they are to give three Cheers, which are to be returned by the Admiral, and one Cheer to be returned by the Captain so saluting.

If the Royal Cork contributed little to the sport of yacht racing or to yacht architecture, it established the concept of the Yacht Club and the gathering together of amateur seafarers to practise navigation and to meet socially.

The Cumberland Fleet, fifty-five years later, began organized racing for cups presented by the Duke of Cumberland and by the proprietor of Vauxhall Gardens on the River Thames, which, as the Fleet had no clubhouse, were its headquarters.

It is to the Cumberland Fleet that we owe the introduction of the word 'Regatta'. It was borrowed from the Venetians who so described their annual gondola races held on the Grand Canal with the whole populace *en fête*. The Fleet's Regatta took place on Friday, 23 June 1775, on the Thames. Guns were fired, church bells rang. There were rowing and sailing races. Thousands of people either lined the banks, crowded the bridges or were afloat: '. . . everything from a dung barge to a wherry was in motion. . . . There was feasting and dancing.'

Racing rules were primitive. Competition was keen and, at times, tempers ran high. It is recorded that, as a result of a collision, the crew of one yacht slashed away the rigging of another with cutlasses. Smaller yachts such as those taking part in these races were armed with muskets and cutlasses. The flags of the Cumberland Fleet are still preserved in the Royal Thames Yacht Club in London.

The next club of note was formed by some forty-five noblemen and gentlemen in 1815 in London at the Thatched House Tavern in St James's Street. It was known as 'The Yacht Club'. It held its first 'Meetings', later known as 'Regattas', at Cowes, where a house on the Parade, now the Gloster Hotel, was leased. In 1857 the club moved into the Castle, which is its present headquarters. It was granted the title 'Royal' in 1820, the first club to have this distinction, and eventually became the 'Royal Yacht Squadron'.

The Squadron's yachts, built to race, contributed to the art of naval architecture, for they outsailed the smaller Naval vessels and revenue cutters with ease—this was recognized by the Admiralty because, at that time, Britain still relied for her naval power upon the 'wooden walls'. In time of war the Squadron's yachts would have been invaluable as despatch vessels.

During the remaining part of the century yacht and sailing clubs were formed on rivers, estuaries and around the coast of Britain, and in 1897 eighty-one of them were recognized by the Yacht Racing Association. That body was formed in 1875 to codify the yacht racing rules. These, with various modifications, served the world until 1959 when a new universal rule was adopted. It was based upon the old and those of the North American Yacht Racing Union, which had broken away around 1950.

The YRA served yacht racing interests until after the second World War when, by a logical process, it became the Royal Yachting Association, which now embraces over 1,500 clubs.

By the mid-nineteenth century, yacht racing was centred mainly at Cowes on the Solent. It was a pastime of the wealthy, and vessels of 100 to 300 tons were commonplace. Design had made but little progress since the early part of the century, when the arrival of the schooner *America*, built by a syndicate of the New York Yacht Club, shook British yachtsmen out of their complacency and revolutionized yacht design in Britain. Her hull, rig and sails were so much in advance of the Squadron Fleet that she completely outsailed them all. She won the RYS Challenge Cup, afterwards known as the America's Cup, which still remains in the NYYC Clubhouse despite all attempts to dislodge it.

The next great step in yacht design was made when the Clyde yacht architect, John Inglis, conceived the idea of an outside lead ballast keel blended into the sections of the yacht so that hull and keel were one. It remained for G. L. Watson to go a step further. Doubting the ability of a wooden yacht to withstand the strains imposed by a lead keel of some fifty tons bolted to her keelson, he designed the steel cutter *Vanduara* (90 tons) in 1880. She was a complete success. He then turned his attention to composite con-struction—wood planking on steel frames—and, in 1893, *Britannia* (221 tons) emerged. With her cut away forefoot, bow overhang and perfectly matching counter stern, proportionately low wetted surface and easy sections, she set the form of the modern yacht which, with variations, has persisted until the present day.

She was the greatest racing yacht of all time. Bought by the Prince of Wales, afterwards King Edward VII, she was inherited by King George V and by the uncrowned Edward VIII who, not interested in yachting, had her scuttled rather than allow her to fall upon evil days.

Rigs have changed, weight aloft has been progressively reduced. In 1921 C. E. Nicholson introduced the Bermudan rig which abolished the topsail and spars and much running gear. It was much lighter, more efficient than gaff rig, and easier on the crew. He first used it with great success on the 169 ton cutter *Nyria*. Today, no yachtsman or dinghy sailor would use any other rig.

The first World War killed the huge sailing and steam yachts which, during Cowes Week, lined the Roads or raced in the big schooner class. The steam yachts were replaced by the more efficient and compact diesel vessels. The great sailing yachts just faded away and nothing took their place.

Between the wars the International Classes, from the 5-ton Six-Metre to the 200-ton J boat, formed the backbone of the racing fleets, but the second World War ended all that. These beautiful yachts would have been prohibitively expensive to build and main-tain. The Six-Metres struggled on for a time, but made way for the

Dragons, local one-design classes, and 5·5-Metres, but the last never achieved much popularity.

Just prior to the second World War the younger generation took to dinghy racing, and the planing boat made its debut. The 14-ft International was the forerunner of the vast fleets of racing dinghies which dominate today's racing scene.

It was in 1906 that the Americans staged the first offshore race from Newport to Bermuda. It became a popular annual event, so much so that in 1925 Britain sailed the first Fastnet Race of 600 miles. After it, the Royal Ocean Racing Club (RORC) was formed. Both races now alternate biennially. The sport of offshore racing has become firmly rooted and has many followers on both sides of the Atlantic as well as in the Antipodes and South African waters.

Offshore racing has led to the development of magnificent sea-going yachts, and to the development of sails and gear of great reliability, strength and efficiency undreamed of when the first race was sailed.

Now the chemists, the scientists, and the metallurgists are giving us stronger hulls, better sails, lighter masts and improved running and standing rigging, as well as compact electronic navigational instruments of great accuracy and reliability.

Today, thousands take their recreation on the water, in all manner of craft, and yachts cruise far and wide, cross oceans, circumnavigate the world, and race in gale force winds when a couple of decades ago they would have hove-to. We have come a long way from Charles II's *Mary*. In doing so, the picturesque, the glamour and the embellishment have given way to clean unadorned grace—to purposeful, urgent yachts.

Yachting has become an international sport, bringing men of many nations together with a common love of the sea and in a spirit of friendly competition.

John Masefield's poem *The Ship** sums it up:

> I march across great waters like a queen,
> I whom so many wisdoms helped to make;
> Over the uncruddled billows of seas green
> I blanch the bubbled highway of my wake.
> By me my wandering tenants clasp the hands
> And know the thoughts of men in other lands.

* Quoted by kind permission of The Society of Authors as the literary representative of the Estate of John Masefield.

You will recognize the exact spot, Sir, for I happen to know that you have passed it on one of your birdwatching and photographic safaris to Ethiopia. You will certainly have passed it, but you may not have given it more than a routine glance. There are many such places in Africa. It consists of a small muddy beach about the size of a tennis court, sloping down to an insignificant, dirty yellow stream.

I should have passed it by myself that morning but for a lucky accident. The accident was one of time. I was driving with wildlife cameraman Dieter Plage across the bush to the lake called Abiata—where you have taken pictures also. The time, as we passed the beach, was exactly five past nine.

At four minutes past nine, the sky had been empty of birdlife, except for the odd ibis and cormorant flighting overhead on a fishing trip to another of the Rift Valley lakes, probably Langano—the muddy little stream connects Lake Abiata with Langano. One minute later, the view through the dusty windscreen of the Land-Rover was practically blotted out by birds. The birds flew in two extremely high velocity streams. One passed directly in front of the vehicle's radiator: the other, travelling in the opposite direction, away from the beach, poured back ten yards beyond the tailboard. We were caught, as it were, in a crossfire of birds, thousands upon thousands of birds.

The birds were golden yellow and, from the chortling noise they made—which was quite deafening—there was no doubt what they were. They were chestnut-bellied sandgrouse.

You will have seen these birds in Africa, I am sure, many times and will know very well how they flight in swarms to certain water-holes, in the early morning, to take their only drink of the day.

Having taken a few sips of water, the sandgrouse fly back to the dried-up savannah, or often into the desert, where they spend the rest of the long hot day. The arrival of a hundred sandgrouse is something you barely take note of. Even a thousand is nothing to get excited about. But it now became clear that we had driven by accident into one of the greatest concentrations of these birds that has ever been seen.

You, Sir, will have seen many fantastic wildlife sights. The migration of a quarter of a million wildebeeste on the plains of Serengeti

COLIN WILLOCK

is certainly one of these. Like you, I have seen these things, but what was taking place now, literally round our heads, was easily the most exciting event I have ever witnessed in the wild.

We climbed out of the Land-Rover and stood by it, ducking involuntarily as parties of birds arrowed past our heads. The sand-grouse took no notice of us or of our vehicle. The water on that one small beach was all that they were interested in.

After a very few minutes, the last bird had drunk and disappeared into the blue and burning morning sky. The waterhole was silent again. It was clear that we had arrived in time for only part of the performance and then, being taken by surprise, had not really appreciated its finer points. We determined to come back next morning with film cameras and to arrive in plenty of time.

We were at the beach by eight o'clock. There might not have been a sandgrouse in the whole of the Ethiopian Rift. We set up cameras, including a remote control Arrieflex down on the sand where we hoped the birds would land.

For half an hour we waited with growing impatience. Were the birds coming? Was their previous performance a fluke, a one-off event which would never occur again? At twenty-five to nine there was a welcome chortling in the sky as about thirty black dots appeared against the distant mountains. They circled over the mile of thornbush-dotted savannah that lay on our bank of the stream. But, instead of heading for the water as we had expected, they landed half a mile back in the grass.

It seemed that at least a few sandgrouse were going to oblige. We need not have worried. In the next half-hour, flights, squadrons, whole wings of sandgrouse arrived, wheeling round like starlings—only much faster—whirling like those dense formations of knot one sees over the salt marshes in winter and then landing, every one of them, on the open savannah.

This mass arrival was impressive enough. By nine o'clock, the savannah for a mile back from the water was golden with birds. At last they all fell silent. No more were coming. Then, as if a signal had been given, the first parties were up and calling. Almost at once the whole mass was in the air.

The speed at which a bird's reflexes must work to keep formation in such company defeats the human mind. Often the parties appeared to fly through each other, or to veer off in a vertical bank at the last split second to avoid collision. We guessed that there must be at least forty thousand birds in that one comparatively small patch of sky. At five-past nine, at precisely the same moment as on the morning before, the first tentative party of about twenty came in to see if the bar was open.

56

This time we were under an acacia tree at the waterside, on one side of the beach, so we could watch every detail of the drama at twenty yards range through viewfinder and binoculars. Drama it certainly was. The beach was most conveniently shaped from the birds' point of view. It favoured a perfect air traffic system. The sandgrouse seemed to understand when they were in the circuit.

About thirty yards from the water, and precisely in the centre of the bank leading down to the beach, stood two acacia trees. The parties made their approach through the gap on the far side of these trees, landed, taxied down to the water's edge to refuel. When they took off, they left the airfield by the gap on our side of these trees. During the first minute or so of the flight, the need for this one-way system did not seem especially important. There was plenty of air space for all.

But the situation quickly altered. All those airborne thousands first had to get the drink they had flown anything up to thirty miles for. They all seemed determined to drink at once. As soon as two or three hundred sandgrouse had touched down, five hundred landed behind them, and a thousand beyond them. The front rank of birds were now scooping up water as fast as they could go. Each bird took not less than four sips though not one that we watched appeared to drink more than nine times. No sooner had one finished, than it took off vertically, its place being taken by the bird behind, the whole vast concourse moving forward like a rippling golden carpet down the beach. Few human crowds are so orderly.

The process had by now become continuous, with birds pouring out past us with a roar of wings as replacements came rushing out of the sky on the far side of the trees. The noise was deafening. The feeling that the sandgrouse were actually pressing down on you by sheer weight of numbers was, in a ridiculous way, slightly frightening. It was like a scene from Alfred Hitchcock's thriller, *The Birds*, only far more so. Towards the end it was impossible to see beach or much of the sky above it. Sandgrouse obliterated everything.

At ten minutes past nine, the pace slackened a little. A minute and a half later, the last bird had gone. The beach was empty and silent save for some mourning doves and a speckled pigeon. The entire explosion of life might never have happened. It had, in fact, lasted exactly six and a half minutes.

Of course, we did not get all the film we would have liked on that first occasion. Even had we done so, I believe we would have continued to get up early and drive the twenty miles across country just to see the whole thing happen again and again, for as long as it continued.

We did come the next five mornings. Each time the flight happened exactly on the schedule. It never lasted less than six minutes and the whole mighty concourse of birds never required more than nine minutes to get their one drink of the day.

One morning we were able to bring Leslie Brown, one of the most distinguished ornithologists in Africa with us. Leslie, as you know, Sir, is not given to exaggeration and is rightly inclined only to believe the evidence of his own eyes. So we briefed him with caution and some trepidation. 'Possibly as many as 30,000 birds,' I told him. 'Nonsense,' he said, or words to that effect.

When the assembly on the grassland began, I could see that the great birdman was impressed. 'At least 40,000,' he admitted, though I noted that later on he talked about 50,000, which was the estimate both Dieter Plage and myself had arrived at independently. Fifty thousand birds all drinking their fill in well under ten minutes. Even for a self-service restaurant, it is something of an accomplishment!

By the sixth morning, we had shot three thousand feet of film and had every aspect of the matter covered and 'in the can', including the assembly out on the grass. We would go back to record all the sound effects just one more time. But at five o'clock on that last morning it rained for an hour—hard.

We waited by the magic beach for a long, long time. Not a sand-grouse appeared. Nor did they come at any time during that day or even during the next week. The birds were getting their refreshment elsewhere, out in the no longer dried-up bush. There was no need to fly twenty or thirty miles to our sloping beach.

Some time, when conditions are dry enough, it will undoubtedly all happen again. In the meantime, we have it all on film. Luck had been with us, for once. And that, when it comes to taking pictures of wildlife, is a phenomenon, I'm sure you will agree, almost as rare as blundering into a cloud of 50,000 sandgrouse.

DAPHNE DU MAURIER

A Winter's Afternoon, Kilmarth

It is the idle half-hour succeeding lunch, when having written a number of unnecessary letters all the morning, I can sip black coffee and smoke the first cigarette of the day. The back pages of yesterday's newspapers are still unread, and it is my whim to contrast the current weather report with the advertisements for winter holidays in Cornwall. 'The ridge of low pressure now approaching our western seaboard will deepen, and the showers at present falling on the Scilly Isles and Cornwall will become heavy at times, turning to hail and thunder on higher ground. Winds will increase to gale force, veering south-westerly to west, and later in the day temperatures may fall to 28 degrees. Outlook for the next two days cold and unsettled, with gales locally.'

I glance out of the window. My informant on the radio was right. The pine-trees beyond the garden wall, planted by some Victorian predecessor in the belief that whatever suited the Scottish climate would defy the elements equally well in Cornwall—and how wise he was—are beginning to sway, while massive clouds, driven by some demon force, bank the far horizon, reminding me of a rather too elaborate production of *Macbeth*.

I turn to the advertisements in the newspaper. 'Double your Sunshine and Come to Lovely Looe.' Looe is a few miles along the coast, and that foremost cloud, vast as a witch's trailing cloak, will be upon it in exactly four minutes. There are, however, further blandishments westward across the bay. 'Visit Mevagissey, the Fishing Village with the Continental Touch.' Mevagissey is already blotted out with rain, but doubtless some winter visitor lured by summer memories of the Côte d'Azur, is now scurrying from the quayside in search of a Casino with an affable croupier in charge bidding him '*Faites vos jeux*'. There may be one or two slot-machines still in action but I doubt it.

The hotels along the coast offer more tempting vistas still. 'A gleaming jewel on a sun-drenched bay. Balconies to every bedroom . . .', but enough. Being myself no visitor to these shores, but an inhabitant, on and off, for over forty years, and having recently moved from a sheltered house in woodlands to my present home on 'higher ground' threatened by that same hail and thunder announced over the radio, I am anxious to prove my mettle. There is, perhaps, an 'Award Scheme for Courage In The Over-Sixties' brewing in the minds of princes, and I could qualify. Besides, the dog needs exercise.

Dressed like Tolstoy in his declining years, fur-cap with ear-flaps, padded jerkin, and rubber boots to the knee, I venture forth. Moray, my West Highland terrier, taking one look at the sky, backs swiftly into the porch, but brutally, I urge him on, and we cross the garden to the fields beyond. Where I lived before, at Menabilly, there was a shaded path known as the Palm Walk, and on rainy or windy days, flanked by tall trees, I could amble along it peacefully, snipping at the drooping heads of blue hydrangeas still in bloom. Here, at Kilmarth, I know no such lassitude. The sloping field I am bound to traverse, if I walk at all, is under plough, and the herd of South Devon cattle who tramp daily across the as yet unsown soil, having first satiated themselves with roots a little further down, have turned the field into another Passchendaele. 'This,' I tell myself, 'is what Tommy endured as a subaltern in the first World War' (Tommy being my late husband), and inspired by the thought, I sink into craters made by the South Devons, wondering if Mr Mitchell the farmer could have cross-bred his prize herd with Yaks from Tibet. The cattle, less courageous than myself, did not linger long on the 'higher ground' but have already sought shelter in the farmyard out of sight, having advanced milking-time by at least two hours.

Shaking my feet clear of Passchendaele, and avoiding the electric fence which guards the roots, I climb over the stile that leads to the grazing-land above the cliffs, thinking how closely I must resemble a veteran at the Battle of Ypres. Moray, flicking his ears, runs like a greyhound to a favourite molehill which he is wont to anoint as a matter of routine. This ritual, if nothing else, will make his day. Mr Mitchell's flock of sheep, taking him for a marauder and mistaking the action, begin to scatter. Heavy with lamb, some of them strangely decorated about the head with brambles, they have a bizarre crowned appearance of beasts bound for some sacrificial slaughter.

Remembering the doomed flock plunging over the cliffs to destruction in the film of *Far from the Madding Crowd*, I hold my breath; but after a brief and hesitating pause, they labour up the hill in a north-westerly direction making for home, and I breathe again. It is Moray and I who turn seaward to brave the full force of the gale.

It is a stupendous sight that meets my eyes. Thirteen ships are anchored in the bay, rolling their guts out in a cauldron sea. I can make out a couple of Dutchmen, a Dane, a German, and I think a Norwegian flag amongst them, but the shelter of Par Harbour will not be theirs this night, for it is already high water, and the docks are full. What if their cables drag, scarce a mile distant, off this lee-shore? The only hope up-steam and out of it, rounding the Gribbin Head to the Fowey estuary.

I put up my arm in salutation, not to the courage of the seamen on board, but in a vain attempt to ward the hail out of my eyes. Below me the sea thunders on Bûly Beach, so called because of the white stones—Bûly—that lie upon it. Rounded, flat, scattered here and there upon the sand, these stones make excellent target on a summer's day for the anointing Moray while I swim. Now, as the incoming rollers break upon them and lash the cliffs, only to withdraw with an ominous sucking sound, the white stones have a ghastly resemblance to drowning ewes, and for a moment I fear that my vision of the scene from *Far from the Madding Crowd* has in part come true. The stones do not loll though in the surf, but remain submerged, and I am spared winning an award for gallantry and plunging to the rescue of mangled carcasses; indeed I could not have done so, for the descent to the beach itself is swept by a sea at least six feet high. This is disappointing. There is a cave on Bûly beach into which the hail would not have penetrated, and although damp and eerie and smelling of old bones, had it been half-tide I could have stood there like Prospero, watching the storm, the faithful Moray Ariel at my side. Which reminds me, where *is* Moray? I look about me, shouting in vain against the wind. Seized with sudden panic I climb up the stony track, away from the beach, to the cliffs above. I can just see his white rump disappearing along the muddied path in the direction of the only shelter known to his dog instinct, a hedge of thorn about a hundred yards distant that overhangs a drop known locally as Little Hell. The place is aptly named. God only knows what drowning seafarer in centuries past caught a glimpse of it from an upturned boat and cursed it as he sank. Or, perchance, an irate farmer, a predecessor of Mr Mitchell from Trill Farm, driven to a frenzy by a scolding wife, hurled himself and her to merciful oblivion. Either, or all three, dubbed the spot thus.

The ravine is cut out of the cliff face, and the potential suicide is only spared from the goal he seeks by a strand of barbed wire, and what appears to be the single bar of an old bedstead—doubtless forming part of the frenzied farmer's connubial couch—with three straggling thorn-bushes beyond. He cannot see the depths below, so steep is the incline, and a torn sack masks the final sickening drop, but at high tide, as it is today, an evil hiss surges some two hundred feet beneath him, fair warning of the fate awaiting trespass. Moray has sense, all the same. The thorn bushes, bent backwards over the muddied path, make an effective arbour in a space of about three feet square; it is, in fact, our only haven in a world gone temporarily mad. He awaits me, hunched and disapproving.

We crouch side by side above Little Hell, enduring some of that same discomfort that political prisoners experienced in that torture chamber of the Tower of London known as Little Ease, but at least the hail is no longer in my face and the rain is driving slantways above my head, missing my humped knees by a few inches. It is some comfort to think of all the things I would rather *not* be doing. Ringing the front door bell of people I don't know well, but whose invitation to drinks has been reluctantly accepted, and as the door opens being met by the conversational roar of those guests already arrived. . . .

Standing in the Model Gown department of a smart London store, endeavouring to squeeze myself into an outfit designed for someone half my age, and as I grapple with a zip fastener that will not meet, becoming aware of the bored and pitying eye of the saleswoman in charge. . . .

Circling any airport in a fog, or worse still, waiting for the fog to lift and sitting in the airport lounge hemmed in by bores, all of them bent on exchanging their life history. . . . Meditation, after twenty minutes or so, is cut short by the realization that a stream from the field above, which disappeared mysteriously under the muddied path on which I crouch, is pouring its tumbling waters into a miniature Niagara behind my back, before descending to Little Hell.

It is time to move. Struggling to my feet, and glancing upward, I perceive, miraculously, that the hail has ceased, the black pall of the sky has parted into jagged shades of blue, and the sun itself is breaking through, gold, all-powerful, like the face of God. The scene is utterly transformed. The rollers in the bay are milky white, boisterous, lovely, even wilder than before, and being graced now with the sun's touch all malevolence has gone. The vessels plunging at their cables dance as if to a fairground's tune, and one of them, the Dutchman, lets forth a siren blast of triumph, and begins to move slowly, majestically, towards Par Harbour. The port is jammed with shipping. Every berth seems full. Derricks appear to intertwine, criss-crossed at every angle, and now that the wind has shifted a few points west it brings the welcome sound of industry, power plants at work, engines whining, men hammering, chimneys pouring out great plumes of smoke, white and curling like the sea. Pollution? Nonsense, the sight is glorious! Later the remaining ships at anchor will dock in turn, load up with china clay, and plough back across the Channel to their home port destination.

The white waste from the clay, bemoaned by some, scatters a filmy dust upon the working sheds, and the bay itself has all the froth and dazzle of a milk-churn spilt into a turbulent pool. Tourists may seek the golden sands of holiday brochures if they like, but to swim in such a sea is ecstasy—I have tried it, and I know! Suddenly, out of nowhere, the birds appear. Oyster-catchers, with their panic call and rapid wing-beat; curlew, more mysterious, aloof, the whistling cry surely portending sorrow; and then like leaves uptossed in all directions, but swerving, dipping, to their leader's flight, a flock of starlings, soaring for the sheer joy of motion, their ultimate destination the ploughed fields of Passchendaele above. Which coward-like I cannot face. Not for a second time this afternoon those crater muddied depths. Nor the climb itself, so easy to descend, but seen from Little Hell, the peak of Everest itself.

So, for Moray and myself, the more easy gradient of the cliff path that will finally lead us in roundabout fashion to a little wood of about four and a half acres, which forms part of Kilmarth domain. My lease made mention of certain 'sporting rights' and for this splendid bonus I pay a shilling a year.

I am not quite sure what I had in mind when the lease was signed. Possibly sons-in-law wearing tweeds, armed with Purdey guns and calling 'Over' as pheasants swerved above their heads, the same pheasants gracing the dinner-table at a later date. Or, on a less ambitious note, the more doubtful pleasure of lunch on pigeon pie. (I read once that pigeon eaten on three consecutive days brought certain death.) Be that as it may, the pheasant's call and the pigeon's flutter is absent this afternoon, the only thing to stir except the trees themselves is a ragged crow, who launches himself from a dead branch at my approach, and croaks his way to Passchendaele.

It is not everyone, however, who is sole tenant of sporting rights, and as Moray plunges into the wood, and I pitch after him, I must admit I walk the narrow path with a certain swagger. Possession is short-lived. As I trip over a rhododendron root and round a corner, I come upon an elderly man leaning against a tree, a gun at the ready. As Moray barks, he turns and stares. Is this the moment to stand, as they say, my ground? One of my predecessors at Kilmarth, a formidable lady by all accounts, who held sway some fifty years ago, and was said to commune with the spirit world, and had for escort when she walked a flock of peacocks and a pack of collie dogs, also a donkey wearing a beribboned hat, would have handled the situation with aplomb. Not so her present-day successor.

I advance timidly, forming appropriate words of welcome.

'Any luck?'

He shakes his head. I shrug in sympathy. 'Too bad, it must be the weather. Well, don't shoot yourself instead of the absent birds.'

I wave a cheerful hand as I pass, and the slow smile that spreads across his features suggests the impression I have made is poor. Ah, well. . . . He must have walked and shot that wood, man and boy, for nearly fifty years himself. I am the intruder, not he, and as I shuffle along beneath the dripping trees I no longer swagger. Moray, of course, is disgusted with me. The ankles of all strange men are suspect, and the elderly sportsman promised easy game. He follows me, muttering, and I 's'hush' him under my breath, relieved when the wood is left behind, and I climb through the fence to the immediate plot of garden surrounding the house itself. Here, at least, I am mistress of all I survey, and I can relieve my sporting inclinations by fetching a long pruning implement, during the ten minutes fine weather that remains, and beheading the grotesque tops of a clump of bamboos, which shaking in the wind and masking the sea view from one of the windows, have the horrible appearance of African witch-doctors, engaged on some tribal rite.

I attack them with ferocity, and then, arms aching, honour satisfied, make my way indoors before the hail strikes. The thought of tea is doubly welcome after these efforts, legs stretched out before flaming logs. I fling off my Tolstoy outfit, replace the pruning implement, and open the door of my living-room, known as the Long Room and so named with nostalgic memories of my former home. I am driven back by clouds of evil-smelling smoke. The pile of logs, balanced with such loving care before setting out for the walk, the paper beneath them gently touched with a lighted match, instead of welcoming me with the roaring blaze I had expected, have turned jet black. Not even a tongue of flame arises from them. I kneel beside the grate, bellows in hand, but not so much as a spark glints from the stinking ashes. I sit back on my heels in despair, remembering all the remaining logs, their fellows, awaiting transport from the old boiler-room in the basement. These were to see me through the winter, and I have no others. Hewn from a giant fir laid low in the autumn by a cross-cut saw, they were my pride and joy as much as the sporting rights.

I hurry to the nether regions to bring up kindling wood, but this has also been cut from the same fir, and when laid upon the corpses of the blackened logs, emit one protesting spark, sigh, and are extinguished. Too late to double back to the wood and search for twigs of stouter brand. I would lose yet more face before the sportsman with the gun, and anyway the heavens have burst again, what momentary glory shone from the sky has gone for ever.

> Pear logs and apple logs,
> They will scent your room.
> Cherry logs across the dogs
> Smell like flowers in bloom.

Somewhere, in a desk, I have the whole poem about logs, sent me by an obliging friend and expert, recommending those that give warmth and scent, and those that do not. Feverishly I search for it amongst a heap of papers, and run my eye down the printed page.

> Fir logs it is a crime,
> For anyone to sell.

I never thought to read the poem before having the fir-tree felled. . . .

> Holly logs will burn like wax,
> You should burn them green.

I can bear no more of it, and go to the kitchen to make tea, but as I drink it in front of the non-existent fire, wearing dark glasses to protect my eyes from the festoons of smoke hanging like Christmas decorations about the panelled room, I think of the many stunted hollies in the shrubbery behind the house, and plan destruction.

Tea passes without further incident, and supper on a tray watching television—a play showing teenagers making love on one channel and a very old film about the American Navy in Korea upon the other, offering doubtful entertainment to my jaded palate—takes me up to bedtime.

The increasing sound of the gale without and lashing rain against the windows gives warning that there is one remaining hazard to face before I climb the stairs. Moray must be put out, not at the front door where he would be blown over the wall and never seen again, but down to those same nether regions where the logs are harboured, and through the hatch-door of the boiler room opening on the 'patio' where he can do his worst in comparative shelter. The winding stair to the basement does not deter me, nor the memory of those characters, dead for centuries, who may have walked the basement in days gone by. Fourteenth-century yeomen, sixteenth-century merchants, eighteenth- and nineteenth-century parsons, squires, are shades that I can brave with equanimity. The idea of the Edwardian lady, however, who communed with the spirit world flanked by her peacocks, is more disturbing. It was in the basement kitchen, no longer used as such, that she used to give her orders for the day to the trembling cook, and I have it, on good authority, that a parrot, chained to its perch, let fly a torrent of abuse at her approach. I stand shivering at the hatch-door of the boiler-room, while Moray sniffs the cobbles in disdain, and then, to test both our nerves, I switch out the light. This surely should bring an Award for Stamina.

Nothing happens. No clatter of a cane upon stone flags. No screech from protesting peacocks. No cry of 'Pieces of Eight . . . Pieces of

65

Eight . . .' from the parrot. A door bangs in the distance, but this is probably the draught. My formidable predecessor of more affluent days may be a silent witness to my challenge, but thank heaven, she does not materialize. May she rest in peace.

The door is bolted, Moray scampers ahead of me up the winding stair, and we proceed to our own quarters, and to the bedroom that was, I am glad to say, built on in later years, after the peacock lady's day. It faces seaward, and thus receives the full force of the sou'westerly or indeed of any gale, but the effect of this is stimulating, like being on the enclosed bridge of a ship, without the rocking. I look out of the window and see the riding-lights of those vessels that have not yet sought refuge in Par Harbour, and the thought of the seamen possibly battened down below, at the mercy of every lurching sea, makes me turn to my own bed with a sense of well-being, even of complacency. Moray retires to his lair next to the night storage heater, and leaning back on my pillows with a sigh of satisfaction I open the unfinished newspaper I was reading after lunch.

'You too can enjoy the thrills of camping in Cornwall.'

Brushing the advertisement impatiently aside, I turn to matters of greater moment. The thrust and parry of political parties, the feuds and international problems of our time.

Something splashes upon my pillow. An ominous drip. It is followed in a moment by a second, and then a third. A tear from an unseen presence? I look up to the ceiling, and perceive, all complacency gone, that a row of beads, like a very large rosary swinging from a nun's breast, is forming a chain immediately above my head and fast turning into bubbles.

Drip. . . . Drip. . . . The water torture, practised in the Far East and said to be more swiftly effective than our own medieval rack. Hypnotized, I watch the row of beads expand and fall, its place immediately taken by another, meanwhile my pillow taking on the sodden appearance of the sack cast away at Little Hell. This is the end. . . . I will *not* be forced out of the double-bed I have slept in for thirty-five years and seek asylum elsewhere. No heating switched on in the spare-rooms, beds not aired, lamps lacking bulbs.

'You too can enjoy the thrills of camping in Cornwall.'

I leap out on to the floor and, risking hernia, proceed to drag my double-bed into the centre of the room. The floorboards groan. Moray, disturbed from sound sleep, sits up and stares at me, a look of intense astonishment on his face. 'What on earth?'

I fetch towels for the cascade to splash upon, and then, marooned on a flat surface, head-board gone, pillowless, install myself on the desert island that has become my bed. Moray continues to look astonished, even aggrieved.

Tommy's photograph, beret at the familiar jaunty angle, smiles at me from the dry wall opposite. I am reminded, only too well, that it was always my berth, in our old sailing days, and never his, which suffered the inevitable leaks from the deck above. My discomfort produced delighted chuckles, and although the following day the leaks would be stopped, with each successive craft we owned the one wet patch would invariably form itself, in an otherwise perfect boat, over my head.

The smile is infectious, and whether a happy echo from an unforgettable past, or a signal from the Isles of the Blest, it has the required result. Sense of humour returns. I make a long arm and switch off the light, reckoning up the follies of one more useless day, yet knowing in my heart that, but for the absence of the departed skipper, I would not change it for the world.

Sir Arthur Bliss—Master of the Queen's Musick

HENRY WILLIAMSON

Genesis of Tarka

The first otter I saw was at Stratford St Mary, a village in Suffolk, on a summer's day long ago. I, a schoolboy of fifteen, was bicycling from Kent, on my way to East Runton on the Norfolk coast, where my mother and sisters had already gone by train.

Men in blue and red uniforms, and carrying long poles, were walking beside a deep slow river near a mill. I lingered there for hours, not interested in the hunting, but looking for old nests in the reeds and bushes of an islet. And suddenly I was gazing at a small brown seal-like face, with small eyes and bristles, staring at me from the water. I said nothing, feeling myself to be on the side of the animal.

Five years later, in the winter of 1916–17, I saw my second otter. It sprang out of an old German field-gun emplacement in the swamps of the river Ancre. A glimpse only: but it brought back, in that most desolate place of charred stumps of poplar, the East Anglian sunlight of that day a world of time lost, it seemed, for ever.

And four years later, when the Great War was a soundless, viewless wraith also lost in time, and I had withdrawn myself to a remote village on the Atlantic seaboard of North Devon, I saw my third otter, one destined to alter the course of my life.

One morning a stranger called at my cottage, where I was writing at a table, to tell me that he had seen a dead otter hanging outside a farmhouse door in a neighbouring village. The otter had been shot the evening before. A smallholder had seen it crossing his pasture, near a stream, while rabbiting at twilight. Why had he shot it, I cried hotly. 'Well,' replied my visitor, 'when I asked the farmer the same question, he replied, "What good be it, anyway?"' He went on to tell me that the otter had been an object of curiosity in the Ebrington Arms the previous night, and also of considerable argument about it being able, or unable, to breathe under water.

'You and I know, of course, that it is a land beast that gets its living in the water, usually in darkness.

'But here's my point,' he continued. 'The otter was a bitch otter, and there's a litter of cubs somewhere by the riverside. I believe I know where they are—in a drain running down from a marsh. Now you will be wanting to know why I have come to you. I'm a crock, I was hit at Thiepval above the Ancre valley, which you probably know; so I can't dig. I wonder if you would care to lend a hand, in the hope of saving the cubs? I can give you a lift in my jingle....'

This was a local type of small governess cart, drawn by an Exmoor pony, which at that moment was regarding my green currants which hung over the garden wall, and being scolded by a blackbird to which the bush apparently belonged.

I left my writing table, stroked the little black and white cat which was watching the blackbird from the top of the wall, and with the spaniel pups leaping and frisking around me, went with my caller to the jingle. There weren't many motor-cars in Devon in those days, and our journey along the sunken lanes to the valley where my new friend lived took the best part of an hour for the three miles.

It was early spring, and the stony surface of the lane was running everywhere with water. The shaggy pony went down the last steep descent very slowly, leaning back against the shafts, while I walked behind, ready to pull the jingle backwards if the outfit showed signs of tipping out the driver; while the spaniel pups, forbidden to go into the fields because of rabbit traps, often stopped to stare reproachfully at me.

My household at this period (1921) consisted of the dogs and myself; Pie, a small black-and-white cat with one kitten; and a pair of white owls. Various young birds had lodged with us for short periods—magpies, a carrion crow, and a diving bird called a razorbill which I found on the shore one day with its feathers clogged by oil-fuel. It was a wild little community, and the warden (myself) was commonly said in the district to be mazed, chiefly because the cottage windows were open by night and by day; but we went our own way happily, writing at night before an open hearth burning driftwood, and wandering down the lanes and by the sea at all hours.

That morning we had an addition to the community. My spaniels wagged their tail stumps, while whining anxiously to know what it was I was holding in my hands. The dogs had never seen or smelled such a creature. When it was put on the ground, they didn't know what to do about it. They gurgled, yowled, barked with puzzled excitement, pushed it with their lips, licked it and stared up at me, for it was like a mole without a snout, with tiny beady eyes; but it could not crawl. And it made slight, snuffling, mewing noises as it sought around blindly with its wide flat head and minute blunt nose.

The dogs had watched excitedly while I had opened an old earth-choked field drain with careful blows of a pick, often kneeling down to listen to the small mewing cries; and when at last we came to the 'bed', there lay two cubs, one of them lukewarm, the other dead.

72

The immediate thing was, how to feed the small, soft animal, pushing so languidly against my hands. We gave it cow's milk, diluted with warm water, in a fountain-pen filler, through a hole nipped in the rubber squeezer. The cub sucked several fills, and then fell asleep upon some cotton wool.

I returned home on foot in the evening, to be greeted by the little pied cat mewing as she ran along the top of the garden wall, her tail fluffed up. She always waited on the wall for us, and showed her affection for the spaniels by arching herself against one or t'other, although both pups ignored her.

I lit a fire, cooked myself some eggs and bacon, and sat down to supper in my tall-backed Windsor chair (2s 6d at a local auction), cat on one side, pups on the other, looking up and awaiting tit-bits. Afterwards I drowsed before the teak wood fire—there had been a wreck on the sands recently, after a south-west gale—spaniels asleep against my feet and cat curled on top of them beside her kitten.

Next morning I was sitting at the table, laughing as I wrote *Dandelion Days*, a satire on my schooldays, while Pie suckled her kitten and our tame chaffinch hopped about the floor for crumbs. The finch arrived every morning, but Pie knew the bird, and never tried to catch it. As I was writing, both spaniels sprang up and rushed barking into the drang, or stone-set passageway outside: the chaffinch flew away: while Pie, all fluffed up, fled to the dogs' help. I shouted for them to shut up, for my new friend had arrived in the jingle, and was making his way slowly to the open door.

'I'm afraid the cub is going to die,' he said, as we looked at the mite now feebly moving on the table. It was cold. The spaniels stood on hind legs and whined, glancing at it, and also at our faces. Then Pie cat leapt lightly on the table. She arched her back, and growled. We watched, as she swore undecidedly at it. When its mouth opened but no sound came, she moved slowly towards it, and after drawing back, in hesitation, she got near enough to sniff it. Again she drew back, made as if to stroke it with her paw, but altered her mind just before touching it, and merely tapped it, holding her head on one side when its mouth opened and uttered an inaudible mew. It was inaudible to me; but Pie must have heard it, for she put her head on one side and quizzed it with new interest. I noticed that the pupils of her eyes were round and very black. Then she sniffed it again, glancing furtively about her as though thinking of escape; cocked her head sideways again; and suddenly swore, jumped off the table and ran up the wooden stairs to the bedroom above, where her kitten was lying in the dogs' basket.

I followed her up, quietly. She mewed pathetically at me. Her eyes were still very dark and round. She was less than a year old, little more than a kitten herself. . . . I took her kitten downstairs and put it on the table beside the otter cub. I rubbed their noses together, and then their tummies. I put them on the lime-ash floor, side by side. Immediately the kitten began to cry out, feeling the cold.

Chirruping anxiously, Pie came pattering down the stairs, and giving a mew of reassurance, went straight to it. She made several attempts to pick it up by the scruff, but she was too small, and, looking up into my face, appealed to me, with the faintest mew, to carry it for her. I picked up cub and kit together and sat on the edge of the table, and she sprang up lightly beside me, rubbed her ear on my hand for thanks, and then lay down on my lap and purred happily while both snuggled into her warmth.

Thereafter the cub was fed and washed and enjoyed equally with her own kitten, until it was strong and well enough to go back to its owner. For there was no question that my friend wanted the cub for himself.

It had short, thick fur, brown as a mace reed, which most people call the bulrush; and Devonians, who work at the freshwater dykes on the marsh by the estuary, call oolypuggers. (A word admirably describing the thick white roots of the mace-reed being lugged by long rakes from the mire at the bottom of the freshwater dykes intersecting the bullock grazing meadows behind the sea-wall of the estuary.)

As summer advanced, the long low body of the young dog-otter seemed to glide over the ground, so short were his legs. He had a long tail, thick and strong, tapering to the tip; his head was wider and flatter than a cat's head. Small ears hidden in its fur; and the wide mouth was set with whiskers. His feet were like a dog's feet, but sturdier, more splayed, and there was a web of skin between the five toes of each paw.

How he loved a watering can. Or better, the garden hose turned into a zinc washing bath on the lawn under the apple trees! He would roll on his back in the bath, trying to clutch and bite the jet of water. The spraying smoothed his hair, and gave him resemblance to a small seal. He was most affectionate and faithful, knowing no fear of the spaniels and Pie the cat; indeed he would run to the gate and stand up whenever he heard the beats of my Norton motor-bicycle arriving, I with an old Army pack strapped to my shoulders and holding Pie and her grown kitten; and two spaniels sitting one behind the other on the tank between my arms extended to the low handlebars.

As soon as we stopped, the dogs were leaping down, and the cats struggling to escape from the khaki pack. A chase of the otter would begin all over the garden and even into the house, in a conglomeration of animal spirits. The cats, unexpectedly chased, sometimes hissed and clawed their way up trees: to descend when all was clear, and begin to stalk the otter.

But of strangers, the young otter was suspicious; gliding away on its almost invisible legs and returning and stopping again, perhaps to open its mouth and utter a growling hiss. It had two cries for its friends—a noise like that made by human fingers being drawn down a pane of wet glass, the other a happier cry like *tuckatuck—tuckatuck*.

He was fed on milk, fish, and part-cooked rabbit flesh mixed with dog biscuit and vegetables. All that summer he ran about in the garden, or followed his master on his slow hobbling walks by the river. I feared my poor friend was dying.

And so it was; and I promised him to look after his otter, which came to live in the cottage. It was September, most of the summer visitors had gone back to their towns. Even so, we kept clear of the sands, and the dogs to be seen there; and confined ourselves to inland fields, and the sunken, hillside lanes, which had been scraped during the centuries by the sleds drawn up hill and down by ponies during the centuries, until, in places, the rock had been worn down several feet in the underlying bed of shale. Rains scoured out the *detritus*, washing the rock clean. In some places these sunken lanes were many feet below the fields they divided, so that the branches of thorn and ash growing at the verges above met, and in summer one walked along a tunnel of green gloom.

We went down to the sea-shore when, at last, the sands were vacant, save for gulls and curlews. Sometimes in dimmit-light (twilight) we crossed the fields lying to the west of the village, and went downstream, where the otter splashed about, hunting eels and small trout. And one night, when he had strayed farther from us than usual, I heard a sudden hissing, chattering, chain-rattling coming from a distant hedge-bank with the excited yelping of a spaniel. The otter was caught in a rabbit gin.

It rolled and twisted as he bit the iron, his paw, the chain, while hissing and blowing in fear; snapping at the spaniel, until a sudden agonized yelping told that the sharp, incurved teeth had met in its body somewhere.

I took off my jacket and threw it over the otter, whose frenzy of strength was amazing, while trying to hold it still and with my right foot seeking to tread on the spring, and so release the serrated steel jaws which held the paw. It was not easy to do this; the spring, about ten inches long, and doubled like a narrow U on its side, kept reversing under my tread. And then abruptly the jacket was empty, and the trap lying free.

For an hour or so I waited, calling and listening, while the spaniel shivered near, sometimes whining. And returning at first light, I found, near the gin trap, two broken toes of a front paw.

I never saw the otter again; but spent many hours, indeed days and weeks, walking down the coombes of Exmoor and Dartmoor, searching the scours beside flowing water, for a three-toe'd 'seal', or spoor.

I never saw him again; and yet, as I write, I wonder if he had visited Dartmoor; for on a grey day of January, 1926, I found the imprint, or spoor, of an otter's 'pads' by the lonely, half-dry bog of Cranmere, near the Great Kneeset, where five rivers have their beginnings. One impression was marred. Could it be my otter? On that vast silence of water and heather only the startled chirrup of a solitary pipit answered my thoughts.

By this time I had already written about a dozen short stories, which I called *The Otter's Saga*. Two were accepted and printed; later knowledge told me that they were only partly true. So I withdrew the other four and rewrote the series; but all the while, as I followed the otter hounds in the valleys, I learned how inadequate the first drafts had been. Every day on the moors, usually alone, I saw something new. Thus I was able to replace a defective incident or details of an otter's life; and every day when I followed hounds, aloof from the genuine sportsmen, I wondered, Will they find and kill my otter. . . ?

I had seen many killed after long hunts during the days of summer, when the rivers were low and the hunted beast could swim no more, but in final desperate fatigue took to the land of its genesis (for the otter, like the seal, was once a land beast) and was overborne and its head crushed and its body pulled and broken apart in deep-growling worry: I saw many killed thus—but never a corpse with a maimed front paw.

One of the North Devon friends of my youth, a doctor whose knowledge of wild flowers and moths and butterflies of the district was absolute, told me that an otter had been found drowned in a crab-pot at Combe Martin, on the shore of the Severn Sea, and thither I went, to seek and find the fisherman; but it was not my otter.

One night, as I sat by the fire in my cottage, I heard a sound as of curlews flying over—and yet more flute-like—soft and gentle, and oft and oft-repeated, in the darkness outside. The cat, now old, heard it too, and as she stood up before the hearth her eyes grew sudden large and dark; and the spaniels ran whining to the round cat-hole near the bottom of the door. Telling them to lie down, I went to the door, opened it; and listened.

The churchyard elms were seething, Atlantic rain lashing down.

I moved slowly towards the stream below the churchyard wall, to see, dimly, the stream running spread over the path. O, why had I not replaced the old battery in the torch? Was that an extra swirl in the water, with a twin glint of eyes, and then—nothing.

Had my otter chanced this way, to his old home, following down the little runner which, rising out of the middle of an upland field, fell through hedge-bottom to the sunken lane winding down the hill, and ran, with its plants of watercress and brook-lime in summer, to disappear through a drain under the road at the bottom, and become the little stream passing through the rectorial garden and so below the churchyard wall, on its way down the valley to the sea?

Had my otter come back—perhaps with a mate—and cried out in the night, briefly, before disappearing for ever, in the flesh?

Then there was that otter caught in another rabbit trap on the high ground of Down End, overlooking the sandhills of Santon and the estuary of the Two Rivers. Hearing of it from my neighbour 'Revvy'—he had once worked in the Rector's garden—I went down to Cryde village and spoke to the trapper who had beaten it to death with a stick. But the 'girt mousey-coloured fitch', he said, had no sign of any broken paw. The skin was worth ten shillings—a bit of luck for him. Times were hard in those days, with no dole for the workless labourer.

On another occasion the stationmaster of one of the little Great Western Railway stations—gay with flowers and rambler roses in season, and lit by paraffin lamps with bulging globes set within lanterns on iron posts, told me he was trouting one evening, by permission, when he noticed he was being followed by an otter as he cast his Red Spinner fly upstream at evening. For more than ten minutes, he declared, as he went slowly upstream casting his fly, it followed him, 'snorting at me like a seal'.

He thought it was after the fish in his creel. I wondered if it could have been my otter, once so faithful and affectionate, disturbed by a feeling within itself which it did not understand.

And again I wonder—that otter I saw, in the summer just before I was married, lying in the sun on a rock below Baggy Hole, that cave running under the precipice three hundred and ten feet above sea-level, where the peregrine falcons used to nest, where their fore-bears had nested for centuries, on the same ledge, the ancestral eyrie, was it once my familiar? The long brown sleek shape with spiky salt-dried hair, which ran towards me around the big grey boulders at the edge of the sea-fret; and hesitated; and stared, and was perturbed by apparent curiosity, even as I was—but would approach no nearer, but ran away when I went towards it.

The years went on, wearing the flesh as the sea frets the land, and it was 1930—but no, it must have been dead by then—but very strange it was, as in summer twilight I passed the Peal Stone falls, roar of white surge under, dark heads moving there—was my otter among them, climbing up and sliding over the falls with his cubs, again and again, whistling and fluting in the joy of life—until suddenly one gave the alarm, and I was alone once more.

And was it, perhaps, my otter which came upon a thousand yearling trout, so carefully reared and tended in the little hatchery at the bottom of the garden at Shallowford, where I lived with wife and children in the valley below Exmoor? I heard fluting cries of joy in the night as I lay in bed, worried because I had not started a book on the life of a salmon, and the years had passed since signing the contract—while outside in the night came the joyous cries—an otter or otters had come upon the pond, and finding sudden wealth had spent it royally, according to its nature, so that only seven yearlings were left alive next morning?

And early on another morning, as I was walking by the dawn-silvered river Bray up by the railway viaduct, I heard a great splashing and furrowing in the gravel shadows of the Fireplay Pool, accompanied by 'hurring' noises—and there was an otter dragging a salmon by one of the forward fins. It must have hunted the fish about the pool, and driven it upstream in the shallows just as I arrived, for in its terror the fish had beached itself on the shillets, as the flattish stones were called. I watched the otter tearing at the flesh of one shoulder—and then the otter saw me.

It seemed to flatten and spread itself into the water, like a bag of brown oil, and went down with the current, its back an inch or so under the surface of the water.

I waded across the stream, and reaching the twitching fish, was about to bang it on the head with a stone when the otter returned, pattering up the fast flow of shallow water. I stood still, staring. Wasn't that brown, flat head, back-sloping, familiar?—surely the front paw seemed foreshortened: *tuckatuck—tuckatuck* I called, *tuckatuck—tuckatuck*.

Was there an answering cry or was it the cry of the river, the cry of water striking rock and stone and gravel-bed, which it utters in all its valleys from the moors to the sea, wherein all is forgotten. . .?

That lower half of a flat skull found in the gravel scours of the North Tail at the mouth of the estuary of the Two Rivers, half-hidden in shingle, most of the teeth fallen out of an otter's jaw.

I wonder . . . I wonder.

Was this the end of 'Tarka's joyful water-life and death in the Country of the Two Rivers'?

PAUL GALLICO

In Praise of the Ball

No one to my knowledge, with the exception of the *Encyclopaedia Britannica*, has lavished any prose in celebration of the ball and the part it has played down through the ages from man's earliest civilization to this day.

This importance has been reflected largely in the entertainment field and as far as one can determine its impact upon history has been negligible, except for the fact that Louis X of France in exaggerated pursuit of a tennis ball, caught a chill when the game was over and was carried off by it at the age of twenty-seven, before he could work any further mischief politically. Whether the country would have been any different today but for this intervention, there is no saying.

My edition of the *Encyclopaedia* lists and presents pictures of some twenty-seven balls in use today, namely: Lacrosse, tennis, billiards, snooker, bagatelle, Eton fives, Rugby fives, large squash rackets, golf, small squash rackets, table tennis, equestrian polo, baseball, cricket, hockey, lawn tennis, lawn bowls jack, rounders, rubber stoolball, football, softball, crown green bowl, crown green jack, croquet ball, basketball, soccer ball, volley ball.

To which, off the top of my head, I can add *boule* or *Pétanque*, bowling, hurling, Irish handball, American handball, French handball, water polo, pelota squash tennis, Gaelic football, shot-put, marbles, the 'ski-ball' of the amusement parks and fun-fairs, and the beach ball that every child manages to bounce off the heads of sunbathers on the strand.

Of these only one cannot be considered a ball in the true sense of the word, namely the Rugby or American football which is egg-shaped and thus given to mad and irresponsible bounces.

The aberration was the responsibility of one William Ellis, a student at Rugby School who, in 1823, playing in an inter-class soccer match, is said to have committed the shattering breach of picking up the ball and running with it downfield. While Ellis was practically consigned to The Tower for this crime, the novelty of his action aroused interest, the kicking and running game was tried and Rugby—father to American football—developed. But nowhere can I find the reason for the change in the shape of the ball and why it has continued to be called such. The object which Ellis picked up and personally escorted downfield was a round soccer ball. At

79

some time, as the game grew in popularity and acquired a special set of laws, the Rugby ball became oval.

There must be dozens of yet unnamed kinds of balls used in esoteric games played by esoteric natives in esoteric countries, but the classic games' missile from very ancient times has always been a perfect sphere, varying only in size, weight or material: solid, hollow, stuffed or pumped up with air.

The origin of the ball is, of course, lost in pre-recorded history but one may conjecture that two things must have contributed to the development of the shape, namely the structure of the paw or hand which could be cupped so as to fit comfortably and with a curious kind of satisfaction about something spherical such as a stone, a fruit, a seed, a dinosaur's egg, and the tendency when confronted with a loose object on the ground to kick it with the foot. When such an object was round, it rolled excitingly for some considerable distance, inviting one to chase it and kick it again or leading a brother troglodyte to have a go at returning it. The human skull was probably the first football. Thus in one case the object was thrown from the cupped hand and in the other given a blow with the foot.

Simultaneously our cave brothers must have discovered that a round missile, either thrown or projected from a sling, had greater accuracy than any other shape. The flat stone was likely to sail off line and others neither fitted the grasp nor were controllable in flight.

It is not too difficult to picture the scene near Choukoutien, north of Peking, in the year 1,569,387 BC, when little Fu and Chu, playmates, come across the egg of a then rare, twenty-foot saurian, the Spherosaurus, which laid an egg some four inches in diameter covered with a tough leathery skin and absolutely spherical.

Fu, who discovers it, is examining it and Chu asks, 'What have you got there?'

'Here, catch!' says Fu and throws the object to Chu who, to his surprise, finds that he is able to pluck it out of the air and hold it.

'Chuck it back,' says Fu. Chu does so. Fu makes a nice shoe-top stop and throws to Chu who is now covering the wicket.

At this point their father Mu appears and in the local Sinanthropian dialect inquires, 'What the hell do you two think you are doing?'

Chu bowls a googly at Fu and both boys chorus, 'We're playing . . .' For a moment they regard one another blankly as Fu rubs the shine off the object to get a firmer grip on it and then for want of a better name, since none exists at the time, they say, 'Ball'.

'Bless me,' says Mu, 'why so you are!'

And the ball has been invented.

The striking of it with a stick developed later, since concurrently with the discovery of the basis of every ball game, namely the use of it as a missile, Fu and Chu's elders were emerging from their caves every so often, happily to club other rounded objects such as the heads of their neighbours.

Symbolically the striking of a ball with bat, racket, mallet or fist may still be an expression of that wholly enjoyable form of aggression. Whacking a ball unquestionably yields human relief from tensions. The golf ball sits inoffensively propped up on its tee, or nestles submissively and motionless in the turf. Lofting it into distant pastures leaves the lofter with a delicious feeling of satisfaction, the same that is experienced by swatting the tennis spheroid out of reach of an opponent, punching a volley ball or hitting the offerings of a famous bowler for a series of fours and sixes. In a sense in each case one is knocking someone's block off, with the aggressive spirit most highly developed and released in the body contact games involving the use of a ball, where the coach sends his team onto the field with instructions to commit everything short of murder or mayhem to gain possession of it, keep it, kick it, carry it or score with it.

One of the most curious features of the ball is that the passionate pursuit of it in almost every age led to excesses so that games played with it in centuries past, such as golf, tennis, football, had to be forbidden by Royal decree so as to keep their subjects' minds on the more important occupation of earning ducats destined for the King's treasury via the tax collector, or practising the arts of killing other subjects in other lands.

The ancient Hebrews played ball, so did the classic Greeks and the pre-Christian Romans.

Isaiah (22, v. 18) in cataloguing the calamities about to be visited upon his countrymen by the Lord in punishment for their sins says, 'He will surely violently turn and toss thee like a ball into a large country; there thou shalt die and there the chariots of the glory shall be the shame of thy Lord's house.'

Isaiah, brooding over the recalcitrance of his people, must have seen the small fry of Judah throwing a ball back and forth and he saw the Jews tossed in the same manner into the maw of the Persian war machine. Archaeologists, in an Israeli strata dating back five thousand years BC, have unearthed a child's game of skittles along with balls of clay and cone-shaped 'pins' to be knocked down.

Blind Homer knew the ball and was probably the first man to celebrate the *lost ball*, since it was he who reported that Nausica, playing at catch with her handmaidens, dropped it; it rolled under a bush, and searching for it she found there and roused from his sleep none other than Odysseus.

There were at least a half-dozen ball games played by the Greeks including one akin to lacrosse, in which the sphere was thrown from runner to runner, and others resembling soccer or Rugby in which it was thrown but never kicked. And, on the Themistoclean ring-wall at Athens there is a sculptured relief showing the details of probably the earliest known hockey match. Two youths with sticks are engaged in a bully for the ball which is on the ground in the middle, and on either side of them stand two other pairs of boys with sticks, waiting for the capture and the pass. Another relief represents a very modern throw-in from the touch-line. One player is preparing to throw and the rest are waiting either to pluck it out of the air or to tackle whoever catches it.

Seyffert's *Dictionary of Classical Antiquities* lists some nine different games played either by ancient Greeks or Romans with five sorts of balls: the small, the middle-sized, the large, the very large and the inflated, and notes that in throwing the little one the rule was that the arm should not rise above the shoulder. It also reports the presence of the first professional in the gymnasia and thermae of Rome. A room (*sphaeristerium*, from the Greek *sphaira*, 'ball') was set apart for the purpose, in which there was a teacher in attendance to give instruction in the art. If there was a room, there must have been four walls. Was the game played here the forerunner of our modern four-wall games, such as handball or squash?

Plautus in his *Truculentus*, written circa 200 BC, used the metaphor, '*Mea pila est*'—'I have got the ball', meaning 'I have caught it', or 'I have won'. If he were writing today he might also find himself 'having something on the ball' (baseball); or to be told, 'Come on, get on the ball' (soccer or football). Likewise 'The trouble with him is he won't play ball', and 'Let's get the ball rolling'. He might also have borrowed from tennis to say, 'Okay, chum, the ball's in your court'. And, of course, that acknowledgement of finding oneself in an impossible position or situation derived from the game of pool, or pocket billiards—to be 'behind the eight ball'.

Shakespeare knew the football made of hide and blown up with air, as in *The Comedy of Errors*, Act II:

> Am I so round with you as you with me
> That like a football you do spurn me thus?
> You spurn me hence and he will spurn me hither;
> If I last in this service you must case me in leather.

And again in *King Lear*, Act I, Scene 4:

> STEWARD: I'll not be strucken, my lord.
> KENT: Nor tripped, neither, you base football player.
> LEAR: I thank thee, fellow.

Not to mention the more cryptic one from *The Tempest*: 'Mistress line is this not my jerkin? Now is the jerkin under the line.'

The clue to this last bit of Elizabethan punning is to be found in the *Proverbs* of John Hayward (1562), 'Thou has striken the ball under the lyne', the origin of which was derived from tennis, the line being the equivalent of today's net stretched across the court. To have hit the ball beneath this line meant one had failed in one's purpose.

In the year 1721 an unknown Irish bard who was also the Master of Ceremonies at a Gaelic football game between the townships of Lusks and Swords, celebrated the ball to be used with the following classic:

> Ye champions of fair Lusks and ye of Swords,
> View well this ball, the present of your lords,
> To outward view, three folds of bullock's hide,
> With leather thongs bound fast on every side,
> A mass of finest hay concealed from sight,
> Conspire at once to make it firm and light.

Following upon this he ran for his life, since no referee who remained in the middle of a Gaelic football match could be expected to survive, the game then being quite different from that of today with the size of the team unlimited. All the able-bodied in one town played against those of another. The membership of the teams scaled between twenty-five and a hundred, and in some of the earlier centuries the rules provided that a game start at a point in dead centre between two rival parishes, which might have been anywhere from two to ten miles from either parish line. The team which advanced the ball across the boundary line of the opposing parish won. There were no restrictions placed on methods of advancing the ball and the late Frank Menke, describing the game in his *Encyclopedia of Sports*, writes:

'Because punching at the ball was permitted, many eyes were blackened, noses broken and mouths cut by players who seemingly aimed their punches at the ball, but actually drove them into enemy faces. The real strategy of the game, as explained by an Irish player, was to mess up the other man's face as soon as possible, because a man with two swollen eyes couldn't follow the ball so well as one with clear vision. Players often started the season by getting a pair of black eyes, and they remained discolored until the season was over. About a hundred years ago Gaelic football had no official name, and the innocent bystanders classified it as a free-for-all fight.'

My one-time colleague, Mr Menke, has also listed some thirty-five varieties of esoteric and little-known ball games such as: Captain's ball, end ball, newcomb ball, drive ball, toss ball, punch ball, bee ball, tom ball, speed ball, fist ball, long ball, bounce ball, pin ball, score ball, bottle ball, curtain ball, cabinet ball, recreation ball, playground ball, lee ball, beat ball, line ball, one o'gang, corner ball, post ball, bounce hand baseball, triangle ball, hit ball, sprint ball, stick ball and others such as: tether ball, cork ball, field handball, paddle tennis and code ball.

Tether ball is an English invention. A tennis ball attached to a string is tied to the top of a maypole and you try to slug it with a racket so that it winds around to a certain mark before your opponent can do it to you.

But code ball is strictly an American innovation, the brainchild of Dr William E. Code of Chicago, and you might enjoy playing it some Sunday afternoon, the variation called codeball-on-the-green, if you have a bit of land, your son's old soccer ball and a supply of washtubs or apple baskets. You lay out a five-hole course exactly like in golf, some long some short, over varied terrain depending on how much you have or whether your neighbour is co-operative or an old grouch. The apple basket or washtub becomes the hole. The idea is, as in golf, to get the ball into the hole with the least number of kicks. So team up in a mixed foursome, tee off from the front lawn with a mighty boot and you are playing code ball, with no more danger to life or limb than throwing out your hip trying to kick the ball out of a cabbage patch or ravine. (Soothing note: you may lift out of the brook; penalty one kick.)

Incidentally, the only square ball used in all the history of sport was in the first game of ice hockey, played somewhere around 1879 on river ice, by some of the students of McGill University, copying field hockey on a frozen surface. The round rubber ball would not do and so they tried a square one. That was not too satisfactory either, so eventually they cut off the two sides of a hard rubber ball, retaining the centre slice and the hockey puck was born. But at least it is still part of a ball.

Yes, that blessed ball, contributor to man's leisure hour pleasure, pastimes and relaxation. Has anyone a conception of the number of millions of persons on any given Saturday or holiday afternoon who, in every quarter of the globe, are following the flight of some type of ball as it is thrown, kicked or hit? Literally billions in currency of every kind come pouring through the box office as fans shell out to see some sort of spheroid maltreated by anywhere from two to an indeterminate number on a side, or used as an excuse to maltreat one another.

If you were blind and deaf, you would only have to finger the ball in use at any time to know what was the time of year: cricket, soccer, rugby, tennis, polo, etc., follow the seasons.

Nations have borrowed the ball from other nations and cultures and made it their own. The West took the polo ball from the Indians; the Japanese, baseball from the Americans and the Americans adopted lacrosse from the native Indians of Canada.

In a survey conducted in nineteen foreign countries, large and small, inquiring into the most popular spectator sports, fourteen were played with a ball of some kind, with soccer leading in popularity to the point where in India, games in Calcutta were known to draw as many as two hundred thousand or more persons to a match. A tiny South American Republic such as Costa Rica reports an average single game attendance of between sixty and seventy thousand in soccer; between thirty and forty thousand for baseball and twenty thousand for basketball. The Lebanese love that soccer ball, so do the Peruvians and the Turks. If you are fed up and want to get away from that ubiquitous object, spend your holiday in Saudi Arabia where horse racing comes first, camel racing second and soccer only third, and the most popular participant sport is falconry.

And finally, anthropologically speaking, only in the most recent times did man discover that he lived on a ball, plaything of the gods, hurled eternally about the universe in what must surely be the biggest and most mysterious game of all.

CLEMENT FREUD

How Far Down Under Can You Get?

There was displayed in my Melbourne hotel room a publication entitled *This Week in Melbourne*—a surprisingly short book considering the length of a Melbourne week. On page five I was enjoined when in Canberra to read *This Week in Canberra*; also to take a brown and white bus to the Botanical Gardens, and under a heading that asked WHAT To Do it promised that the NICEST ideas come from Vic Tours.

This left the rest of the page at the mercy of four advertisements from Escort Agencies. Two of these, Black Orchid and Marie Claire, simply list telephone numbers, the second of these prefixed by the letters A.H. which could mean Australian Housewives but probably stands for After Hours. The Right Escort Service stated that 'hostesses were available for interstate overseas visitors and businessmen' which is like saying 'not suitable for children or persons of a nervous disposition'. The Blue Venus Agency, taking a column inch more than its rivals in the field, offered 'local and overseas executives the company of models and entertainers for luncheon and dinner engagements'.

Being at rather a loose end it seemed to me a splendid idea to hire myself an escort . . . and in view of my inexperience in such matters I decided to play it safe and get myself one from each agency. If one escort is good, I argued, four escorts must be better; so I telephoned

BLACK ORCHID

The listed number rang half a dozen times and a man's voice deliberated on my escort inquiry and suggested I ring another number and ask for Len. The other number was Lord Ted's In Shop and Len turned out to be a woman. She said there would be no trouble finding me an escort for that evening, just wait till I get a pencil.

Pencil getting seemed to be a little more difficult but she came back on the line and said 'Now. . . . How tall are you?'

She did not desire to know how many heads I had, how old I was or whether my intentions were honourable or otherwise; but she did mention that there was a 25 dollar fee which should be given the lady on arrival and that this entitled me to the exclusive services of a dinner companion up till midnight. 'After this it is up to the lass if you wish to go somewhere or take her to a nightclub—if there is a nightclub in Melbourne.' Having asked Black Orchid to have her lady on parade at 7.30, ask for Mr Smith and come up to my apartment I rang

RIGHT ESCORT SERVICE

The telephone was answered immediately, a pleasant sounding woman said, 'May I tell you about the service. . . . It is for interstate and overseas visitors who often find Melbourne to be a very lonely place.'

She added that the hostesses were picked with extreme care, many of them having been overseas; they were also selected for their abilities to listen and provide companionship. The fee is 20 dollars paid in advance to the girl who will ring your apartment on arrival at the hotel.

The Right Escort agency were entirely disinterested in my height, age or intentions, wished me a pleasant evening and confirmed that the lass would be there at 7.45.

BLUE VENUS

A rather business-like lady listened to my inquiry, asked where I was staying, what room, what was my age. She then mentioned that 'all my girls are selected not only because of their looks but for their personality . . . and that immense care had been taken to ensure that customers were entirely satisfied. I have a lady in mind,' continued Blue Venus, 'of whom I am sure you will approve. . . .' It sounded strangely like a one gal outfit.

After a short pause Blue Venus said that 25 dollars entitled me to her services from 8 p.m. to midnight and in a slightly breathless paragraph she told me that this was the way that most escort agencies were run. I assured her she was probably correct and she checked on my name (Smith), room number and rang back fifteen minutes later to confirm that the hostess would arrive at 8 p.m.
This left

MARIE CLAIRE

The phone rang three times before being answered by a lady who was clearly fairly New Australian, though the accent had taken a firm hold. She was without doubt the least switched-on of the agencies and had some trouble getting the name . . . as did her hostess, who called me Byron. She asked what age-group I had in mind and when I said 'youngish' she said 'about twenty-five'. Having told her that

88

I would like the hostess to be at my hotel at 8.15 she confirmed 8.30, said 'Oh yes, 8.15', and there followed a longish silence which I broke by saying 'About money?'

She said, 'Oh yes' or possibly 'Jawohl . . .', 'the charge is twenty-five dollars put in an envelope and handed to the girl on her arrival.' On this happy note we bade each other farewell.

So, as I was instructed by the Sydney *Daily Telegraph*, my scene was set; the hall porter was informed that if anyone asked for Mr Smith mine was the room to send them. The floor waiter prepared the sitting-room, advised me that 'the ladies' would probably drink brandy and ginger or gin and tonic and stocked the bar and refriger-ator. The thermostat kept switching itself on and off and I jumped and sat apprehensively watching 'This Day Tonight'. Black Orchid telephoned from the foyer and arrived a few minutes later—7.35; she shook hands and I perceived a lady in her late twenties, of statuesque proportions wearing a black and gold culotte suit with gold sandals. She asked for brandy and ginger, made herself com-fortable on the divan, eased off her sandals and lit a cigarette. She then asked whether anyone else was coming and I said yes.

The telephone rang . . . in fact the phone kept ringing because every escort phoned when she left home to say she was leaving home and then phoned from the lobby to say she was in the lobby. I gave Black Orchid her envelope containing 25 dollars and hoped that the others would arrive in the correct order. I should hate to overpay Mrs Right—or for that matter underpay Blue Venus. Mrs Right came next. A small lady in her thirties, she wore a violet mini-dress which could have been worn as a commercial for underwear. She also had on a leather-type coat and on her head she had what might once have been the bottom of the dress and was now a sort of Little Violet Riding Hood bonnet. Immensely ill-at-ease at seeing Black Orchid, she perched on the side of a sofa, refused to remove her coat, said that she did not care for a drink and seemed to light three or four cigarettes simultaneously.

Black Orchid and I did our best to make her at ease but it was an uphill struggle. And then the doorbell rang and Blue Venus arrived —tall, fair-haired, in her twenties, sort of surprised to see other people there. She too took her envelope and slipped it unopened in her handbag. She took off her black wrap and disclosed a full length silk—or possibly crêpe—light blue evening-gown that could have doubled as a nightshirt. The atmosphere in the room was now a bit tense . . . and it transpired in hardly any time that the reason for this was that Blue Venus knew Black Orchid. As Right was not doing anything about this, other than lighting cigarettes like crazy, it was up to me to try and make some sense out of the situation, which was that Blue Venus had gone to Black Orchid for a job, been refused and opened her own agency.

They both looked at Right and asked whether she was Mrs Right; Right (who did not even look as if she would suit Mr Right) said no she was not.

'Is there,' said Blue Venus, 'anyone else coming—perhaps a business acquaintance?'

The phone rang and Marie Claire from the lobby asked whether I were Mr Byron. I said come on up. She stayed down.

About fifteen minutes later, with Right relaxing sufficiently to take a brandy and discard her coat, the phone rang again.

'Mr Byron?'

'Yes?'

'You did not come down.'

I said, 'Please come up . . .' and some minutes later there was a knock on the door. My three guests looked eagerly and there came in a girl of about twenty, prettily dressed with a sweet intelligent face described by soft brown hair. I smiled and said Good Evening, noticed a look of acute apprehension on her face as she saw my other guests and then stammering something about 'I thought it was just going to be the two of us' she fled down the passage.

Black Orchid, who was fairly smart, asked if that had been Marie Claire. I said yes. She said, 'Go after her and bring her back . . .' but Marie Claire had been too fast. When I returned Blue Venus had opened her envelope and was counting her money, and Right said in a plaintive little voice that one did not get the full benefits of an escort agency if one used more than one. The waiter came in to take the order for dinner. Black Orchid was really the lead escort. She said, 'I want pork crackly . . . you've got it in one of the restaurants downstairs,' and prawns to start and white wine, and Right said pork crackly sounded interesting but could she have a steak, like a fillet, and Blue Venus said she didn't eat pork, but she would have some oysters and then some other meat. Right said she would have Claret, perhaps I would care to choose it and Blue Venus decided to stick to spirits and, as for being escorts for me, I found myself acting the part of duty butler and cigarette lighter to three women who began, after three or four drinks, to warm to each other and refer to mutual friends as Bill and George and (from Right), 'I get a lot of repeat bookings; repeat bookings are beaut.'

The first deviation from complete ladyhood arrived around 9.30 when Black Orchid told the waiter that the coffeespoons were like bloody soupspoons, Blue Venus went to the full length mirror, eased off her white court shoes and tugged at her petticoat, and Right said that men from Adelaide were fantastic . . . like there were those two fellers and I would go out with one of them one night and the next night I'd get a repeat booking from the other.

They then started talking about the occult (Blue Venus thought it was someone called Fred Occult from Brisbane) and Right said she always clicked with Leos but fought like crazy with Geminis.

I said it was nearly eleven. Right said 'I'm just beginning to enjoy it' and sent down for some more cigarettes on my account, and shortly after eleven they left, barely bothering to say goodbye—except for Black Orchid who was beginning to see that I was not the perve she had feared I was at 8 p.m.

I suppose Right was right. You *don't* get the full benefits of the escort service if you engage more than one—but you get a pretty interesting evening if you care for girls' talk. When I was a Scout I learnt that a Boy Scout smiles and whistles under all difficulties. That is where the escorts failed. Their conversation was dull; they never even offered to pour my coffee and, for what I consider pretty substantial payment—even if Right was five dollars cheaper than her rivals—they made no effort to amuse me. I am afraid that my suspicion that if one escort is good, four must be fantastic, has become 'if one escort is sad, three are pathetic'.

I expect by the time you read this Right will have upped her price to conform to the escort norm; Marie Claire's pretty girl is probably still running and I hope the others have repeat bookings until they are old and happy.

As for me, I spent the rest of my evenings in front of the hotel television set.

Keats and Cricket

It would be remarkable indeed if the poet John Keats were not a cricketer. His interest in all manly sports, his small but tough-knit frame, his quickness of hand and eye, the 'dexterity' he himself said he displayed as a medical student, all make it likely that if he had gone to Harrow, as his parents at first wished, he might have surpassed Lord Byron's record there. As it was, he went to a school where cricket was combined with poetry in a very personal way. The headmaster's son, Charles Cowden Clarke, was an enthusiast for all types of poetry. As Keats wrote of him:

> Who read for me the sonnet swelling loudly
> Up to its climax and then dying proudly?
> Who found for me the grandeur of the ode,
> Growing, like Atlas, stronger from its load?
> Who let me taste that more than cordial dram,
> The sharp, the rapier-pointed epigram?
> Shew'd me that epic was of all the king,
> Round, vast, and spanning all like Saturn's ring?

Yet, as well as being the first inspirer of the poet, Clarke had another distinction, in which literature was mixed with cricket. It was he who 'ghosted'—to what degree will never be known—the reminiscences of one of the most famous of the old Hambledon cricketers. When John Nyren's *Cricketer's Guide and Recollections of the Cricketers of My Time* appeared in 1833, Leigh Hunt, friend of both Nyren and Clarke, wrote: 'Mr. Nyren remembers, and Mr. Clarke records, every thing with a right taste, masculine as the game, and pleasant as the punch after it.'

The Clarke school at Enfield, which Keats attended officially from 1803 to 1810, and unofficially for a few years more during his medical apprenticeship in the neighbouring Edmonton, was a friendly and humane institution. Its atmosphere was created by its enlightened headmaster, John Clarke, the father of Charles Cowden Clarke. His object was to give a balanced education. The senseless cramming and the ignorant brutality of the big traditional public schools had no place in Clarke's régime. Every activity was encouraged, indoor and outdoor. There was abundant music—one of Keats's close friends, Edward Holmes, became an expert on Mozart

93

—and the boys cultivated individual gardens. Another contemporary of Keats was the notable inventor, Edward Cowper, whose experiments were given scope in his schooldays. French was taught by an émigré from the Revolution. In all this, games took their proper place, not regimented, but played for enjoyment and the exercise of skill. Cricket, in any case, was a relatively unsophisticated game at that time; it was only in Keats's schooldays that the off-break was invented, the 'cursed twist' that defeated so many batsmen, until they adapted their style to meet this new menace. Yet it is clear that it was played and regularly enjoyed from the way that Clarke's schoolboys use cricketing terms as a matter of course. There is a striking instance from Charles Cowden Clarke himself, who acted as pupil-teacher for his father. He describes how he used to go to the theatre—yet another activity encouraged by the school— walking twelve miles to Drury Lane or Covent Garden, and then another twelve back late at night after the performance by Sarah Siddons or Edmund Kean. Remembering this in his old age, Clarke wrote:

> Dark and solitary enough were the 'Green Lanes', as they were called, that lay between Holloway and Enfield—through picturesque Hornsey, rural Wood Green, and hedge-rowed Winchmore Hill— when traversed in the small hours past midnight. Yet I knew every foot of the way, and generally pursued that track as the nearest for the pedestrian. I seldom met a soul; but once a fellow who had been lying under a hedge by the way-side started up and began following me more nearly than I cared to have him, so I put on my cricketing speed and ran forward with a swiftness that few at that time could outstrip, and which soon left my would-be co-nightranger far behind.

After that, one would certainly have liked to have seen Clarke actually in the field, displaying the 'cricketing speed' which, even after about twenty miles of walking, and the free-for-all of a Regency theatrical audience, could still leave a footpad panting behind.

What is notable, of course, is the way in which Clarke uses a remark about cricket as a normal part of ordinary description; for this is the manner too which his most remarkable and in some ways most abnormal pupil, John Keats, uses in his own descriptive writing. It is true that he uses no metaphor from cricket in his poems, but nor does he import any image from what was well known to be his favourite sport, boxing. Football and bear-baiting, the latter in a cancelled passage of *Endymion*, appear in his poetry; but it is in his letters that his pleasure in cricket is shown. In fact, he first mentions the game in association with the word 'pleasure'. Some of Keats's finest letters, those in which he displays his whole self, witty, wise,

playful, profound, and even youthfully plain silly, are those written
to his brother George. George at the age of twenty-one had married
and emigrated to America, where he hoped to join one of the new
pioneer land schemes in Illinois, eventually settling down as a
general merchant and respected citizen of Louisville, Kentucky.
He had also been to the Clarke school, where his greater height had
made him generally mistaken for the elder brother. Keats wrote to
George as he must have talked to him in their schooldays; these are
family letters, sometimes even in a private family language, and
though they incidentally contain some of the most memorable
statements on poetry and life ever written, their basis is a deep
shared personal understanding. In the first of such long journal
packets, marked A to distinguish this fact in the erratic transatlantic
posts, Keats uses this example to show how much he intends this
understanding to continue even in absence:

> I intend to write you such Volumes that it will be impossible for me
> to keep any order or method in what I write: that will come first
> which is uppermost in my Mind, not that which is uppermost in
> my heart—besides I should wish to give you a picture of our Lives
> here whenever by a touch I can do it . . . this I am certain of, because
> I felt so much pleasure from the simple idea of your playing a game
> at Cricket—

George, on landing at Philadelphia, had evidently played cricket
there, and communicated the fact to John in his own first letter from
the new continent, as something that would please his poet brother.
It also provides evidence of that famous club, the Gentlemen of
Philadelphia, a fact that has not escaped the ever-questing eye of
that poet and cricketer Edmund Blunden, who writes, 'Formerly
the Americans, like Keats's American brother, had some room for
cricket.'

At all events, cricket was one of the parts of life which the poet
John Keats considered far from trivial, and fit to serve as a picture
of his own life in England. So, in his next-but-one journal letter to
his brother, the enormous package marked C, containing among
many other things the first draft of *La Belle Dame Sans Merci* and a
complete transcript of the *Ode to Psyche*, we find the poet himself
playing cricket. This was, it must be remembered, Keats's annus
mirabilis so far as poetry was concerned. Between September 1818
and September 1819 he wrote nearly all the poems that now make
him famous—*Hyperion, The Eve of St Agnes, The Eve of St Mark,
Lamia,* and, of course, all the great Odes. It is, in fact, with two of
the Odes that this cricketing account is curiously but closely connected. To Keats, however, much of this year was a time of despair,

frustration, and dissatisfaction. 'Nothing', he summed up, 'could in all its circumstances have fallen out worse for me than the last year has done, or could be more damping to my poetical talent.' We may now guess, as he afterwards came to suspect himself, that the first stages of tuberculosis were beginning to erode his otherwise powerful and robust constitution. March 1819 found him in a state which he himself described as 'an uneasy indolence', to which other witness, perhaps not inaccurate, has added an account of relatively heavy drinking. His one hope was that the fine weather, unusually early that year, would rouse him to renewed poetry. What happened was that the weather roused him to cricket, and that cricket—or rather one of the accidents of that extraordinary and wayward game —was indirectly a source of poetry. This is how Keats describes the events of Thursday, 18 March.

> Yesterday I got a black eye—the first time I took a Cricket bat— Brown who is always one's friend in a disaster applied a leech to the eyelid, and there is no inflammation this morning though the ball hit me directly on the sight—'twas a white ball—I am glad it was not a clout—

One may ask how, even on the bumpy improvised wicket of Hampstead Heath, one could get hit in the eye while batting to underarm bowling. The answer is that Keats, compact and muscular though he was, barely stood five feet high. The same accident had happened a few years earlier to his friend 'the little lawyer', Richard Woodhouse, reader to Keats's publishers, who was equally short. The real mystery is what 'a white ball' and 'a clout' mean in this context. Edmund Blunden once more has put forward the theory that there was a maker of cricket balls called Clout, and that the terms indicate a soft ball and a hard ball; but the clue may be some form of Regency sporting slang that still eludes us.

What is certain is that the phrase 'the first time I took a Cricket bat' does not mean that he had no previous acquaintance with the game. Later in the year, in another letter, he uses a cricketing phrase as a matter of course, writing 'I . . . can but go over the same Ground with you in a very short time, it not being more in length than the ordinary paces between the Wickets'. Keats's accident was an occurrence common to many batsmen early in the season—it was only the middle of March—when he completely mistimed the ball; it does not necessarily imply lack of familiarity or lack of skill. Its importance for us was its indirect effect on him as a poet. The next day saw him lying in bed until eleven in the morning, in a state which he himself quietly mocks—'if I had teeth of pearl and the breath of lillies I should call it langour—but as I am* I must call it Laziness', adding '*especially as I have a black eye'. In this state, he remarked, 'Neither Poetry nor Ambition, nor Love have any alertness of countenance as they pass by me: they seem rather like three figures on a greek vase—a Man and two women—whom no one but myself could distinguish in their disguisement.' Then, hearing of the family distress of a friend, he remarks, 'Circumstances are like Clouds continually gathering and bursting—While we are laughing the seed of some trouble is put into the wide arable land of events—while we are laughing it sprouts and grows and suddenly bears a poison fruit.'

Readers of Keats's poetry will at once recognize here the origins of two of his Odes. The first, and lesser-known, is the *Ode on Indolence*, beginning

> One morn before me were three figures seen,
> With bowed necks, and joined hands, side-faced;
> And one behind the other stepp'd serene,
> In placid sandals, and in white robes graced;
> They pass'd, like figures on a marble urn. . . .

The whole poem goes on, as Keats's musings in the letter had done, to identify these three figures as Poetry, Ambition and Love. Less often observed is the connection between his continued musings and the better-known *Ode on Melancholy*, or at any rate, parts of its second and third stanzas.

> But when the melancholy fit shall fall
> Sudden from heaven like a weeping cloud,

and again

> aching Pleasure nigh,
> Turning to poison while the bee-mouth sips:

It was some time, probably a few weeks, before the sensations of the morning after his cricketing misfortune turned into poetry; but we may safely add, as somewhat curious by-products of his love of cricket, the inspiration of these two poems. He himself once wrote elsewhere, concerning the habit of taking a piece of literature and meditating upon it, that 'A doze upon a Sofa does not hinder it, and a nap upon Clover engenders ethereal finger-pointings'. It may take a Keats, however, to transmute an injury on the cricket-field into the stuff of great poetry.

Orienteering

A faint feeling of despair forced its way through to me as I squelched through intractable mud and tried vainly to decipher the sodden map in my hand. My muscles ached, my eyes strained in vain through the beech wood in an effort to see a small red flag. War? An impending battle? No, only orienteering undertaken for fun, I reminded myself grimly.

This was the first meeting of the Sussex Occasional Orienteering Club of which we were founder members. Half an hour earlier fourteen families had been briefed, bravely accoutred from gumboots for six-year-olds to stout staves for those in their sixties. In each heart there throbbed the keen conviction that brain could win over brawn and enthusiasm over both and here I was half an hour later utterly baffled, being swiftly overtaken by a knot of jubilant children, their eyes so eager, their faces so triumphant, that I could not help forgiving them for the swift look of pity they threw in my direction. On I squelched until, suddenly, out of the wood, over a gate and in the lee of the hill, I momentarily forgot all about the clues and the scurrying figures of my competitors ahead. The sight of rolling hills stretching out to the sea struck me with full force—a sight so glorious that all action seemed to stop for a moment. Then with renewed optimism and the sweet smell of spring in my nostrils I stretched my legs along a firmer path and speeded up. The sheer pleasure of gathering speed was suddenly enhanced by the sight of my daughter gleaming exultantly; she was the other half of my team and had found the elusive red flag.

For the past ten years I have tasted many different sports as, goaded by four increasingly active children, I have searched for a solution. Now I have the answer—orienteering.

This sport hails surprisingly from Sweden, not from Gordonstoun (though the privations of some of its more rugged variations would certainly appeal to Kurt Hahn). In Sweden ten per cent of the population claim to be regular orienteers and I have no reason to doubt the claim of dedicated Swedes.

The general idea is that competitors must find, in the correct order, a number of red and white flags scattered about some wild, inhospitable, but probably beautiful, part of the country. The clue to the sites is a description and a grid map reference on a $2\frac{1}{2}''$ to the

99

mile map. The description is usually deliberately inadequate (for example, 'a re-entrant'), occasionally oblique ('after the last muddy path you will have need of this!'), more occasionally witty or erudite and needing something of a *Times* crossword mentality. The courses can be varied in length and difficulty to suit age and energy or lack of it over three to seven miles with a dozen checkpoints. Experts have been known to cover seven miles and find all the points within an hour!

The skill lies in always knowing where you are. Your actual surroundings have to be fitted to some landmark so that you are never completely lost and if you miss a checkpoint you can retrace your steps to a known mark and try again. In time you can gauge your stride length with precision and reach a point within a few yards of your target. Then, even if the course setter has hidden the flag in a yew tree that has been thickening up nicely since 1066 you may still find it. The quickest route may not be the most direct, unless you are prepared to swim an icy river holding your compass and map aloft in one hand. Other competitors have to be misled as much as possible. The late Stephen Potter would admire the nonchalance with which the experienced orienteer gets away very quickly from a checkpoint and without speaking gives the impression to his rival that the checkpoint is in a totally opposite direction.

No competition is without its problems. Once I came dangerously near to facing a firing squad. We were on a stretch of land used for war games and followed, or more likely preceded, by my children I was concentrating so hard on small red flags in thickets that I missed a large red flag fluttering overhead. As the twigs snapped underfoot there was a louder cracking sound in the distance which my children asked me about. Still absorbed in my map, I excluded the sound from my consciousness and told them to concentrate on map reading. Minutes later I met the firing party returning from practice, which had nearly included a live target, and realized that I had made one of my commoner mistakes of reading the compass wrongly by 180°.

After the competition is over everyone gathers round the starter who has laid out the course and comes in for a whole host of cheerful rebukes from those who had found the course and clues impossibly hard and from those very superior few who thought it all too easy for words. Then best of all in our Sussex Club, everyone drives to a home of one competitor for steaming tea, rock buns and fruit cake in front of an open fire. Everyone is arguing about clues found, points gained, difficulties surmounted and advising the winner, who will have the task of setting the next course. There is a sporting camaraderie as tired limbs are rested and friendships are renewed. As I looked at the group with small children sitting on the hearth so glowing, so eager, so full of rock cake, I thought of the ancient philosophers who gloomily tell us there is no such thing as complete happiness—but they did not know about orienteeering.

I have written as though I had achieved some measure of success but I confess that this is really more of a Walter Mitty dream, though in time my experience will doubtless enable me to write a preface to The Awful Orienteer's Guide. Now I am a veteran scarred by many a piece of unexpected barbed wire and toughened by the exigencies of impossible courses and impossible English weather. Now a talented new generation has arisen. Orienteeering, as a sport, has what the sales advertisements would say 'faster growth than its rivals'. New clubs are mushrooming all over the country. There are now eight regional associations affiliated to the National Federation and it even earns its grant from the government Sports Council.

One word about its most diabolic variant—night orienteering. I happen to be a brain specialist and at one time of family crisis we had a splendidly cheerful Cockney home-help. One morning, seeing a heap of muddy clothes in the corner, my wife tried to explain to her that I had just come back from a night orienteering competition. My wife talked about torches, maps, forests and mud. There was a pause and Elsie said: ' 'E examines other people's 'eads. 'E ought to 'ave 'is 'own 'ead examined!'

But I shall not give up; one can enjoy it and still be fairly bad at it and this is more than you can say for many other sports. The cricketer who never scores will soon condemn cricket as a game for two played by twenty-two. The golfer may struggle on for the rare pleasure soon of smiting the ball on what P.G. calls 'the meat', but he will find the game costly, especially at the bar. I have always had a theory that the person who really appreciates a sport for its own sake is one who is bad at it! A good orienteer may get tied up with the success of the game; a bad orienteer *must* love orienteering for its own sake. I have never to my knowledge won any orienteering contest or even been placed, but the orienteer can go on learning and can muddle round with his family, giving point to a day in the countryside, sharpening his powers of observation.

Orienteering has a short history in Britain but I am sure it has a rosy future. The countryside of Britain offers an escape that will become more important as working lives become increasingly restricted. Yes, a 'royal' sport.

Cottages on a Norfolk Byroad
Edward Seago

RAYMOND BAXTER

The Shrinking World of Tomorrow's Taverner

An anniversary is, by tradition, a time for looking back. But for forward thinking people like Lord's Taverners, and notably the Twelfth Man, an anniversary must also be an appropriate time for looking ahead, and there can have been few periods in history when competent crystal-gazing has been in greater demand, but presented a more difficult challenge to the soothsayer.

Without delving into the realms of mysticism, however, it is possible to obtain an accurate preview of, at least, the 'hardware' which will be at the disposal of Tomorrow's Taverner.

The time-lapse between the drawing-board stage and the everyday use of any device clearly depends upon its complexity. But one of the more interesting phenomena of contemporary technology is that, almost regardless of the scale of the operation, the period involved tends, paradoxically, to be increasing. In the days of craftsmanship and cottage industry, a few hours might separate the birth of an idea from its execution in durable material. The blacksmith, after pondering over a pint or two at the local the squire's requirement for new entrance gates for the manor house, would translate his imaginative concept into wrought-iron as fast as he could swing his hammer. The new pattern which the weaver dreamed after a particularly rich harvest-supper would emerge in glowing colour from his loom as soon as he had recovered from his hangover. The carpenter who invented the gate-leg table doubtless had the chips flying off his first prototype within hours of his wife's request for more space in the dining-room.

But the demands of mass production soon put a stop to all that. When something has to be made by a machine, its design has to be modified accordingly. The more stringent and complex the demands made upon the finished article, or dictated by its manufacturing process, the longer the period of what has come to be known as R and D—Research and Development—and all that this entails. The Wright Brothers built their first aeroplane in days. The fact that the first two Concordes are numbered 001 and 002 speaks for itself. Production Prototypes will be numbered from 01. The first fare winner will be Number 1, and at the time of writing, that is still four years and a £100 million or so away.

What this all means in terms of practical soothsaying is that what is happening in the laboratory today gives us a preview of the market place ten or more years hence. Therefore, if the object of the exercise is not so much to keep up with the Joneses but to get one step ahead of them, the compulsory reading is not the popular Press, nor even the 'glossies', but the technical papers presented to learned bodies and specialist groups in the ever-growing calendar of symposia and conferences which keeps the practising technologist busily on the trot from country to country with his briefcase in one hand and an airline schedule in the other.

Of course there are many forces which bring their influence to bear. Politics for one, although it is not intended to occupy any of this valuable space on that subject. The Writer is in no way qualified so to indulge himself, and the Reader, officially at any rate, is disbarred from that pursuit. Nor is it the intention to allow this particular crystal ball to become fogged by the complexities of Big Business. It is accepted, for example, that shareholders' money should not inevitably be devoted to the construction of the better mousetrap until an adequate return has been won from the investment in the original, if inferior, model.

Personally, I find much more sinister the attitude, not unknown in influential circles, which suggests that technology is a bore and that science is a dangerous threat. From this it follows that anyone indulging himself in either is some kind of nut, or at best a necessary Evil of Our Time not to be entrusted with any serious responsibility in the conduct of business affairs or civil administration. Even in the modest—or should it be immodest—realms of popular television, it has taken those in control of what we see 'on the box' an unconscionable time to realize that technology can be comprehensible and that quite normal people find it a fascinating subject.

There is considerable evidence to suggest that the principal recipient of this book has himself played a not unimportant part in the conversion to this more enlightened point of view. But there clearly remains much to be done. How often are we told that we cannot afford this or that investment in our technological future, when the relevant question must surely be whether we can afford *not* to develop, encourage and harness in every possible way our national genius for invention.

Take, for example, the urgent problem of strangulation by congestion which threatens virtually every city centre in the Western world. It so happens that international co-operation between a leading British company and a Swiss research trust has produced what may well be the most attractive and practical solution. But few people have ever heard of it. The popular stock answer to the question of what to do about city traffic congestion is to apply still further restriction—to 'price out' the private motorist, to ban the commuter car, to outlaw the petrol engine, and so on. But the Anglo-Swiss idea, which is already attracting active interest in the United States, is more positive in its approach. Given that mobility for the individual is the requirement, but that the continued mobility of vehicles is the problem, then instead of allowing vehicles to move on static roads, why not provide moving roads for the use of individuals? The idea is not entirely new. The principle is precisely that of any conventional escalator, or the type of horizontal passenger conveyor which has made its appearance during the last decade in such places as airports, major exhibitions and the like. The difficulty has been that the speed of movement has been restricted to less than two miles per hour because of the necessity to accelerate the individual user as he steps on to the conveyor and, by the same token, to enable him to dismount at the far end without having to indulge in a major feat of acrobatic agility. This problem has been overcome by the invention of an ingenious accelerating-feeder which, stepped upon at $1\frac{1}{2}$ mph at the receiving end, will within the length of a football pitch deliver the pedestrian at 10 mph at the far end without requiring any physical effort from him. Thus smoothly and effortlessly accelerated to the target speed, the individual can then step on to the main belt of the conveyor which, travelling at 10 miles an hour, will whisk him towards his destination at a point-to-point speed currently unattainable in almost any city centre. The system can be installed to work at ground level, below the surface, or elevated on a superstructure. The main 'walkway' and its 'feeder accelerators' would of course be covered and air conditioned, and preliminary designs suggest that the layout could be aesthetically attractive as well as offering immense practical advantages. Passengers are, of course, at liberty either to stand still on the moving conveyors, or add the speed of their own pace. Thus a point-to-point average speed approaching 14 mph would be an entirely practical proposition from, shall we say, Waterloo Station via Trafalgar Square and Piccadilly Circus to Oxford Street, in the thick of the rush hour. And even a police car in a hurry is unlikely to be able to match that today! During his journey by passenger conveyor the Taverner of Tomorrow may enjoy the view, pass the time of day with a casual acquaintance, do a spot of window shopping (albeit somewhat briskly) or merely admire the mini-skirts, or whatever other attraction the fashion of the day might provide.

Offering freedom of mobility to the individual at a price calculated to be extremely competitive with any conventional mode of transport, fumeless drive, silence, and many other social advantages currently under pressure, it is difficult to see how the 'Moving

Walkway' will not win its place in the city centres of the world during the next ten to twenty-five years—depending on the foresight and imagination of the City Fathers concerned.

Less revolutionary, but every bit as important, is the recent discovery by engineers of British Rail that worn rolling-stock wheels are more efficient than new ones. Based on the 'worn wheel profile', as it is called, they have already designed trains capable of cruising at up to 150 mph on existing main lines without the expense of having to lay special high speed track as did the Japanese for their New Tokaido Line. The highly streamlined carriages will 'bank' into turns in the same way as aircraft, thanks to an automatic system of hydraulic rams built into an extremely efficient and completely new system of suspension. These Advanced Passenger Trains, APTly named, will make mincemeat of the journey times from London to Glasgow or Penzance before the 1980s.

However, spurred on by the financial success of the New Tokaido, the Japanese are now designing 250 mph trains based on the linear induction motor and magnetic hover suspension, both British discoveries. The linear motor, pioneered by Professor Eric Laithwaite, enjoys the magnificent advantage of employing no moving parts despite its immense performance capability. 'Magnetic hover' uses the fact beloved of every schoolboy that 'like poles repel', instead of Sir Christopher Cockerell's cushion of air on which rides the now conventional hovercraft. But interestingly enough, a man-carrying magnetic hover 'train' was built in its inventor's garden in southern Buckinghamshire five years ago.

The Japanese plan to be carrying 12,000 passengers per hour between Tokyo and Osaka by 1985 at 250 mph is not lost upon the planemakers. Hence the current emphasis on VTOL (vertical take off and landing) and STOL (for 'vertical' read 'short'). If aviation is to stay in the short-haul passenger business against such competition, it has to have more airfields nearer to city centres. Not least because of this, the noise factor is now a primary consideration in civil aircraft design—an interesting example of the effect of public opinion upon what had been heretofore a purely technological parameter. In fact it is this same question of noise which may decide, literally, the shape of things to come in vertical take-off.

There is every indication that a major battle will develop between the protagonists of the rotor for lift-off, and the direct thrust of jet engines—as used in the world's first operational jet VTOL, the Hawker Siddeley Harrier, with its remarkable vectored thrust engine.

Rotor-lift aircraft have more limited performance, but are quieter. The American helicopter industry is, not surprisingly, backing the rotor. The European consortia are working on multiple, direct-thrust jets. In Britain there are design studies in progress for both configurations, as well as aircraft with advanced STOL capability.

But whatever way this particular cookie will crumble the point-to-point navigational system, which currently obliges aircraft to fly in narrow corridors between radio beacons, will have to be abandoned if the mounting crisis of air traffic congestion is to be overcome. The alternative Area Navigational Systems call for electronic aids capable of telling pilots precisely where they are 'on the map' from second to second, and more than one such system has already been on display at Farnborough.

From all this it will be apparent that although journey times between city centres will be halved in the next two decades there is a wide variety of choice available. It seems that Tomorrow's Taverner may still have to make agonizing decisions, though these will no doubt be ultimately governed as ever by the quality of the freeze-dried bitter served aboard by those competing for his patronage.

Apart from that, the question of who is to pay his fare becomes of increasing importance. When the supersonic transports come into service—and they will, whether the anti-Concorde lobby likes it or not—tickets for them will cost about 40 per cent more than for the subsonic Jumbos which will still be flying twenty years and more from now. But the record of the travel business as a whole shows that reduced journey-time increases traffic. People in a hurry are prepared to pay for extra speed. Already, however, it is also clear that the tourist will sacrifice speed for economy. Therefore the development of a two-tier service seems inevitable, with the alternative of ultra speed and luxury available for those to whom time means money.

But the businessman who now spends so much of his valuable time flying from conference to conference already has alternative means of communication at his disposal. A telephone call to a London number can book him a multi-channel video conference circuit with complete facilities supplied by the GPO. It may tax his patience to the limit to get an answer from Directory Inquiries in order to obtain the correct number in the first place, but the facilities are there, and the potential is clearly enormous.

Perhaps of even greater significance are recent achievements in the techniques of data transmission. We are all well aware of the ever-widening role played by computers in our everyday lives. They are handling much of the daily routine of banking, and their application in business can now be taken to the level of the cash register in the department store, but since computers depend fundamentally on the information which is fed into them, it has become increasingly necessary for them to communicate directly with each other. This they can now do at incredible speeds, measured in thousands of 'bits' (of information) per second. What's more, advanced machines are capable of spewing out this exchanged information, and conclusions based upon it at equally astonishing speeds, and in almost any form desired—from charts and graphs, to visual presentations on television screens, and even working blueprints and drawings.

Given these facilities, literally at his fingertips, and with the ability to enjoy face-to-face confrontation with the people he wants to contact almost anywhere in the world, it's difficult to see how Tomorrow's Taverner is going to be able to drum up any effective excuse ever to leave his office.

Travel, it seems, may therefore assume in the near future a new dimension. It will be strictly for fun. Of course most Taverners have known this all along anyway. And is it too much to hope that chopped down to size as our Earth will be, its inhabitants, with time at last on their side, will make it a place as happy as it is beautiful?

JOHN SNAGGE

Travail by Train
A TAILPIECE TO THE TOKYO OLYMPICS

One of the many prides of the Japanese is that their trains, whether suburban, long distance or super-express, run exactly on time. With some confidence, therefore, I decided to make my way from Tokyo to Enoshima by train. Enoshima is the coastal town of Sagami Bay where the yachting events of the Olympic Games were taking place.

I had found from practical experience that it was more comforting on such occasions to have a colleague, for four hands are better than two when it comes to attempting a conversation in Japanese. Alun Williams had completed his immediate task of reporting the swimming events the day before I was due to go, so I suggested that he might like to journey with me. As a Welshman he at least had another strange language which might be useful, as well as a forthright and expressive approach to any awkward situation that might arise.

The most excellent (and, I might add, attractive) Japanese English-speaking secretary told us that the train left for Enoshima from Shinjuku station. To be there on time we had to catch the 7.35 a.m. train from platform 4.

We had railway passes, so at 6.30 a.m. we set forth from the Diamond Hotel by taxi to Shinjuku and arrived in plenty of time. Breakfast seemed important, so Alun strode to a fruitstall and procured two large apples and two bananas. After a short conversation in Japanese on the one side and Welsh on the other he paid the princely sum of 50 yen (9*d*).

Now it seems that even the Japanese have some difficulty in finding their way around, so it was not surprising that it took us a little time to establish our starting line. But by virtue of the bold strategy of Wales in passing barriers with passes which later were shown to have no bearing at all upon our set course, we found platform 4 and saw to our relief '7.35—Enoshima'. We joined an orderly group of other travellers lined up across the platform. The train drew in and disgorged a vast concourse of people, but before the tail-enders were out our fellow passengers were in. We were a little late on the draw, not quite knowing the form. So by the time we were aboard there was standing room only.

On the dot of time we left platform 4. In the next half-hour the train stopped at about five stations. Nobody got out, but a horde of people swarmed in. We would not have thought it possible for one undersized hamster to creep in, but by taking a run at it, and with the help of professional shovers-in on the platform, the commuters came aboard. Alun and I had by now lost contact with each other. Occasionally, through momentary gaps in the swaying multitude, I glimpsed the towering figure of Alun with glasses slightly askew and perched on a very determined expression.

Saturation point was reached, and then gradually from station to station the pressure became less until breathing was possible. Eventually we could sit down. Over an hour had gone by and we were due at Enoshima at 8.45 a.m.

At 8.55 a.m. I tentatively suggested that either the claim that Japanese trains were never late was an exaggeration or, alternatively, we were on the wrong one. Alun, with supreme confidence and wholly undisturbed, took charge and said that all was well—it was just that we were a little late.

At about 9.20 a.m. we seemed to be very lonely travellers and the train came to a halt. We looked out and found that, short of ramming Fujiyama, the train could go no further. The platform indicated 'Hakone'. The buffer indicated a terminus.

At least we knew now that something was wrong. Undisturbed and unhurried Alun approached the train conductor. In an animated conversation in no known language, heavily interlarded with Welsh, the conductor was led to the conclusion that we did not really want to go to Hakone and that our target was Enoshima.

At this point the conductor disappeared and Alun suggested that we should sit it out, for surely, he said, the train must go back whence it came, and the worst that could happen would be an eventual return to Tokyo. So we settled down to apples and bananas. Presently the conductor returned and said in clear and unmistakable English, 'Car'. Puzzled, but feeling that at least here was action, we followed the conductor to the other end of the train where we were signalled to sit down. We did—and we waited.

Very soon we were off in the opposite direction. The conductor then conveyed to us by means of a few English words, a couple of timetables in Japanese and much mime, that we should change trains when he told us. Relaxed, we awaited instructions. At Fuji Sawa station he pointed to the door and then to a stationary train some three platforms away. With much bowing and much smiling we left him, climbed aboard the other train, and some twenty minutes later arrived duly at Enoshima. The time by now was 11.10 a.m. Happily the yacht racing was still in progress and we saw the end of all the races.

I went again next day by train to Enoshima. This time, to my regret, Alun could not come, so I had an expert bilingual guide. We *did* get the 7.35 a.m., and it *was* from platform 4. But on this occasion we (*a*) got into that part of the train which exclusively went to Enoshima, and (*b*) by swift and nimble movement at Shinjuku got seats before the stampede was properly under way. *And* we got a proper breakfast of bacon and fried eggs at a café when we arrived, right on time—8.45 a.m. at Enoshima.

There are two morals to this story:

1. Never travel to strange destinations when the language problems prevent any communication with officials, unless you have Alun Williams with you;
2. Never have bacon and fried eggs at a café in a small seaside town in Japan unless you have completely mastered the art of using chopsticks.

JAMES FISHER

Man and the British Environment

My father, James Fisher, was asked by the Lord's Taverners if he would contribute something to Prince Philip's birthday book. He was most honoured by this invitation; but he died before he could write anything. I offer here what I think is a fair distillation of his concept of conservation in his own country. This is my own arrangement of the words. Anyone who knew him, or read his work, will know how much better my father himself would have arranged them; I hope they will be indulgent.

Crispin Fisher

> Accuse not Nature, she hath done her part;
> Do thou but thine, and be not diffident
> Of wisdom, she deserts thee not, if thou
> Dismiss not her.
> Milton: *Paradise Lost*, VIII, 561–64

Man belongs to a species of sophisticated ape, distinguished from other animals by a certain power to store and communicate experience, by certain skills with tools and engines, and by certain capacities for abstract thought, pure curiosity, spiritual values, and both altruistic and viciously aggressive behaviour. He has existed in his present species form for only a quarter of a million years, and has made more of a mess of the face of the earth than has any other agent in the thousands of millions of years of the planet's existence.

The first Old Stone Age man was a food-gatherer and a skilful hunter (for the pot) of all things of the land and of shallow waters. It is a characteristic of life to press its distribution to its utmost limits, and men learned to master their foremost rivals, usurp their homes, and dominate the hunting-grounds. As his skills improved, man became an exterminator, and huge elements of the Pleistocene fauna, particularly heavies like forest-elephants and hippos, disappeared for ever. At some point Stone Age groups of men must have encountered the effects of their over-kill, and developed a lore of self-denying ordinance. They probably evolved cropping and rationing rules, and came to understand the value and significance of sharing space and prey with other animal species.

There is evidence that, much later, the Vikings too imposed self-denying ordinances. They founded most of the northern sea-fowling communities and their systems, and we may be pretty certain that they soon arrived by trial and error at a crop-limit custom in the outlying Scottish islands.

With the beginning of agriculture, man adopted a new defensive and offensive attitude towards wildlife; he became suspicious of animals in general as possible takers of what he owned or was growing. The measures which he took to pre-empt an imaginary enemy heralded his discovery of hunting for fun.

In furtherance of his sport, he evolved artificial methods of raising stocks of prey, and 'game' was as sanctified as 'vermin' was execrated. Between these two groups lay most of Britain's animals, sometimes gaining from the protection of game, and sometimes losing in the suppression of predatory animals.

In the nineteenth century Britain's wildlife was threatened by the Industrial Revolution. Man's actions produced myriad reactions by the creatures and plants whose habitats he made untenable, and nature adapted itself strenuously to the changes in the country's environment. We may accept that during the period of industrial expansion, wildlife must have benefited by the jealous guarding of hunting areas by the privileged landowners. These landowners were not preserving wildlife as such; but they were preserving its habitats, and that was of immense value.

But 'shotgun man's' most important early mistake was the loss of respect for his believed rivals, the animals of prey. Skilful and ruthless in assailing these rival predators, shotgun man had by the beginning of this century, for example, depressed to very small populations all but the most tenacious of Britain's birds of prey.

Happily, a reverse process got well under way by the middle of the current century, and it has become a definite part of the British sporting tradition to kill only in certain ways and at certain times. Thus hunting does not now destroy the wildlife of its area: it merely takes a toll like any other predatory animal.

But if wildlife was protected from the imbalance which would have arisen out of uncontrolled hunting, an entirely new factor, the premature large-scale use of chemical pest-destroyers, put the clock back again. Intensive propaganda, backed with scientific measurement, was necessary before wildlife could begin to be protected from the consequences of chemical farming, and despite new sense and improvements in this sphere protection is not yet nearly adequate.

After 250,000 years of the activities of man the hunter, man the farmer, and man the industrialist, the British countryside shows now a face which is paradoxical. Smoke, fumes and chemicals from our industrial areas do untold harm to the plant life which is the basis of our 'ecosystem'; yet various living things thrive alongside the masses of humanity and their effluent. Even industrialisation has something to offer in the creation of stretches of water, of reservoirs, canals, gravel-pits, sewage-farms, and so on, which attract and support abundant wildlife.

Fields are now so large that there is not that profusion of hedges and thickets which made a safe home for small creatures; mechanised arable cultivation tends to deplete the numbers of ground-breeding animals; chemical farming tends to upset whole inter-relating faunal structures by its random destruction of balancing components in nature. Yet Britain still contains stretches of deep rural country, commons, fens, wastes, moors, mountains, and thousands of miles of sea-coast, which maintain a wildlife as magnificent of its kind as any in the world.

As a nation, we coldly note the ribbon development of our marvellously varied scenery, and laconically accept the rash pollution of our living space by selfish interests unable to see beyond their short-term greed. Yet no other country has lived through so many decades of multiplying public enthusiasm for wildlife. And no other comparable country has dedicated, as we have, more than a tenth of its area as National Parks, Areas of Outstanding Natural Beauty, National Forest Parks, National Trust Areas, Nature Reserves, Geological Monuments, Greenways, Trackways, Wildfowl Refuges and Bird Sanctuaries.

Our standards of care for domestic animals are high, and our rich and distinctive literature of natural history shows us to be observant and compassionate. Yet, despite our philosophy of respect for all forms of life, despite urban man's burning nostalgia for the rural tradition, many people find it hard to see that the ultimate protection of nature and all its ecological systems demands a plan whose core is the management of the environment, and an enlightened exploitation of its wild resources, based on scientific research and measurement. Many people cannot understand that such a plan does not seek to repress man the hunter: Europe is networked with a complex array of public licence systems to foster hunting and at the same time the populations of the hunted. It is when the rules are unknown, or lost and forgotten, or ruthlessly ignored, that a situation of over-kill develops.

The modern over-kills are 'investment over-kills', like over-whaling and over-fishing, with expensive tools and heavy capital investment behind them. Such investments run contrary to the public good and even to the interests of the investors (let alone the future of the animal species concerned), unless they can be planned and controlled by ecological criteria.

An ecologist sees and understands an environment in which living things share the same ground and make, maintain and break equilibria, co-operate and compete. Man, with his intellectual superiority, is at the top of the environment's pecking-order, and wields a strong sword and a heavy responsibility in the lives of the rest of the living world. His fecundity and his movements produce changes that have a profound effect on the wildlife which shares the countryside with him.

The study of nature was formerly undertaken by the naturalist, a compassionate, sincere explorer of truth, with the seeing eye, and the love of his habitat. An ecologist is a naturalist whose work has acquired a new vigour through his analytical approach to the problems of wildlife. He is in no circumstances indifferent to the beauty of the subject which he studies; but his role is fundamentally that of a searcher for knowledge, his function to report objectively in order to focus the nation's attention on wildlife in a state of crisis. Because there is no such thing as pure research, the ecologist becomes from his application of immediate truth a forecaster of consequences, for he knows that the survival of the human species is inescapably linked with the survival of all other forms of life.

This knowledge in itself is not enough to conserve and regulate the wildlife of a changing countryside; but it evokes with its message of alarm a positive will to make provision for our living neighbours by setting aside reserves and sanctuaries. Such reserves are not effective, in a small and heavily populated country, without 'scientific game-keeping', the intelligent application of growing scientific evidence of cause and effect. To this application the public attitude is crucial, for laws made ahead of the will of the people rarely achieve their intended result. The fate of wildlife in a land of surging humanity devolves on all of us as individuals. We cannot have reserves and National Parks without spending money for them and on them; but such areas have immense social value for the recreation of the community, quite apart from their value as wildlife sanctuaries.

A sanctuary as such is ecologically futile. There is no advantage in a vast reserve from which only one species, man, is excluded. Within National Parks, agriculture, forestry, and other human works must continue, and the areas must pay their way. But an emphasis must be laid on giving wildlife its chance. In these areas, man is a part of the ecological complex, his development not to be stopped, but to be steered; his influence neither to be deplored nor exaggerated, but to be self-controlled.

At a national level we cannot look forward to a continuing enjoyment of Britain's natural resources unless we take the long view and organize their protection and preservation wisely. This is conservation. And unless we attend much more closely to the conservation of our worldwide environment, the future for our own species looks grim.

Before our generation mingles with the universe, our prayer for nature must be: For what we once beheld in awe, make us truly responsible.

. . . and one Dodo, with Birthday Greetings to H.R.H. Prince Philip from H.R.H. Prince Bernhard. Sign here, mate . . . .

Happy Elephant
David Shepherd

'And do you have any particular hobbies or outside interests, your Highness?'

PATRICK BERESFORD

Polo Reflections

From the Chiswick flyover traffic bursts out of London like fish escaping from a net. Ahead stretches the wide ribbon of the M4, sweeping on past London Airport and Windsor Castle, beyond whose imposing bulk lies that magnificent area of woods and paddocks that is Windsor Great Park.

In the midst of the Park shimmer the broad fields of the Guards Polo Club. It would be an ungenerous soul that did not warm to the sights and sounds surrounding their No. 1 ground on a fine summer afternoon. Above the stands the flags of many nations fly proudly in the breeze. In the pony lines gauchos from Argentina, seises from India and cowboys from Texas mingle with the English girl grooms, whilst out on the field an ever-flowing tide of men and horses surge backward and forward in a kaleidoscope of colour and action.

For those who rejoice in a ball struck cleanly, and in the courage of a horse in conflict, there is no parallel to polo. It is the fastest game in the world and naturally possesses that small but alluring element of danger without which no pastime is wholly satisfying. It is truly international, but through being mainly amateur and confined to a comparatively small community, there is not that intensity of feeling that sometimes mars other international sports. For in this age it often seems that the battlefield has been replaced by the playing field as an outlet for nationalistic fervour.

The polo champions of the world are the Argentinians, who because of their natural advantages in climate and terrain, plus their seemingly inexhaustible reserves in players and ponies, have reigned supreme for over thirty-five years. Except by quirk of fate, it is unforeseeable that they will ever seriously be challenged. Nevertheless, the game is equally enjoyed in over seventy other countries.

In many, home-bred ponies are hard to come by, simply because in terms of time and expense they are uneconomical to produce. For this reason the vast majority of ponies playing in England are imported from Argentina, though most players actually prefer the small, well-trained English thoroughbred. He has the balance and the courage and that extra turn of speed which can prove vital.

Every player recalls with pride and gratitude the ponies that have served him best. Two of the highest class that have played at Windsor in the last decade were both English thoroughbreds, one known as

Gussy, the other named Joxer. The former was a big brown mare with a white face and rather a lot of white about the eye—reputedly a sign of temperament, and sure enough she was not particularly easy to handle. But she was blessed with a smooth and majestic stride, and to watch her sweeping down the ground, challenging the wind for speed, was a sight not easily forgotten. In 1963 she went with the British string to win the American National Handicap in Chicago, in the finals of which it was said that 'like a great ship gathering sail, she soon had the opposition toiling in her wake'. Soon afterwards she was retired from polo to the more peaceful atmosphere of Her Majesty's stud farm on the edge of the Great Park.

The second was a supremely elegant chestnut gelding. Because he was bred and trained in Ireland he soon came to be known as 'the Irish pony'. Never once did he fail or fear or falter, and at the close of the Ascot Week Tournament of 1966 he was the judges' unanimous choice for the cup awarded to the best playing pony. A great cheer went up when the result was announced, and the crowd surged round as Joxer was led from the pony lines to the Royal Box. As always he stepped forth firmly and boldly, his coat gleaming, his head held high, the master of all he surveyed. Later that year he went to Argentina with the English international team. There, ridden by Patrick Kemple in a critical period of the Open Championship, he met a hero's death. The ball had come to them in mid-field. With two men to beat, Joxer called upon that sensational reserve of speed to which the crowd at home so often thrilled. He outran them both, and Kemple's stick made good the goal. Less than a minute later the pony was dead. In mid-stride that gallant heart had ceased to beat. Like so many of his countrymen, the Irish pony had fought and died for England, far from home and on a foreign field.

On this occasion the English side won through by a single goal. For many this was an unqualified triumph, but for those who knew and loved him best, it simply meant that Joxer had not died in vain.

There are many facets that add lustre to polo—the attractions of team play, the lure of competition, the incomparable sensation of striking a ball at speed, but above all it is the thrill of riding a pony that is fast, fearless and obedient. For such, it is the breath of heaven that blows between their ears. Gypsy gold, they say, does not clink and clatter, it gleams in the sun and neighs in the dark.

High in the Himalayas, near the natural arena which was the cradle of polo, there stands a rough wooden sign which reads:

> Let other men do other things,
> The King of Sports is still the Sport of Kings.

A sentiment which anyone who has played polo is bound to share.

LAURENCE OLIVIER

My Life in Cricket

In December 1940 I sailed home from America and arrived back in England during the first week of January 1941. Thanks to splendid staff work by some of my friends, one of them being Ralph Richardson who was already in the Service, I was able to present myself at the Admiralty without any delay—and joined the Royal Navy. For the next two years I flew aeroplanes in the Fleet Air Arm.

I owe a tremendous amount, as an actor, to those two years of flying, for they taught me, more than any other experience of my life, the true value and importance of co-ordination—of the balance of mind and body. It is the essence of good flying and, to my mind, it is without doubt the essence of good acting too.

I have often been asked what I consider to be the most important physical attribute for an actor. There is, I think, no such thing. One *could* be tempted to say that the eyes are *almost* the most important—for me, at any rate, that is near the truth—or that, on the stage, it is the voice. But the answer really is that an actor is, or should be, a finely balanced piece of machinery. And since one part cannot work without the other, it is idle to speculate which is the most important bit of the engine. If one word were essential, that would be 'stamina'.

One of the best co-ordinated of men whom I have ever met is Douglas Bader. At a time when his life seemed for him, as he would say, somewhat unpromising, it was this nice balance of mind and body which enabled him to face it with a rare blend of courage and audacity, and make of it a triumph of good humour and distinction. I met him only once during the war—but not for the first time, for we had been at school together. In fact he figured in a most memorable day of my life.

He was a natural athlete and very good at all games, whereas, as a boy, I had a very poor physique—very poor indeed. All my life I have been at great pains to improve and develop it, and to this day I still go to a gymnasium at least twice a week, to relax and keep me strong. I may be wrong, but I have always imagined that a strong body means a strong heart.

Despite my lack of natural endowment I had every schoolboy's longing to excel at games, and of them all I craved most earnestly to be a fine cricketer. My father whom, all my life, I had sought to emulate, was a very, very good cricketer. He played for his college at Oxford and was a triple Blue when he came down and went to Durham. He later played for Hampshire and for the MCC, so it was natural therefore that both my brother and I were keen on the game and longed to play it well. We rather regarded it as part of our heritage. I have often thought what a pity it is—how much a better life I would have had, what a better man I would have been, how much healthier an existence I would have led, if I had been a cricketer instead of an actor. But it was not to be. I don't know what it was—the finger of God had not touched us with a stump or something. It just wasn't there.

It was not until my final term at school that, to my utter joy, I was picked to play for my house. At this school 'houses' were called 'sets', and there on the set notice-board was my name—Olivier, L., Number 11. It is true that there were some six or seven sets in the school, but here I was, in my last summer term, maybe eightieth in line for my First Eleven cap. The full glory of my selection was not immediately apparent to me, indeed it was still swimming into focus when I found myself putting on my pads and my batting gloves, taking my bat firmly in my hand and stomping out to the middle. Seven runs were needed to win, and as I walked out to the wicket I thought—'This is the moment I have been dreaming of'. I reached the crease, requested the umpire for 'middle 'n' leg', surveyed the field as I had been taught to do, and faced the bowler. To the first ball I played a somewhat defensive stroke, and as I did so I thought—'This will not do. Time is running short—I must be bold. This is my great chance—none of that cagey stuff,' I thought, 'I must be bold and resolute.' I made two runs off that over.

The field changed over and it was my partner's turn to take strike. This gave me time to dream a little. Only five more runs for victory. Now I was beginning to have that glorious creepy feeling, a tingling behind the ears. I knew that triumph was within my grasp. Already I could see myself being marched up through the dining-hall, having been sent for by the senior prefect, to be congratulated on winning the day. Not only that—to be told of their deep regret that they had never before appreciated my talents and that it was time to put me in the First Eleven straight away. We ran a single bye, and I faced the bowling again. Four more for victory. The full glory was now upon me. In my mind I was already beginning to shape the first century that I would make for the First Eleven . . . and I was clean bowled by Douglas Bader. He ended my cricketing career.

The Mark of St George

When I first went to Hollywood, I was extremely short of cash and twenty-three years old. I had just registered with Central Casting as 'Anglo-Saxon type, No. 2008'. I had been doing a fruitless round of the studio casting offices and my last port of call was the United Artists studio on Santa Monica Boulevard. So that the sanctity of the studio could be preserved, the entrance to the Casting Office was separated from the main gate by a twelve foot high wall of wire netting. I was walking out—'Nothing doing just now. Call next week'—when I was hailed from a large limousine on the other side of the fence. 'Hi! How's the golf?' It was the great Douglas Fairbanks himself. I had once played at Sunningdale with him in palmier days.

He never forgot a face but he had the greatest difficulty in coming up with a name to match it. However, I was soon on his side of the barricade and setting him right that I was not Bobby Sweeney. He asked what I was doing in Hollywood and I told him. He thought for a moment and said kindly, 'Gee, I hope you make it. . . . I'm here with Sylvia at the Beach House and we'd love to see you any time you like. I'd like to take you to play at Bel Air—it's a great course. Come around any time; I mean it. But please don't ask me to help you with your career.'

This was the completely honest expression of a completely honest man and a breath of fresh air in a place where the empty promise was the easy way out.

'Now,' he said, 'I'm going to take a steam. Come on in and join me.'

Actually, I would have preferred the offer of a good hot meal but I gratefully tagged along. He greeted everyone he passed with a wide smile and 'Hi! How are you?' It was obvious that he was greatly loved but he was never quite sure of the identity of the person who was loving him.

Inside the steam room, I was introduced to various mist-shrouded figures and I found myself sitting stark naked on a marble slab between Darryl Zanuck, the head of Twentieth Century, a thrusting new company which he was just forming, and Joe Schenck, his partner. Opposite sat Charlie Chaplin and Sid Grauman, a famous theatre owner. Present too were Bill Goetz, another associate of

Zanuck's, Lew Schreiber, his casting director, Bill Dover, Sam the Barber and Aiden Roark.

The sight and proximity of these great men, combined with the intense heat, was almost too much for me. They were used to these steam baths. I wasn't, but I decided to sit there if it took all night. It might lead to something. After ten minutes, my lungs felt scalded and my head was spinning.

Fairbanks, above all, loved jokes of any sort, funny jokes, practical jokes, any jokes. He had, of course, caught on that I was practically broke so he couldn't resist saying, 'Oh, Niven, what are you planning this winter? Playing polo or bringing the yacht round?'

'Polo . . . polo,' I croaked and made for the exit. Sam the Barber grabbed me before I fell to the marble floor and put me forcibly into the ice-cold plunge. I was reviving when the others came out of the steam room.

'Doug says you played for the British Army,' said Zanuck.

'Well, I played a bit in Malta,' I said.

'Come and play a few chukkas on Sunday. We'll have a good game.'

'Er . . . my clothes haven't arrived yet, I'm afraid.'

'Aiden here will fix you up.'

Aiden Roark was a ten-goal international. He and his brother Pat both played for Great Britain. Now he was employed by Zanuck in some capacity or other and organized Zanuck's polo team. A quiet, dark-haired, olive-skinned Irishman, he looked more like a South American. I decided to tell him the truth, and in a corner I explained my limitations.

'Don't worry about it,' he said. 'I'll lend you all the stuff you need. Just play a couple of chukkas—you'll have fun.'

So it was arranged. I was to play polo at the Uplifters Club the following Sunday afternoon with Darryl Zanuck! How many two dollars and fifty cents 'extras' were getting that break?

On the fateful day, Aiden Roark lent me some jodhpurs that were much too tight, and drove me to the ground. The first thing that worried me was seeing that the stands were full of people. Douglas Fairbanks, who had landed me in this mess, and the gorgeous Sylvia Ashley were, I noticed bitterly, safely in a box. The second thing, which unnerved me even more, was the sight of the other players. Among them were 'Big Boy' Williams, a formidable performer, Elmer Boseke and Cecil Smith, both ten-goal internationals. The final thing, and this nearly completed my disintegration, was the sight of 'St George'.

St George was a white Arab stallion. He bit savagely at everything in sight, and at that moment a groom was struggling to put him into a muzzle.

'You can play St George,' said Aiden. 'Play him in the first and fourth chukkas. It's only a pick-up game. You play at number one and I'll hit the ball up to you. . . . Mark Darryl, he's playing back on the other team—wear the red vest.'

The bell went. It was a nightmare. I didn't know who was playing in which position on what team. Those great experts were hitting the ball like a rocket from every direction, but during that first chukka I was far too busy stopping St George from leaving the ground altogether to care. When Aiden passed the ball up to me, I made vague flourishes at it with my stick but quickly needed both hands again to control the brute. It was during one of these mad dashes that St George kicked a goal!

Zanuck I tried to cover, but generally St George and I passed him at high speed without making contact.

At the end of the first chukka, Aiden was laughing so much he could hardly change ponies. 'Come back in for the fourth one . . . you'll find St George easier now he's worked some of it off.'

I toyed with the idea of slinking from the ground but I still hoped that I might impress Zanuck and further my movie career, so I waited apprehensively for my next appearance. The last time I had been on a horse was two years before, when I had been dressed as Buffalo Bill in the Municipal Auditorium of Atlantic City. Now my riding muscles, suddenly forced into violent action, were reacting and causing me to shake like a leaf. This did not go unnoticed by St George when I mounted him for the fourth chukka.

But I was determined to make my mark on Zanuck, so I stayed as close to him as St George would let me. I even hit the ball a couple of times which encouraged me enormously. The experts continued to charge about, playing a spectacular game and shouting oaths and instructions at each other, but Aiden, I suspected deliberately, had stopped sending the ball up to me. It all seemed more peaceful.

Suddenly, 'Big Boy' Williams, renowned as one of the longest hitters in the game, connected from the far end of the ground and the ball sailed over Zanuck's head towards the goal. Zanuck turned fast and galloped off to backhand it away. I chased after him to try to ride him off the line and, if miracles could happen, to score. The two of us were now the focal point of all eyes. People were shouting and clods of earth were flying up into my face from Zanuck's pony's hooves.

St George was the faster and we gained inexorably. As we drew almost level and I was getting into position to bump Zanuck off the line of the ball, St George leaned forward and through his muzzle sank his teeth into the seat of Zanuck's breeches. Zanuck roared with alarm and pain and in the ensuing shambles, his pony trod on the ball. It became embedded in the turf. I caught a momentary glimpse of the white mushroom top passing below us and, trying to ignore the embarrassing action at the front end of my steed, I made a vague swipe at it as it fell astern. I missed, and my stick passed beneath Zanuck's pony's tail. His mount, being extremely sensitive in that area, with a maidenly reaction clamped its tail to its behind. The head of my stick was thus imprisoned. I was attached by a leather thong around my wrist to the other end of the stick. St George had a firm grip on Zanuck's buttocks and our horrible triangle galloped past the stands.

Zanuck was good about it. I was not invited to play polo with him again but to this day he mentions it when I see him.

With the help of St George, I must, after all, have made a mark.

HUGH FALKUS

Salmo

He comes in from the deep dark sway of the sea; from the distant tide-race; from lonely conger-haunted reefs and the bones of dead ships hairy with weed. At the estuary mouth, where tide and river meet, he scents the water of his homecoming and leaps in the sunlight, a brief, curving flash of lilac and silver—the Atlantic salmon, in full magnificence, with the sea lice itching on his flanks.

There is no mention of a salmon by the early Greeks, but the invading Romans knew him well enough. He was leaping in the Thames when Agricola marched north. From the banks of many rivers they glimpsed his flashing beauty, and they named him *Salmo* —which means 'the Leaper'.

The Romans came and went, as others have come and gone, and to *Salmo* it was a flicker of time. But now in so many streams where since the Ice Age he has leaped on his homecoming, *Salmo* leaps no longer. Disease, pollution, water abstraction, over-fishing and indifference threaten *Salmo* as never before. His future hangs in the balance, and each day of his life seems a tiny miracle of survival.

It all starts in fresh water, when the eggs are laid during November or December in the gravel bed of some well oxygenated and fairly fast-flowing stream.

A salmon egg takes between three and four months to hatch, and the product—known as an alevin—is a tiny, translucent creature with an umbilical sac hanging below its throat. During the alevin stage the little salmon lives on the contents of this yolk sac—which contains upwards of a month's rations. And when the yolk sac has become absorbed, the alevin becomes a fry.

Now, forced to fend for itself, it hunts actively for food, gradually acquiring a form of camouflage in the shape of dark 'finger' marks along its sides. At this stage of its development it is known as a parr, and in looks is very similar to a small brown trout.

Parr feed on insects, nymphs, fly larvae, tiny crustacea and other forms of life, depending on the food supply available. And in turn are preyed on by a host of enemies. Otters, feral mink, cormorants, mergansers, goosanders, herons, kingfishers, pike, chub, perch and eels are all enemies of the salmon during some stage of its fresh-water life. But its biggest enemy is probably its cousin the brown trout. It is on record that 134 identification tags, which had been attached to salmon parr by research biologists, were recovered from the stomachs of 20 brown trout ranging in length from 9 to 13 inches!

When the parr are anything between one and four or five years old (usually two) certain physiological changes take place to fit them for a new environment. Then, during May or June, as slender forked-tailed, silvery little fish about six inches long (now known as smolts) they migrate to salt water.

In the estuary the young salmon meet further enemies: pollack, coalfish, congers, shags, herring gulls and many others. The survivors hurry on towards the rich feeding grounds of the sea. And they go there in order to grow.

Young salmon grow very quickly. By the end of their first year at sea they will be twenty to thirty times their original weight. Some return to fresh water as grilse: fish of three to seven pounds that have stayed little more than a year at sea. Some may return as thirty or forty pounders after an absence of four years. But at whatever age and weight they return to the river—whether as grilse after one year at sea, or as maiden salmon of two sea years or longer—return they must, since salmon cannot spawn in salt water.

From the recapture of tagged fish it seems that returning salmon move in from the Atlantic at many points. Then, on arrival in coastal waters, they swim close inshore up or down the coast until they reach their destined rivers. A small percentage find their way into strange rivers, but the majority return to spawn in the rivers of their birth. It is not known how a salmon navigates from the distant ocean to the coast, but experiments have established that it selects its destined river by the particular scent of that river. A salmon 'homes' by sense of smell.

On his return from the ocean, in addition to the many animal predators which beset him from the moment of his birth, *Salmo salar* runs the gauntlet of every device for his destruction dreamed up by man. Commercial fishermen lie in wait with drift nets, draft nets, seine nets, stake nets, haaf nets, hang nets, bag nets, coops, garths, weir traps and cruives. Poachers lurk with leisters, stroke-hauls, gaffs, click-hooks, snares, trammel nets, poison and explosives. To say nothing of the anglers—with their rods and lines.

To fishermen, fair or foul, the salmon has long been a fish with a high price on its head. William Scrope, in his book, *Days and Nights of Salmon Fishing on the Tweed*, gives the most vivid account of a night's poaching on Tweedside a hundred and fifty years ago. 'Burning the water' (or salmon spearing by torchlight) was a popular pastime in those days. It seems to have been a rather blatant form of poaching, but certainly not without excitement. At least, in Scrope's account, it was an affray carried out by men of high spirit and *joie de vivre*—which is more than can be said for most poachers and poaching methods today.

It is unfortunate that such a large proportion of the British public regards the poacher with the sentimental affection usually reserved for dogs and bears. He is pictured as a romantic individualist victimized by the minions of some wealthy riparian owner. There is nothing so popular as the story of Little Man being hounded by Big Man—and finally doing him down. A great quantity of romantic literature is based on this simple plot, and the story of the poacher is no exception.

The very word 'poacher' evokes the picture of a shining moonlit night with wind in the trees and the sound of a rushing river, our salmon-snatching hero outwitting brutal bailiffs by river lore and homely guile—eventually flogging his meagre haul to feed his starving children.

The truth is somewhat different.

Poachers using poison can destroy all living creatures in a considerable stretch of river downstream of their operations, in addition to many hundreds of fish, in a single night. And frequently they do. At, say, fifty pence a pound, sold at the back door of the pub with no questions asked, the average salmon represents a five pound note, and there are few rivers on which poachers are not active. At his worst, the poacher is an organized gangster who works entirely for profit and does not hesitate to injure anyone who attempts to interfere with him. At his best he is a local bumpkin who sells his 'clicked' salmon at the pub for booze.

A favourite old country pastime used to be the miserable sport of gaffing salmon from the spawning redds, the salmon roe being used in the manufacture of an illegal fishing paste. And sometimes it still is. (It is droll to consider that a Scottish edict of the year 1400 stipulated that three convictions for killing spawning salmon constituted a capital offence.)

But to the salmon it hardly matters whether he is taken on the poacher's gaff or on the angler's fly. From this viewpoint how does the angler fit into our list of predators?

Well—as one early angling writer observed:

> As fish are the inhabitants of an element which man cannot live in, and have unlimited motion in the water, with innumerable retreats, it is evident they are to be taken only by strategem. In rivers, they retire to pits and holes, lie concealed under the roots of trees and in a thousand close places, so that nothing is to be done but by *alluring* them out of their retreats and bringing them to hand by the art of a skilful workman—and thus they are sometimes surprised and made prisoners.

A delightful, if somewhat vague, dissertation on the angler's art. And yet, salmon fishing has advanced very little from this simple philosophy. Modern tackle, of course, is considerably more efficient than that of bygone days; nevertheless, when considering the chances of capturing a salmon on rod and line we face a certain fundamental problem.

Just suppose that the salmon was a fish entirely unknown to you. And suppose that I invited you to come and fish my beat of river for this strange fish. Our conversation might very well take these lines:

'This salmon,' you ask. 'Is it a fish worth catching?'

'Oh, yes. Very much so.'

'A strong fighter?'

'Very strong.'

'Good to eat?'

'Most excellent to eat.'

'You tell me it returns from the sea to spawn in fresh water and that we fish for it on its way up the river?'

'That is so.'

'On rod and line?'

'Yes.'

'Splendid!' you exclaim. And, full of enthusiasm, you would at this stage want to know *what* to fish for this salmon *with*. In other words, what sort of bait or lure to offer it. And in order to find out you would obviously ask me:

'What does this salmon *eat* while in the river?'

And I reply:

'Nothing.'

'Nothing! You mean it doesn't *feed*?'

'That is precisely what I mean.'

Well—after such an exchange you might be excused for thinking me a lunatic. How on earth can anyone expect to hook a fish that has no appetite and eats nothing? But that is the problem which confronts every salmon fisherman: for what in effect he is trying to do is to catch a fish that is not hungry, that while lying in the river waiting to spawn lives on the supply of nourishment stored in its tissues and has no need of food. On the face of it angling for salmon is absurd. And yet every year a large number of salmon are caught on rod and line. For some reason they do occasionally take a lure. Why? Nobody knows. Various theories have been propounded: habit, curiosity, anger, irritation, playfulness or even boredom. Perhaps there is truth in all of them. Perhaps in none. There are times when salmon will take a lure, and times when they won't. Which is just about all that anyone really knows about salmon fishing.

The salmon's abstinence from food is not surprising. Few rivers could supply more than a fraction of the meals to which the fish have become accustomed while in the sea. If salmon retained their normal desire for food the river would soon become depopulated of all small fish, and the hungry salmon would exterminate themselves by eating the young of their own species. Indeed, they would have eaten themselves out of existence long ago.

As we should expect, nature makes provision for this enforced fast. The returning salmon bring their rations with them. They enter a river with sufficient fat on their bodies to sustain them for as long as twelve months, in addition to supplying the food necessary for their developing milt and ova.

Of course, not all Atlantic salmon endure so long a period of waiting. There is no month of the year during which, in one or another of our rivers, fresh salmon are not running. And while those that arrive in winter and early spring will wait for many months before spawning, others have only a short time to wait after their late summer or autumn arrival.

By the end of October, many of the salmon have arrived in or close to those parts of the river where they are going to spawn—perhaps in some quiet glade among English water-meadows, or high in a moorland burn below raven-haunted crags and heather slopes where the red grouse call. Now, with the autumn leaves drifting overhead, the salmon's silver streamlined beauty has quite vanished. The once sleek females are dark, almost black, with bulging bellies; the males rust-red, their heads ugly and misshapen with huge pointed knobs—or 'kypes'—curving upwards from their lower jaws.

After a period of exploratory wandering in a stretch of clean, shallow, streamy water with a bottom of gravel and small stones, the female prepares the spawning bed by movements of her tail. Meanwhile, the male fish waits in close attendance, ready to drive off any intruders.

Eventually, perhaps after days of preparation, the male joins her on the bed. During the mating act he quivers violently—which stimulates the female so that eggs and milt are extruded almost simultaneously. Immediately afterwards the male swims some little distance downstream; while the female, by going a foot or two above the bed, covers the eggs with gravel by vigorous movements of her tail. Several more similar sequences may be carried out before she has deposited all her eggs. Nature prepares for huge losses during the salmon's life cycle, and a hen fish carries an average of 700 eggs per pound of her body weight.

By the time spawning is finished the fish are emaciated and very weak. These spent fish—or 'kelts'—are little more than two-thirds of their original weight. The once juicy pink flesh is pale and flaccid;

and often enough their hollow-flanked and ragged-finned bodies are smothered in fungus.

Only a few survive. Once their all-important task is done, most salmon die of exhaustion and disease. For reasons which are unknown, surviving females greatly outnumber the males. Those fish that regain the rich feeding pastures of the sea recover their condition surprisingly quickly. On their subsequent return to the river for a second spawning, their fat content is as high as or, in some cases, even higher than that of virgin fish. The proportion of fish that survive for a third spawning is very small indeed. Only an exceptional fish returns to spawn for a fourth time.

Surviving kelts don't all leave the river together, even when seemingly able to do so, but separately over a period which may extend into several months. Again, as with the incoming fish, it seems that nature insures against total disaster. Were all fish to enter a river during the same week or month, some catastrophe such as river blockage, drought or disease, might wipe out a complete annual run. As it is, those fish still at sea, destined to make their homecoming during a later month, or even another year, form an insurance against total loss. And so with the returning kelts. Should some meet with disaster at the river mouth there are others to follow, and there are those that have already gone ahead.

But gone *where*? What *is* the Atlantic salmon's destination? Where, for instance, do the young smolts go, to put on weight so rapidly?

Until a few years ago the story of the salmon's pelagic wandering was unknown. Recently, however, two of the main feeding grounds were located: one in the Baltic, and the other, a much larger area, off the west coast of Greenland. The result of this discovery has been appalling.

Commercial fishing started on the salmon feeding grounds along the Greenland coast in the 1950s. According to published figures, the 1957 catch of 2 metric tons rose astronomically to 2,200 tons (667,000 salmon) in 1969.

In 1966, the Baltic nations agreed to limit and prescribe conditions for taking salmon in the Baltic Sea. Alas, so far no similar agreement has been reached to protect the Greenland feeding grounds from being over-fished. Unless a limit can be placed on the number of salmon taken annually from Greenland waters, over-fishing is inevitable, and the effect will be disastrous.

If *Salmo salar* is to survive, conservation is essential—both at sea and in the rivers. And in support of this we must put our own house in order. In the past our husbandry has been abysmal. There were once huge runs of salmon in the rivers of Britain. Salmon figured

largely in the commissariat for military campaigns. Edward II
ordered thousands of dried salmon to feed his army. Farmers shovelled
salmon fry to feed their swine. Even as late as the Reformation,
salmon were only half the price of pike. Our waters still teemed with
them two hundred years ago, when special teams of horses trans-
ported fish to the London market. But the industrial revolution
destroyed river after river. Unrestricted netting hastened the decline
of their salmon stocks. Abstraction reduced the flow of water over
their redds, and pollution poured from towns and factories along
their banks. Today, the lower reaches of all too many rivers are open
sewers, and the effluent vomits from estuary mouths to stain the tide.

Three hundred years ago, Walton wrote:

> There is no better salmon than in England; and that although some
> of our northern rivers have salmon as fat and as large as the river
> Thames, yet *none* are of so *excellent* a taste.

A century later, Charfy wrote with enthusiasm of the Thames as
being:

> The Greatest and Chiefest of all the rivers of Britain—for the
> *prodigious* quantity of its fish, the *variety* of their sorts, and the *goodness*
> of their kind, preferable to all the other rivers in Europe; and the
> *prime* of the English salmon is found in the Thames.

At about that time a Member of London City Corporation, a
Mr Binnell, said:

> The Thames abounds with salmon, flounders, plaice, mullet,
> whiting, smelts, eels, perch, trout, carp, tench, bream, chub, roach,
> dace and gudgeons, besides *oysters*—the finest in the world.

Look at the Thames today.

In 1816, London had an exceptional run of salmon, so many
being taken that they fetched only threepence a pound in Billings-
gate market. Twenty years later the Thames salmon had almost
vanished. The locks and weirs that made the river navigable blocked
the passage of salmon to their spawning redds, and pollution finished
the job. Today, our London river, like so many others, is a national
disgrace.

Must it always be so? The essential river requirements of salmon
are: water containing sufficient oxygen, and ready access to the
spawning redds. The provision of fish ladders beside lock and weir,
and cessation from using the river as a common drain, would bring
back a run of fish even to the Thames.

Most salmon return from the sea to spawn in the rivers of their
birth. But not *all*. Each year, a small but vital number find their

way to the redds of strange rivers. Quite apart from fresh stocks introduced by man, these wanderers would explore and eventually re-stock the Thames, as they would our other barren rivers, if not repelled by the present outflow of filth.

Nature will stock, protect, and after disaster re-stock, if only given the chance. Must our gaze remain so firmly fixed along our noses that we ignore the beauty at our feet? Is there no place in this world of 'progress' for *Salmo*—the Leaper? Are we so poor in spirit that we deny him even the encouragement of clean water?

E. W. SWANTON

A Club is Born

Overseas travel in 1946 was necessarily organized and controlled by Government. You had to go when it was decreed (and for that matter in a shared cabin, and on a dry ship to boot). So it was that Walter Hammond's MCC team, with its attendant fourteen scribes, found themselves in Perth at the end of September in the very early spring rather before the Australian season had started.

This was not a bad thing, as it gave our side the chance of settling down gradually and getting fit in the mild West Australian climate. It also gave us camp-followers a chance of organizing some cricket for ourselves to while the time away, and in most cases to make up a bit of what we had been deprived of during the war. So we did what all Englishmen are supposed to do as soon as two or three are gathered together in foreign parts, and formed a club. Moreover we naturally recruited our Australian press and radio friends who had come across from the eastern states to cover the tour; journalists and old players hired to give their comments. Not very old were most of them, incidentally, so that the teams we turned out against the schools and clubs of Perth and the other capital cities as we came to them sparkled with such names as O'Reilly, Vic Richardson, Mailey, Grimmett, Fingleton, Oldfield, Percy Beames (captain of Victoria the preceding year), and McGilvray, while we contributed Bowes, Duckworth, Sellers, Vivian Jenkins, and Wellings. I, much junior in fame, was usually ordered to captain this lot, and great parties we had, before, during and after.

Our gala day was a Sunday on the St Kilda ground at Melbourne where fifteen thousand turned up and paid a great deal of money to Dame Mabel Brooks's pet charity to see us play Victoria Past and Present, the only hilariously incongruous moment, I remember, being provided by the ace racing commentator who from a box far up in the stand had kindly agreed to offer enlightenment to the crowd over the public address system. 'And who's going to open the bowling?' he piped up. 'Surely it must be our friend, Bill O'Reilly. Yes, sure enough, here he is, all arms and legs, wheeling away in the same old way. Wonderful to see him playing again. Who could mistake that extraordinary action?' Alas, alone of all present he could, for not unnaturally I had given the first over to Bill Bowes. Quite a contrast in styles! Nothing could have been better calculated to get the match off to a fine guffawing start.

This sporting enterprise, by the way, produced the best part of £2,000, in reward for which I was presented with a scroll designating me as a life governor of the Queen Victoria Hospital of Melbourne. Since it was a maternity hospital and I, for some years following, remained a bachelor, I was not able to avail myself of any gubernatorial privileges—but it is fair to add I have never been saddled with any responsibility either.

We played in all the Australian states during that 1946–7 tour, and also, though more intermittently, on the two following ones, and we duly designated ourselves the Empire Cricket Writers' Club. I think I may have proposed the phrase 'Cricket Writers', as covering all of our company whether professional journalists or not. The 'Empire', soon quietly dropped as being inapposite, was insisted on by that most firm of Anglophiles and whimsically endearing of men, Arthur Mailey.

Being the first chairman I found myself organizing our first big function, a dinner given on their arrival in England to Don Bradman's 1948 Australians. Everything helped to make this an outstanding occasion. Because of the continuing scarcity of food, sporting dinners were almost a pre-war memory. The Australians were back, for the first time since 1938, and the greatest cricketer of his generation was returning to the scene of his greatest triumphs. All that was needed was some good speeches—and, of course, all to cloud the evening one or two bad ones. But, leaving my own brief introduction of the Australians out of consideration, here we were lucky.

Don Bradman followed me with a nostalgic speech for the end of which the BBC in those less rigid days held up the nine o'clock news, and which brought him a flood of letters. There followed four speeches of rare wit and excellence, each of which complemented and made the prelude for the next.

Sir Norman, later Lord, Birkett, gave the toast of cricket with that rare felicity of phrase and articulation which so many cricket diners-out soon came to know so well. This was replied to by H. S. Altham, whose great services to MCC and the game generally had scarcely then begun (apart from his authorship of *A History of Cricket* and his marvellous work as a coach at Winchester). It would have been hard if not impossible for anyone to have followed these two speeches in a similar classic mould. But happily the next man in the order of going in was R. C. Robertson-Glasgow, whose oratorical style was as unique as it was uproariously funny. 'Crusoe' proposed the guests. But who to follow that? For the sixth and final speech—

nowadays, of course, six speeches are at least two too many—I had recruited none other than 'Parson', or to be exact the Rev. Canon F. H. Gillingham, a batsman of some note between the wars for Essex and the Gentlemen. He was widely known as an Anglican preacher, a large lantern-jawed fellow with, in repose, a face of un-relieved gloom. What the Australians thought was coming when this avenging prophet got up in his clerical rig goodness knows, but within a few seconds he was putting up a performance that would have fetched hundreds a week—in 1948 currency—at the Palladium. His dog-collar and that dead-pan expression naturally enhanced the effect. What he said I have no idea except that there was a story about some Australian so tough that he bound his bat with barbed wire—or perhaps it was that he used it to protect his knuckles. No matter. It was all a riot.

The occasion was calculated to bring the best out of anyone, but the luck was happening on such a selection of speakers and getting the batting order right. A good speech is always talked about, and followed by further invitations, and in two of these cases especially this night was the precursor of, literally, hundreds of others. Between 1948 and their deaths in 1962 and 1965 respectively, no cricket after-dinner speakers were in such demand as Norman Birkett and Harry Altham, and such was their love of the game and natural generosity that they went to the greatest trouble to accept if it was humanly possible. They gave the utmost pleasure to many thousands, and it is one of the things most agreeable to look back on that I was one of those who chanced to start them off.

The Cricket Writers' Club, having earned recognition if not fame in a night, gathered strength with the years, and most would say it has played no small part in promoting a better working arrange-ment, as well as closer personal relationships, between cricket administration and the Press. Moreover the idea that had such a happily fortuitous birth in Perth, Western Australia, has spread into other sporting fields. There followed a Rugby Writers' Club, a Golf Writers' Association, one for soccer, and a Sports' Writers' Association, all apparently thriving organizations with their own parts to play in the body politic.

Now, why did I think the little story of the birth of the Cricket Writers' Club appropriate to this book, to which it is such a privilege and a pleasure to contribute? Ah, yes, I remember. On my right at the aforesaid dinner was not the captain of Australia but the Patron and Twelfth Man of the Lord's Taverners, no less. He had been married only a few months before. His contact with and patronage of cricket lay in the future. He had come as the personal guest of one of our members, the understanding being that he would not be called on to speak. When 'Gilly' sat down to deafening applause I said quietly, 'A word from you, Sir, would just finish things off.' 'I don't think so,' he said. 'They've had some wonderful speeches. Let's leave it at that.' I didn't think I could go further, though I'm sure he would have got up if I had appealed once more. And, as one now knows, he would have said exactly the right thing and rounded off the evening perfectly.

So, it might be said, the dinner lacked its ultimate distinction. But it was pretty good for all that, and I'd be surprised if, despite the many hundred such functions he has attended since, Prince Philip has entirely forgotten it.

'Wal, Mister Missionary, I reckon this game could take on over here—it's a whole new way of feudin''

Twelve is a Crowd

I needn't tell you, of course, now you're so steeped in decimalization that you've practically forgotten that you ever had twelve toes on your feet, that if you still feel a sentimental attachment to temperatures in Fahrenheit it's easy enough to work them out. You just read the Centigrade figure off the nearest modern thermometer, stuck up on a handy wall by some trendy *avant garde* nit, add 9, multiply by 32 and divide by 5.

To take an example, because it's a lot simpler than it sounds, if it's 24 in the shade on Hove cricket ground, which doesn't often happen because of the sea mist—well, let's take somewhere else, in that case. Chigwell, say. No, I'm not going to get into an argument over it. Here we are at Chigwell, then, 24 Centishade in the grade. Centigrade in the shade, I mean. Add nine, that's thirty-three, multiply by thirty-two, which gives you a thousand and fifty-six, and divide by five and you get your answer, 211° Fahrenright, heit? No wonder you can't see the umpire for sweaters. Deep third man's taking his trousers off, a thing not seen in Essex since Trevor Bailey couldn't get the window open in the commentary box.

You've probably spotted a flaw there. I was trying to bluff it out. Even for us old Fahrenheit fans, 211° is too hot. You have to add 9, of course, multiply by 5, and *divide* by 32. Idiot. So that comes to— well, you can work it out for yourself: somewhere around 8½°F, or getting on for twenty-four degrees of frost.

I'm afraid this is what comes of not really applying myself to learning decimalization. I picked up a fair smattering in the early days, from the helpful free conversion tables that kept falling out of my shopping. Particularly packets of tea-bags, for some reason. I don't know why they should be so keen on decimalized tea (ten for each person and ten for the pot), but there they were. But I always seemed to memorize the wrong bits. If you asked me what I had to multiply a kilogramme by to get a ton I'd tell you in a flash: ·0009842. But who wants a ton of tea-bags, being dragged off the muck-heap by the blackbirds and strewn in the soft fruit? Yards into metres, now, that's different. Twenty-two yards, for instance, to take a round figure that's as much a part of British sporting history as arguments with the net-cord judge, is convertible into metres with no trouble at all.

It comes to twenty metres and a bit, actually, so groundsmen with their new metric-system tape-measures may find it a bit maddening. (They're lucky compared with some. Let them think of the batsman, the first time he tries to swing a bat 96·52 centimetres long.) Anyway, if they'd rather have it in inches, I make it seven hundred and ninety-two. And gladly. Because by some strange quirk of the lower mathematics this works out pat at twenty-two yards exactly, and we're back in the snug old familiar world where a cricket ball still weighs a maximum of 5¾ oz. or else: and none of your ridiculous foreign litres, or whatever they put in cricket balls in the Common Market.

But on the whole it's going to be a proper turn-up. You didn't think they'd stop at just decimalizing the money, did you? Anyway, that's bad enough. I don't know whether you remember a character called A. J. Raffles? A born Taverner if ever there was one. Gentleman cracksman and off-spinner. Invited to all the best cricketing house-parties, took nine for twenty-two and all the diamond pendants. I don't suppose many of us go in for his net-practice techniques these days, but he used to get the Lord's professionals to sling a few down, and he put three gold sovereigns on the stumps, and all they hit they had. The last report I had from the bullion vaults, gold sovereigns were fetching around £2 17s 11d per stump. Try that as a bails substitute in the new currency, and after the first good ball you've had it—all the gnarled old pros chasing the rolling fivepenny bits. You mightn't even get a ball, if there was one of those 10 kilowatts-per-hour winds, scattering the little piles of loot as fast as you set them up.

What started me on all this was thinking, for some unaccountable reason, of the Twelfth Man. It's strange, the way things drift into your head from nowhere. I wasn't thinking of any Twelfth Man in particular. Just the whole frustrated tribe of them. I was thinking what a life it is, sitting out of sight in the pavilion, all done up in their best whites, and no chance of a showing unless the thermometer hits 211°F and they have to go out with the drinks tray, with all eyes turned on them expectantly, hoping they'll drop it. The trouble is, with any game you're excluded from by a mere freak of tradition—who the heck ever thought of *eleven* a side?—they have such rotten cricket for you to watch. There they are, your side batting, and coming out right and left to bowling that simply isn't worth the name. Rubbish is the only word. If only you were number eleven occasionally, instead of number twelve, you'd be hammering every ball over the gasworks.

It's just the same when the other side's batting, except that it's your lot's bowling that's so diabolical this time. No wonder they're getting belted through the immemorial elms and the upper windows of adjacent tower blocks. Good grief, if only the captain had enough sense to take you off the orange-squash one of these days and invite you to whirl down a couple of overs—you wouldn't need more—you'd have the computers at *Wisden*'s chattering their teeth out. And as for tomorrow's back pages. Boy! 'TWELFTH MAN TAKES 10 FOR 3: Star is Born at Oval' . . . or Wivelsfield Green, or wherever it is.

But you never get a break like that. Those happy strokes of fortune, such as the team's strongest opener ripping his Achilles tendon, diving to clutch a pint in the pub on the way there—when do they ever happen, except in the school stories? (And not often then, now I come to think of it.) Even the chance of an hour's plain fielding would be some sort of recompense for your dry-cleaning bills, not to mention showing them a thing or two out there: because, honestly, to watch them letting the fours go fumbling through, and dropping sitters you could catch in your shirt pocket . . .

Not that they seem anything but delighted with the whole thing. When a man comes sprinting lithely back up the pavilion steps after somehow scrambling a fifty together in an innings of incredible escapes, his captain's hand on his shoulder smites, as likely as not. 'Great knock, Fred,' he says. And Fred says, 'Watch the chap this end, he's dynamite.' He doesn't say it to you, and that's just as well, because you'd have a job not to come back with, 'What, him? All those slow full-tosses?' He doesn't say anything to you, actually. Just treads on your foot as he goes past. It's the same story when they're in the field. The wicketkeeper only has to find a catch accidentally stuck in his gloves and they're all over him: not literally, perhaps, in the World Cup sense, trying how many congratulators can climb up him before he goes down under the weight, but it's only a matter of degree. Just supposing for a minute that *you* were out there crouched behind, the other chap having missed one and come in holding his bleeding nose, you'd regard it as pure routine to do an efficient job. 'SUBSTITUTE KEEPER STUMPS NINE: "It was nothing"—Twelfth Man with Magic Gloves.'

Ah, well. The maddening thing is that the only time you did get half an hour on the leg boundary this season nothing came near you but the one that a Centurion tank would have side-stepped. . . .

But all this is going to change. Twelfth Men everywhere, lift up your hearts. Because decimalized sport is on the way. Has in some cases arrived. It's years since anyone ran a yard in the Olympics, as you must have noticed: the Yard Sprint, as an event, has gone altogether. Any time now—well, say at Munich in 1972—they'll be putting the metric shot, throwing the metric hammer and the decimalized discus. It's only a matter of time before Wimbledon umpires will be shouting things like 'Twenty-Love', and thirsty golfers are gathering at the twenty-first hole. Going to be a shock at first on boatrace day, watching the tens streaking their crowded craft out of Putney, and it's a good thing, in a way, that public-spirited commercial interests have prepared us a bit for it all—those bunches of duodecimal daffodils, you remember, went down to ten some time back, keeping the price the same in order to lessen the shock; and it's curious, really, that my tea-bag friends, who gave me all that useful free dope about turning miles into kilos, are at the time of writing still selling packs of 36's and 72's; however, if you drop in to tea with me around the time you read this, I expect they'll be handy round figures, like 20's and 40's—and I'm sorry if it's a bit pale and gnatty, but working out at ten new pence a pot, and a metre of milk the price it is. . . .

Still, this is getting away from the Twelfth Man situation. And logically enough, as it turns out. Because that's exactly what he's going to do. Any time now he's going to be through with the whole degrading, superfluous business. Eleventh Man to a team of ten isn't going to make all that practical difference, perhaps, but the moral and spiritual refreshment of never being Twelfth Man again! I think you'll find it'll alter your whole approach to the game. Besides, don't forget that once we're in Europe, all the nations merrily melting their ideas into each other, there'll be this great cricketing interchange. We shall keep nipping over there to play an Italian X, or the Germans will be steaming in with a German X to play an English X.

And all I can say is, if you can't shake off even your new Eleventh Man status, and actually get a place in a side against the Eyeteyes, Wogs, Frogs and Krauts without getting *aus* to your first *boule*, then you deserve the worst that decimalized cricket can do to you. Like, say, leaving you behind in Chigwell, in $8\frac{1}{2}°$F, or twenty-four degrees of frost.

MARY HAYLEY BELL

Mawnan Smith

She walked out of the hotel and onto the beach below. The tide was on the flow and the sea made little gentle lapping sounds against the sand. A few yards away small white boats lay at anchor and beyond them, across the Helford River, the greens and indigos and deep saffron foliage came down in great sweeps to the water's edge—but between her and the other side lay the remains of the Mulberry floating dock, grim reminder of the war that was finished long ago. She shaded her eyes with her hand, looking at the rusty ironwork carefully. How ugly it was; what a great work it had done, and out of sheer sentiment how few would expostulate that it was an eyesore and should be taken away? A great sigh rushed through her thoughts, but she tried to push them all away. She mustn't think of anything else but the sea and the sky and sleeping and eating—that was what Uncle Herbert had said, and he was her doctor as well as her friend.

'Go to Cornwall,' he had said, 'and be a good girl and read and write and eat and sleep and walk—walk a lot every day.'

'Poor Matron,' they had all said at the hospital. 'You're working too hard; you'll have a breakdown if you aren't careful.'

Well, that's what had happened. It was surprising really to herself. She had a strong constitution, could never in fact really remember being ill, not even when Dick was killed in the war. She hadn't cried then, not at all, she hadn't allowed herself to in case she couldn't stop. She'd looked ghastly, only she didn't mind about that. It didn't matter then, and it didn't matter now that there were lines round her eyes, and that her hair had turned grey. There had been little time for tears in those days, there had been too much work at the hospital, and the work somehow accelerated through the years, until suddenly the old engine had worn itself out.

She smiled absently, and pushed the short grey hair back from her damp brow.

Dick would have been fifty-one by now. What would they have held—the years in between! Difficult to imagine. Children perhaps, in some English countryside like this, with ponies and bicycles and dogs running ahead of them through fields to the sea. Twenty-eight years! Her mind flew through all the imagined stages of their schooldays, universities and adolescent love affairs, while she waited in a cottage by the sea for their return. Yet, she hadn't wasted her life, hadn't filled the months or years with self-pity or bitterness. She had decided then and there that the only cure was work, work for people, or go into a convent. The war had stopped all that; the ashen-faced men and women who had passed through her hands had stopped any thought of quiet, selfish withdrawal. She'd been lucky to have chosen the hospital, for the months and years had flown and the girl had developed into a quiet, strong woman.

Two small boys came round in a rowing-boat, their faces tanned, their eyes bluer than the sky. She smiled at them, but they only stared, and she moved away feeling a little foolish.

She turned up from the beach through some stones and up onto the field above Mawnan Smith; a big field full of buttercups and gentians and in the wet hedges ragged robin and bluebells thrusting themselves out at her in profusion. She pulled off a head of sorrel and started to chew it reminiscently. 'I'm glad I never came here with Dickie. I couldn't have borne it if he'd been here. I think—I think then I should have really cried. I could never have crossed the river and climbed amongst the garlic and wild fuchsia and hauled myself up by the lichen on the stunted oak tree if I'd ever been here with Dickie. I'm not one to go back to places and hear ghost voices.' She cleared the brow of the hill and looked far away to where the river met the open sea. What was the old song about the Weary River somehow meeting the sea? 'Now I know that weary river somewhere meets the sea.' She smiled. What a lot of uncollected thoughts were moving slowly through her head. Part of the cure, she supposed, Uncle Herbert's cure—'Just lie about and Nature will do the rest.' The process of relieving the mainspring, letting it go. What did he expect Nature to do?

She stood a moment, nervously crumbling the sorrel between her fingers, sorrel, sorrow—near enough—not much difference in the look of it—brown. A coastguard came up behind her.

'Nice evening.'

'Lovely,' she murmured.

'Yes. Sun's come up warm this arternoon—'

'Yes,' she replied again.

The coastguard stopped, took off his cap, and scratched his head thoughtfully, looking at the woman with the grey in her brown hair and the stalk of sorrel between her lips.

'You know, sometimes it's sorrel and sometimes it isn't,' he hazarded. 'Ye want to be careful ye get it right if you're going to chew it like.'

She smiled at him as he turned to go his way.

After a few moments she followed him down. A notice board pointed out that the beach was private, and there was a long high ugly wooden jetty sticking out from a concrete runway into the sea. This, too, she crossed, pausing to wonder why the owners had made such a big affair of it. A little white gate, also marked Private, led through a valley full of rhododendrons to a tall, austere house at the top.

Everything seemed very private, and yet she felt happy and started to run across the runway and down on to the sand among the big rocks. Choosing a round flat rock, she lay on her back staring up at the sky, the stalk of sorrel still sticking out of her mouth. The great cliff reared high overhead, with twisted gnarled oaks and firs covered with lichen, pink and white may and ivy, apple green against the faded eau-de-nil of the rocks, the curling fronds of fern and the upright leaves of the garlic plants, and all about her the air sweet and fresh after the rain. She closed her eyes, drawing in the scent of firs and rhododendrons.

'I will open the locked gates marked private and let the thoughts of years come tumbling out of their darkness. I will see just how they can hurt me; I will stand as much of them as I possibly can here, lying on my back on the warm flat elephant-coloured rock, and then when I can stand it no longer I will force them back again behind the gate marked private. I will do this every now and then, until the years pass and they don't hurt so much—oh, Dickie. Why aren't you here beside me staring up at the sky? Where are you? If there is anything beyond this life, why did you never try to find me again?' She sat up suddenly calling aloud: 'Dick! Dickie! Where are you?' The only answer came from the sea as it rolled over the flat green stones, murmuring comfortingly as a mother to its child, 'Shush! Shush!'

The sun was hot on her face and she experienced a sudden feeling almost of happiness. Everything in her body seemed to be working in harmony—it reminded her vividly of Dick one summer in Hong Kong that first year when the regiment had arrived; they were sprawling on a cliff, idly picking at the pinks growing on the rocks. 'What's happiness?' she had asked him and he had laughed quietly, rolling his great length over on his stomach and peered down through the pinks to the sea:

'Happiness?' he repeated.

'I mean the sudden overwhelming feeling of well-being and happiness I got suddenly just now. It nearly knocked me over!' she had insisted.

'Harmony,' he replied. 'Health—the harmony of everything working properly—no indigestion.'

She had laughed aloud.

'Oh, Dickie, what a mundane level to look at happiness, from your eyrie in the pine trees.'

Then he had put his hand out and taken hers, 'It's me, too. I am the rest of your harmony and you are mine, dear love.' Then he had rolled over and scrambled to his feet pulling her up. 'Tea! Tea! Beautiful tea!'

Yes, that had been harmony, and health, and the two had made up the word happiness, and with his going she had lost all three. She breathed in the heavy scent of may and remembered the day she had taken it into her mother's house, not knowing.

'Bad luck! Bad luck!' she had screamed at her in that grating well-bred voice. 'Bad luck! Bad luck! Bad luck!' That's what they had all murmured to her in the hospital, those who hadn't known her very well: 'Bad luck, Mrs Carter, bad luck.' Yes, she supposed it could be called that, the good or the bad luck, the draw out of the hat, lucky at cards, unlucky in love. But then she had always prided herself upon being very grotesquely unlucky at cards. Not like Elizabeth, now; she always won everything at poker and her husband, a beast. . . . She smiled ruefully. A beast, and still alive; a beastly, selfish, loud-mouthed man, and still alive, while Dick with his mellow dark eyes and sensitive hands . . . The thoughts were rushing out too quickly now, they must be checked, one couldn't stand too much at one time. She must think of something else, just for a while. She propped herself on her elbow, stirring the sand with her finger. A small hermit crab walked swiftly sideways from her, and the salt water rolled out of a spiral-shaped shell when she lifted it, remembering sharply the small collection of such shells on the mantelpiece in the house where Dick's mother lived.

She took the locket from the chain round her neck and propped it up in the sand, staring at it for the millionth time. How well she knew that small, serious-faced little child with his soft light-brown hair lifted gently by the wind, his rompers, and round his waist his father's Sam Browne ten sizes too large for him. That was in the first war; his father had been killed soon after and now war had passed again over the Carter family—and there would be no more of them. Nothing could hurt any of them again—only her who is left. Were they all together somewhere, the Carter family? Had his father met him and was his mother near by, still giving orders in that fretful, spoiled voice of the rich woman of the 1930s? And did they peer down at her, the three of them, watching where she went and how she conducted herself? She wished she knew about that. There had been a day in Scotland staying with John on Dick's last leave. They had gone for a walk together; the rain had come on so they had sheltered in a church, wandering round reading the inscriptions on the walls. She remembered how quite suddenly Dick had knelt in one of the pews, and just to save him from feeling embarrassed afterwards she had knelt beside him—and how later, standing hand-in-hand on the porch, he had whispered to her:

'Do you believe there's anything else, Lynny? Do you believe we go on, all of us, and are together forever?'

'I don't know,' she said slowly at last. 'I've always *wanted* to believe so, but all the clever people I've ever talked to seemed to make me believe otherwise.'

'You mean they believe it all ceases with the heart stopping?' he asked.

'Lots of people do believe that. Yes, they say when you've seen anything dead it's so finished, so inanimate—so *gone*—so uncaring any more.'

'I've seen plenty of dead.' He spoke slowly. 'I've seen dead that died quietly, sitting, a sort of surprise on their faces. I've seen dead flung impotently into the air. I've seen dead that died in agony, clutching at things, rigid, their faces drawn into ghastly contortions, and I've seen dead that had no faces. . . .'

Her heart beat a little quicker but she hadn't interrupted him, and after a pause he had gone on speaking:

'And yet I believe there is something more. I believe it for the same reason that your clever men don't believe it, for the inanity of it. They weren't there, those people, they were just their coats, flung aside.'

'Didn't it make you feel awful?' she asked.

'I used to remember Bridges' lines about the soldier—"they were England's glory as a common coat". I felt comforted—the two coats seem synonymous.'

'Yes,' she had assented simply, for there had been no more words to say.

Dick went on: 'There were other men, Lynny, who considered life to be only a little gleam of time between two eternities.' He had ended up with a smile, suddenly shy.

The rain stopped after that and they walked off arm-in-arm down the road to Errol, she clinging to him a little tighter than before, he looking down at her from his great height and patting her hand clumsily.

'What is it, my darling? Haven't upset you, have I?'

'Oh, Dickie. I wish this beastly war would end so that I didn't have so much to fear when you're out of my sight.' And they had walked on again in silence, threading their way through a herd of John's Highland cattle.

'I wish I could be like you and *know*,' she had gone on. 'I wish I could believe that if anything happened to you that you would try and get back somehow to tell me everything was all right—*that's*

151

the sort of thing that I find makes it hard for a birdbrain like mine to hold.'

'If anything happens to me—which it won't,' he said, 'I will try. But, my darling, don't be shaken if nothing happens, because it's all so far too big for us to understand.'

They had run into John then, laughing on the old steamroller he had bought in Dundee, and there had been nursery tea in the old Castle with the children and the subject wasn't brought up again.

She lay down on her back once more; the sun was hot and she'd have a red nose tomorrow, but no one would care, no one would be there to tease her. Her youth had been flung aside, too, just like his coat. He had never returned. Not a sigh, not a whisper— and she had listened for nothing else. Once she had talked to Uncle Herbert about it but he had just frowned and taken off his glasses and wiped them carefully with his silk handkerchief. 'As you get older, Lynnette, you don't struggle so to know. You accept everything more easily, without always asking why.' She had almost laughed at that—but it was no use. Everyone, every living thing is quite alone once it has lost its mate, its chosen companion out of all the world—the hands, the arms, the body. . . .

She shivered suddenly in the hot sun, catching again the heavy scent of may. Oh, how he would have loved this place. What a tragedy he never saw this part of the coast, these hedgerows and tall exotic trees. Her heart sobbed, but her face on the stone had almost the same appearance as the granite.

The sun was making her sleepy; she looked at her watch. Nearly time to go, nearly time for another meal, then bedtime once again and—merciful God—another day would pass out of sight. Nor would she even try to recall any of them as they sped past her—not yet anyway, not for years and years, and then she would undo them carefully from their wrappings of moss and Cornish flowers and take them out one by one gently and call them Experience.

A distant rumbling of wheels caught her attention for a moment; a farm cart, she supposed.

Well, it could roll over her for all she cared. She wouldn't lift a hand to stay death.

A man was whistling; she caught herself putting the words to it. 'Ist wir Lili Marlene, Ist wir Lili Marlene. . . .' Would she never escape those tunes! The rumbling wheels were coming nearer; so were voices, and there were men singing now. In the distance she could hear the sounds of motor-boats or motorcycles and the voices were getting louder. More people seemed to have found her little cove. With a sigh of annoyance she sat up on her round, flat rock and was astonished to see coming down the road onto the runway, soldiers in lorries and armoured cars. Behind them were tanks. In the water were landing barges, with motor-boats fussing around them.

'What on earth—' she started, but as the badges on the soldiers' berets gleamed suddenly in the sunlight, she caught her lower lip between her teeth, as she always did when she saw one of those berets, frowning, wondering if she had been asleep and hadn't heard their coming earlier, for it seemed now that they were all about her, shouting orders, laughing, whistling, as they put their brown faces up through the turrets of their armoured cars.

Lynnette might have been part of the rock on which she sat, so still she was, so astonished and absorbed by all she was looking at. One by one the cars ran down the runway and onto the waiting barges, while the rest waited their turn. Some of the soldiers stood about, some were lying, some sitting or standing on the cliff by the road; one man had a big pink rhododendron over his ear, and the others guffawed with laughter and shouted things to him, but the wind caught their words and tossed them out to sea.

A knot of officers on the far side had their backs to her, heads bent together over a map. If she half-closed her eyes she could pretend that the long-legged one was Dick. She'd played this game often before and for a full second, heartsease took the place of pain. She half-closed her eyes, watching him; he turned away from the others, suddenly finishing off what he was saying with a gesture of the hand that made her bite her lip again. Then he strode towards her. She sat there, her fists clenched, her eyes screwed up; then quickly, as he was almost upon her, she opened them wide, a word of joy bursting from her lips:

'Dick!'

But he seemed unaware of her, deep in his own thoughts, his eyes bent upon the sand. She sat frozen to the spot where she sat. What was this? A dream, an hallucination? She looked round quickly. They were all still there, calling things out to each other and loading up the boats. He was quite close to her now. She put out a hand, feeling too weak to do more.

'Dick,' she whispered again, and then loudly. 'Dick!'

But he took no notice, and mounting a larger rock than the one on which she sat, he raised his binoculars to his eyes and scanned the sky. She followed suit, shading her eyes with her hand, but there was nothing save a few clouds come up from the south-west. . . . How beautiful he looked, how magnificent his dark green eyes, his brown, humorous face under the jaunty beret. She longed unutterably to be able to touch him, for him to look at her and know her. Then suddenly he started speaking—he was speaking to her and yet she knew quite definitely that he couldn't see her—knew indeed that none of them could see her, that she was taking part in something unreal and dreamlike and no one, no one would believe her if she even tried to tell them about it.

'Lynny, darling.' His voice was low, as if he talked to himself. 'Can you hear me, I wonder, as you go about your hospital? Will you pause suddenly and look round, sure you heard my voice?'

He stopped speaking, the figure on the rock seemingly carved in granite. He went on:

'I didn't tell you before, Lynny, I didn't want to make you unhappy because I may be wrong anyway, but I don't think so. I've felt it a long time and when we had our orders I knew for certain that I wouldn't be coming back to you, that I shall get no further than the beaches. It will be a beach like this, perhaps, with round flat stones and small yellow shells, and clumps of seaweed and sea pinks on the rocks by the cliff. That will be all I shall see, Lynny. I shan't see death in the sandhills. I shall think of you once with tenderness, then quite gently shall put the thought of you firmly from me and go up the beach.'

He stopped again and she could see the muscles of his face tighten as they did so often when he was upset about anything. He had a stalk of sorrel in his hand that he was rolling nervously between his fingers, then he flicked it away and went back to the others.

The tears were raining down her cheeks, great tearing sobs shook her body, and somehow in the midst of it all she realized it was the first time tears had come. She put her head in her hands and sobbed, swaying this way and that like a native woman in uncontrollable grief, while the great slab of concrete that had tightened round her heart loosened itself and slowly slid away. . . .

After what seemed only a few moments the terrible crying ceased and she looked round. There was nobody there. No sound save the flapping gulls. No movement save the wind in the grass over her head.

'But I saw them!' she whispered to herself. 'That was no dream! I swear I was never asleep! I couldn't have dreamed Dick's words, I couldn't have dreamed the soldier with the rhododendron. I *saw* them!'

But the place was empty, no movement on the cliff road but a piece of dirty paper, nobody on the runway except a solemn gull who prinked pompously towards the water. White and exhausted she leaned back, trying to collect herself, dimly conscious that the pain had somehow left her heart. She got up and climbed onto the runway and started up the cliff road. When she got to the top she turned and looked back. She *had* seen them, but how could anyone account for it? A step behind her made her turn quickly. It was only the coastguard, who smiled in a friendly way.

'Clouds comin' up,' he called as he came on a level with her. She hesitated a moment, then, 'I say,' she began nervously.

He looked at her, waiting for her question.

'This is a private beach, I see.' She hesitated.

'Oh, yes'm. B'longs to thay house up there.'

'What do they have such a big jetty for? Yachts?'

'Oh no'm. Thay runway was built a-purpose, and that haven't never been changed or taken away since.'

'A purpose?' Her voice was faint, and he turned and looked at her again.

'Thay tanks coom up over thay hill day afore D-day and thay go down thay runway to t'barges—I see them coom along o'me own eyes through Mawnan Smith.'

'Tanks . . . you saw them before D-day? Not any more, never since?' Her lips were white.

'Oh, no'm. Thay tanks was goin' to Normandy. Proper noisy things thay was, and thay boys singin' and laughin' and thay girls a-throwin' flowers.'

She was silent for so long that he thought she wasn't listening any more.

'Ah well, it's all over now, all that.'

Still she didn't answer and he looked at her face. Rarely had he seen such happiness, though the eyes were full of tears. And he realized for the first time that she was quite beautiful.

She stood where he had left her, staring down at the rocks, and the sea, and the runway and beyond to the hills and woods nestling green. Her mouth trembled a little and the tears ran unchecked down her cheeks. A slatter of mist blew in from the sea and the greens and blues merged into one.

She was smiling as she turned and walked away.

GARRY MARSH

August Bank Holiday 1932 found the Stage Cricket Club facing an Old Boys' club on a Kentish ground. The wicket prepared for us was as rough as gnarled oak, three times as hard, and bone dry. I won the toss and elected to bat. I must have been mad . . . we should have just tossed and let the winner take all!

Not only was the pitch a disaster but the home attack was made up of eight boisterously healthy youths, all well over six feet tall—and, it appeared, as wide—who bowled at a pace Larwood at his peak would consider satisfactory. Earle Grey and I opened the innings. By going in first I hoped for an early dismissal before these bowlers found their lengths. At least I could sit in the sun and watch the massacre I knew must follow. I took guard a foot outside the leg stump.

In the distance the bowler began his run and thundered up to the wicket. The ball was too fast for me to see but I felt an unpleasant draught around my head and heard a terrible smack in the wicket-keeper's gloves some fifty yards behind me. Despite my sunburn I knew I had turned white. The next ball hit my chest and all but went through me. The bowler screamed 'How's that!' and I did not wait for the umpire's decision. I made for the pavilion as fast as my shaking legs could take me. Then, to my horror, I was recalled as the umpire insisted on giving me 'Not out'. From then on I faced a tornado of hate.

Earle Grey at the other end opened the scoring with a sizzling four leg-byes off his left ear. I realized by now that the opposition proposed to use these eight fast bowlers in relays of three overs each so that the battery, once launched, could be sustained *ad infinitum*. They did not bother about direction or length but just concentrated on the batsman's body, and virtually ignored the stumps.

In the pavilion was Abraham Sofaer, co-founder, with Earle Grey, of the Stage Cricket Club in 1929. Sofi, as we called him, remains to this day a man of infinite dignity, a fine actor, especially in Shakespearian roles, with a voice so resonant that even when he considered himself to be whispering, glasses in the bar would ring or even smash to pieces. In addition Sofi was a man of complete courage at the wicket, facing fast bowlers by creating the impression that he considered them presumptive impediments to be taught a lesson.

He had all that summer been quoting from Prince Ranjitsinhji's book on how to bat. And, as I faced untimely and painful death out there now, I could hear Sofi's penetrating voice from the pavilion: 'On a bad wicket like this, it is a question of footwork and timing. . . . Ranji would never have fallen flat on his face like Garry did just now . . . he would have eased his right foot in the direction of point, put his head in line with the ball and picked it off his nose to the fine leg boundary.'

I had no intention of putting my head or any other part of my anatomy in line with the ball. All I wanted was to get out as quickly as possible. An actor's life was hazardous enough without going to auditions crippled and maimed. Then a full toss landed bang on my big toe joint. My language was florid as I sank down to the ground but my mind was sufficiently agile for me to swing my bat against the stumps and shout 'How's that!' The umpire seemed reluctant to give me out but my ordeal was over.

On returning to the pavilion I was greeted by a very hostile Sofi.

'Why am I batting number eleven?' he demanded.

'Because,' I said, 'you have a wife and God knows how many children.'

'My eight children have nothing to do with it.'

'They certainly have. If you go out there your days as a salary earner will be at an end. I love your glorious Irish wife Psyche dearly, and it is my duty as captain to protect you on her behalf. In fact, come to think of it, when the time comes for you to bat, I shall declare.'

Sofi stamped up and down. The scoreboard now read 4 runs for three wickets.

'Why don't you let me go in?' he ranted. 'I could knock them off their length in no time.'

For the next five minutes he bellowed quotations from Ranji's book, dancing up and down in front of me to show how simple was the art of dealing with the onslaught we were facing.

'Concentration . . . agility . . . use your feet like this . . . down the wicket to the pitch of the ball . . . smother it, hook it, pull it . . . ,' and 'Stuff it', said another incoming batsman on his way to the first-aid tent, having deliberately run himself out. The next batsman was still sitting fearfully in his deckchair looking both disinterested and a nasty shade of green.

'It is time,' said Sofi in his grandest manner, 'that someone stopped the rot and restored our interest in this game. I will take your place and show you how to deal with this aggression. I have read Ranji's book diligently and am confident I can master this attack no matter what they throw at me.'

I made no objection. By now Sofi had me almost believing he was Ranji's reincarnation. He strode to the wicket, like Sidney Carton to the guillotine, a figure of dignity and courage. As he took guard his voice boomed like an organ in a cathedral.

'Two legs!' he thundered and the fielders seemed to quiver.

Forward short-leg moved even closer to within a yard of Sofi's bat. Sofi turned to him and, in his best Shakespearian manner, growled: 'Remove yourself, my good fellow. Otherwise when I play my strokes I could decapitate you.'

The fielder gave ground, appearing to have been blown back!

The bowler had already increased his abnormally long run by some twenty paces, clearly intending to scare this presumptuous batsman—a waste of time even if Sofi had been aware of that intention. The first ball he received he greeted with a magnificent cover drive which, had not the ball been almost a wide outside the leg stump, would have undoubtedly gone to the boundary. Sofi's bravery was of a high order as he continued to face five and a half ounces of solid leather hurtling at him at the thick end of a hundred miles an hour. After a couple of overs, by a miracle of luck and tenacity he had scored 14 runs, earning cheers from us and the home crowd.

So delighted were we that we began calling out to him to show us some more of Ranji's shots. This proved fatal. Sofi waved his bat at us, smiling broadly and confidently. The next ball was short and rearing—and in direct line with his long, prominent, illustrious nose. Just right, according to Ranji, to face the right foot to point and, at the last second, glide the ball away for four.

True the ball did flash to the fine leg boundary but something in the execution of the stroke had gone wrong. It had actually been played with the nose—and Sofi's statuesque figure subsided slowly to the grass.

We collected him from the pitch in a dazed condition and it was some time before he was able to speak coherently.

'What happened?' he gasped at last.

'You've had a bit of a knock, old chap,' I said. 'You know that shot of Ranji's . . . the one you pick off your nose . . .?'

'Yes,' he said faintly. 'Ranji never missed it . . . a beautiful stroke. Did I play it?'

'Without question you played it. . . .'

'And did it go for four as Ranji said?'

'Well . . .' I hesitated. 'Yes. Yes, it did go for four . . . but your nose sort of got in the way.'

'Tell me . . . tell just what happened.'

'You did everything Ranji said . . . foot back . . . nose in line with the ball. Absolutely perfect positioning . . . but your bat was not there. That was the only mistake you made.'

From looking melancholy, Sofi's eyes became stony.

'You know,' he said mutinously. 'Either His Highness Prince Ranjitsinhji is wrong—or I've misread the instructions. . . !'

G. O. NICKALLS

The Megaphoney

ILLUSTRATED BY
JACK BROOME

During my active years as an oarsman a large proportion of my time was spent on predestinate grooves, which took the form of sliding in acute discomfort backwards and forwards on a hard wooden seat.

During that time and since my withdrawal from the active lists I have heard, and I expect uttered, so much sense and nonsense on the subject of rowing as to last me a lifetime.

I can assure my readers that the comparative silence (except of the coxswain) required whilst in the boat is more than made up for out of the boat. Then the arguments and theories advanced twixt active oarsmen and their elders, commonly called the 'heavies', must be heard to be believed.

I have received and given so much criticism and advice, heard and talked so much esoteric balderdash, entered into so much skulduggery and intrigue; felt so much discomfort, humiliation and ecstasy —all, it sometimes seems, to so little purpose, that writing now from a fixed seat and without bearing Professor Higgins any Pygmalice, I honestly believe I could fashion not only a formidable rowing coach but a really full-blown 'heavy' out of someone who had never seen an oar in his life. Allow me to present—'The Megaphoney' or 'Leanderthal Man'.

Your first requirement is a small, faded schoolboy cap. You need never put it on your head. Hold it in your hand, taking care to massage or crumple it beyond recognition. To give it an authentic dilapidated look, it is an advantage if you can manage to break the peak's cardboard foundation in at least two places. A blazer of any colour is recommended, preferably of a rough material that picks up the maximum of hairs and fluff in the shortest possible time. The breast pocket should bear a crest or emblem of an intricate and unrecognizable design. No one will challenge you, and even should they do so, you can always pass it off by saying that you founded the Darjeeling Rowing Club in the early thirties—or, how can you ever forget that day in Rangoon when you rowed ten races in an afternoon with a mulatto cox and an Ethiopian in the bows, 'damn

The Megaphoney

fellow could never keep time'. A scarf is essential, the longer the better. At any rate, it should be of sufficient length to go three times round your neck with enough over to be brought down and tied sash-wise round your waist. Any trousers will do, so long as they appear sufficiently impromptu. Grey bags, blanket bags, twill bags, all are perfectly permissible so long as they have not been cleaned or pressed since you bought them. It is a great advantage if the bottom of such trousers as you may choose are tucked in to the tops of your socks, and permanently enclasped in bicycle clips. It will indicate that you have just come in from coaching. And don't forget: 'It's only cissie dry bobs who care a damn how they look.'

Having got thus far, it would be a fatal mistake to imagine that you are completely accoutred. Before entering the club bar with your host (I am assuming that you are not, as yet, a member of any rowing club), you should arm yourself with a megaphone. Place it on the floor in the far corner of the bar with as much ostentatious clatter as possible. At the same time your face should assume a horrified, half-apologetic expression at the disturbance you are causing.

Your host will now offer you a drink. That's the least he can do. Accept it. Ask for a quart of beer. This never fails to impress, and will show them right away what a splendid, hearty fellow you are. Your companions at the bar will now notice that you have three (no less) stop-watches hanging around your neck. These adjuncts are absolutely essential. They should be slung outside the scarf, and should swing with a sort of bumble-puppy action somewhere in the region of your navel. Don't talk. Sip your beer meditatively, and pretend to be listening. This will single you out as being something out of the ordinary. Amongst twenty men all talking at the same time, you will be the only man who has ever listened—or for that matter, ever pretended to.

When you can't stand it any longer, bring a small but intricate-looking piece of machinery out of your pocket. It need have no significance as regards rowing. It's just a gimmick which goes a long way to impress the semi-initiated. You should previously have armed yourself with this contraption, which can quite easily be picked up for a few pence in the Portobello Road. Handle it with studied casualness. Put your beer down. Move towards the window of the bar room, or go out on to the balcony should you feel inclined. Make it obvious that you want to be left alone.

Gaze upwards at the club flag, flapping on the flagpole. Now twiddle a screw on your piece of machinery. Now stop, and gaze intently at the river. Let your lips move without uttering a sound. This indicates that you're doing some rapid mental calculations.

Next, check your findings by whisking a small slide rule from your pocket. Now get out a pencil and make some illegible marks on the back of a flat and empty cigarette packet. This is all immensely impressive, and is well worth hours of private rehearsal prior to your first public performance.

Should anyone have the temerity to ask what you are doing, mutter disparagingly that it really couldn't be of the least interest to anyone else; it's just to prove (or disprove) some silly inconsequential little theory of your own. This should be muttered in such a way as to indicate that no one except the intellectual élite would be likely to understand it even were it explained to them, and you're certainly not going to attempt that. Sheer waste of valuable time.

A few evenings of these sorts of antics, provided your host continues to persevere with you, should work wonders. He may even suggest that you might care to become a member of the club. Don't be too elated. It may be that your frequent encroachments on his hospitality are taxing his pocket more than his patience. The brutal fact is that he just can't afford you any longer. At this stage you should, whilst making the usual self-deprecatory noises, allow your name to go forward. You may not get another chance. Within a week or so, you may find yourself a fully-fledged member. What a triumph! A fully-fledged member! *You may even be asked to coach.*

All right, you have been asked to coach. Accept. Clinch it straight away. This is the golden opportunity you have been looking for. It may be the only golden opportunity you will ever get. Strike now before it turns to dross in your hands. Don't be frightened. These notes, together with a little over-confidence, should transport you (provided you can ride a bicycle) into the higher hierarchy of successful coaches.

Have the crew assembled immediately. Don't be diffident. Look them up and down with a jaundiced eye. Remember, they're only so much rowing fodder. Don't make any old bones about it. Tell them the going's going to be tough, but that they have an advantage in that they all seem to be quite well equipped physically. This may mean nothing more than that they possess two arms, two legs and a head. You then proceed to play your first trump card. Mention that you must have their complete confidence at all times. That you are as dependent on them as they are on you. Probably not true, but it puts them on a man-to-man basis which they will find quite irresistible. Then you must tell them that if at any time they think they are not making the progress they feel they should, then you are in their hands, and they are at liberty to sack you as they would a defaulting butler. The fact that neither you nor they are ever likely

164

to be in a position to sack a defaulting butler strengthens your case. The effect of this piece of histrionic oratory is electric. They're yours for life, and with limpid, trusting eyes they will cluster round you like a pack of thrashed water spaniels. Show no surprise at this. Keep the whole thing on a brusque, strictly unemotional basis, and announce that they must be ready on the raft at 10.30 the following morning. But first of all make up your mind how you're going to follow the crew.

Undoubtedly the easiest thing to coach from is a launch. This is really 'not on' during the summer because of the wash or waves it creates. It is considered bad form so to disturb the water that it may:

(*a*) Swamp or capsize other river craft;
(*b*) induce seasickness in other users of the river.

The generally accepted coaching vehicle nowadays is the bicycle. If you can get a tandem so much the better. You can then fag the ninth man (same as cricket's twelfth man) to steer and pedal away in front whilst you wield the megaphone with abandon from the rear seat. This has distinct advantages. You don't have to look where you're going, and your propulsive activities are reduced to some occasional and undemanding token pedalling.

Tandems are getting scarce so it is more probable that you will settle for that cosy old animal, the ordinary, common-or-garden bicycle. Buy a second-hand one of a suitably dilapidated appearance. Bicycles of whatever vintage are at a premium before Henley Regatta and your chief concern will be to retain it for your own use. For this, padlock*s* are essential, and here the stress is on the plural. One padlock draped around four or five spokes is useless. A pair of wire-cutters will soon get rid of spokes, and coaches are constantly seen careering perilously down the towpath apparently without any spokes at all.

To prevent the loss of spokes, you must get a second and stronger padlock and chain the framework of the bicycle to some immovable object such as a tent pole. *Only do not lose the key*. One coach of my acquaintance did just this, so that his bike remained chained in holy padlock to the tent pole eighteen days and nights. In fact, I am credibly informed that when the tentage people finally struck the tent and re-erected it at the Farnborough Air Show some few weeks later, the bicycle was re-erected too. A parachute-jumping friend of mine has informed me that it appeared to be none the worse for its experience, and looked perfectly composed and elegant in its new surroundings.

After your crew have taken about half-a-dozen strokes, say: 'Easy

165

You will settle for the ordinary, common-or-garden bicycle

all!' And with any luck their cox will stop them. This should indicate to your pupils that so acute is your perception that in those six strokes you have seen enough to last you a coaching lifetime. It should not only suggest that you've seen enough, it should go further, and make them feel that what you've seen doesn't altogether meet with your approval. Now, fix Stroke with a knowing stare, and ask him: 'Stroke, where did you learn your rowing?' His answer may take the form of giving the name of his school or college coach, or he may content himself by giving the name of the school or college. It doesn't matter, for in every case your reply will be the same. Throwing your head back reminiscently, and allowing a trace of a smile to play around your lips, you answer: 'It doesn't matter—no harm done—we'll talk about it tomorrow.'

'Bow, has anyone ever taught you how to hold an oar?' This should be in the gentlest, most sympathetic manner, as though you fully appreciated that it was not his fault that he started in wrong hands. The fact that he's already holding an oar is neither here nor there. The implication is that he's holding it in the wrong way. You can continue in this vein until the completion of the journey. Then is the time to talk to them confidentially. After they have had their shower and are fully clothed again, gather them round you in the changing-room.

Now is the moment to show that you're pretty well versed in everything that's ever been written about rowing. This, of course, is not the case. You've never read a word about the subject in your life, which is a distinct advantage. It's all terribly confusing. All you need do at the moment is to memorize a few key quotations. Don't have any truck with any modern rowing books. Your pupils probably know them by heart anyhow. Go straight back a hundred years to Dr Warre. That'll fox them, and you won't be contradicted.

All the same, just in case one of your over-eager pupils should show an interest in that majestic personality, it would be prudent to know something of the background of the 'great Dr Warre' as he was invariably termed. In his youth he had rowed for Oxford, and was something of a classical scholar. This came to light in his early years when he entered for the pair-oared race at Henley with a chap called Snow. This was too great a temptation. They entered under the names of 'Bellum and Nivis'. This pawky little joke so enraged a number of the Stewards of the Regatta to whom it had to be translated that they introduced a rule debarring the use of pseudonyms in the future.

Now just one more paragraph, and you will have got Dr Warre in a nutshell. In his later years he became Headmaster of Eton, and coached the Eton eight whilst still nurturing a passion for classical allusion. Thus, still besprinkling his coaching with Latin phraseology, he could never resist a leaning towards the ancient Greek triremes, and relapsed into Greek quotations on the slightest provocation. This became somewhat confusing to many of the semi-educated louts he was forced to coach. On occasions he spoke in English, and many were never certain in which of three possible languages they were being addressed.

Don't be put off. You can soon swot up a few Greek and Latin phrases. After all, what was good enough for him is good enough for you. So, addressing your pupils, you remark: 'I need hardly remind you of what the great Dr Warre used to say. *"Dulce et decorum est* . . ." ' No need to finish the quotation. No object in over-taxing your memory, so you continue: ' "Boys!" he used to say, "Let your rowing be *dulce et decorum."* ' And suiting the words to the rhythm of the rowing stroke, you repeat: '*Dulce et decorum.* . . .

'D'you see what I mean? Of course Steve Fairbairn was after the same thing when he said: "If you can't do a thing easily, you can't do it at all." ' To quote two such great masters in one breath, whose views on rowing were diametrically opposed, should absolutely slay them. In one fell swoop it will prove:

(*a*) That you know it all;
(*b*) that you can see both sides of the coin;
(*c*) that you're not one of those bigoted, biased sort of chaps who would stoop to petty arguments on mere technicalities.

Here you add: 'Of course, rowing, like everything else worthwhile, has had its fair share of disagreement, a Warre and a Steve aren't born every day. And so often it's a question of *"Quot homines tot* . . .".' Don't complete the sentence; nod knowingly, and say: 'After all, you don't have to be reminded of that.'

And now a word about Steve. Whereas rowing doyens invariably dub the Headmaster 'the great Dr Warre', it is quite sufficient to refer to Stephen Fairbairn as 'Steve'. Everyone will know who you mean.

Warre harked back to the days when, quite apart from racing, there was still an element of pageantry about rowing. Processions of boats presenting 'a very lively spectacle' were all the rage. Cannons were fired, and heavily embroidered flags unfurled. This trooping-the-colour approach required precision and uniformity. Nothing slipshod was tolerated. Hence the poker-like straight back beloved by the great Doctor and his followers.

Then a breezy, big-hearted giant blew in from the Antipodes to stir the millpond of our rowing complacency. He formulated the astonishing theory that to propel the boat you should concentrate on working the oar, and that any attempt to position the body in order the more easily to accomplish this feat was a lot of clap-trap.

This was 'Steve', who must bear the entire responsibility for another ludicrous dictum which was that you must enjoy rowing. This was an entirely new conception which infuriated the traditionalists. Whoever heard of anyone enjoying their rowing? No good could possibly come of this sort of nonsense, which was most certainly *not* in the best interests of the sport.

For a whole decade the supporters of these opposing doctrines in rowing bars up and down the country waged a fanatical, verbal, pint-of-bitter warfare. So much so that everyone became so engrossed in proving their various theories as to forget to row at all. This civil war phase is now known as the 'Wars of the Rowses'* which left the rowing kingdom weakened, embittered and confused.

Whereas Warre coached in Latin, Steve coached in parables. For instance, should he require some crew he was coaching to give of their best when overtaking another crew, he would inquire: 'Who is the king of glory? Show them who the king of glory is, boys.' The effect was miraculous. Then again, to emphasize the smoothness and ease with which he required you to extract the oar from the water and row round the turn onto the feather, he would, suiting his action to the words, exhort one to: 'Turn yer mother's mangle, turn yer mother's mangle. More like a dose of salts than a stiff shirt.' Sometimes the effect was miraculous.

Your first contact with the crew has been an enormous success. Beyond question you have established yourself as the medicine man par excellence. However, you have another three weeks to fill in. Don't let it worry you. If you don't know what to say, bicycle behind some of the other coaches as they instruct their crews and you'll pick up enough parrot-cries to last you a lifetime. On the other hand you may decide that silence is golden. Some coaches without saying a word beyond 'Well rowed, boys' have proved staggeringly successful. Should you feel that the repetition of those three words may prove monotonous, remove your teeth occasionally. Don't alter your script. The words will be the same but they'll sound different. Above all, don't take too much out of yourself. Overwork the crew if you must, but *don't* overtire yourself. Remember there's a race in prospect: you are the key man and it is absolutely essential that you are fighting fit for the ordeal which lies ahead.

The great day has arrived. As a keen coach you will obviously

---

* *Rowses, Wars of the:* The first syllable can be pronounced to rhyme with 'thou' or 'low'; both are equally applicable.

Whoever heard of anyone enjoying their rowing?

want to be with your crew those few fatal minutes before the starting of the race. Disdain the offer of a seat on the Umpire's launch, for that would prevent you addressing your crew before the word '*Go*', an eventuality which might well prove fatal to your plans.

So get out your bicycle, provided it has not already been pur-loined by your rival coach, and pedal down to the start. Don't take a megaphone. Anyone addressing a crew through a megaphone during a race renders that crew liable to disqualification. Coaching during the race is definitely *verboten*. This regulation is a compara-tively recent innovation which came to this country from the Conti-nent. Many consider it a most dastardly interference with the liberty of the subject. One of those filthy mid-European tricks designed to ensure that, other things being equal or unequal, the best crew wins. Whoever heard of such nonsense?

In the good old days when men were men and blood pressure hadn't been invented, you could coach your crew through a mega-phone during the race to your heart's content. This coaching differed slightly from that employed in practice. In fact, some unsporting officious busybodies have been heard to suggest that it came nearer to barracking than coaching, its object being to ensure your opponents as well as your own crew should hear every megaphoned comment and injunction. For instance, you could tell your crew that they were all rowing splendidly. Should they have been behind at that par-ticular moment you could assure them that it was all going to plan. This was intended to demoralize and reduce your opponents to a state of jittery incompetence, and suggest that your crew had some tremendous *coup d'état* up their sleeves. Still addressing your own crew, you could then tell them something about their rivals. All such comments should have been carefully chosen to suggest that they were in a pretty bad way. For instance: 'You can go past them whenever you choose' could have the most devastating effect. 'They've had it!' is shorter and equally devastating. To proclaim that their number Five had turned green and was liable to pass out at any moment, or that Two has just lost his slide for the third time, might have been considered to be going a little too far, and was, very sportingly, only used when you realized that your own crew was '*in extremis*'.

Of course, there was absolutely no reason why your rival coach should not indulge in exactly similar tactics. Then the fun was end-less. The only thing to do on such occasions was to manœuvre your bicycle so that your hated rival was between you and the river. Then, by judicious jockeying, and with a few well-judged, by-mis-take-on-purpose swerves you could, with any luck, arrange that he and his machine subsided into the watery depths. This left you as the only coach and virtually in charge of both crews which was a great advantage.

But that is all in the past. It was *not* considered to be in the best interests of the sport. That rollicking British sense of fun is no more. *Sic transit gloria* . . . No wonder so many races nowadays have devolved into grim humourless processions with the best crew always winning. Just how dull can it become?

Do not despair, however. Just before the race there is still an awful lot a clever coach can do to ensure victory.

You have pedalled down to the start, and your crew have turned round to get on to the start. Dismount, and advance to the water's edge. By this time they will be divesting themselves of their sweaters or track suits, and you're there to collect them. Just put them in a neat pile on the bank. You need do no more. It's just possible that someone will collect them and return them to their rightful owners. However, that's no affair of yours. You've done all you can.

See that your crew are on the mark well ahead of time. It is no business of the Umpire's to chivvy your crew on to the start, and if you leave it to the last moment he will hate you for it. Don't forget he's working to a very tight schedule anyway, and if you're late he'll probably miss his second dry martini before lunch. So don't let the Umpire hate you. It never pays. (N.B. Nowadays a steward on the bank does the chivvying, much to the relief of all Umpires.)

The crucial moment is when your cox has just got them on to the stake boat, and the other crew are alongside. Don't say the obvious thing like 'Remember what I told you.' That's old hat. A curriculum is essential. A curriculum, moreover, which merits a good deal of careful rehearsal. You must have a password, which suggests to your wretched opponents some sort of private joke. Any gibberish will do so long as it's completely unintelligible. So just before your crew come under Umpire's orders, say in a loud, clear voice: 'Remember, boys, Lucy, Lucy, poisoned arrows.' Their response to this must be immediate. The whole crew should go into gales of maniacal laughter, and at least three of them give the 'thumbs up' sign. The effect of this is miraculous. It establishes beyond doubt :

(*a*) That you are one of the boys, and that between you and your crew there is complete *rapprochement*;

(*b*) that your crew are so full of buck and self-confidence, so happy amongst themselves, that they've hardly had time to consider the opposition.

The combined effect is to give your crew a psychological advantage and to spread gloom and despondency in the hearts of your opponents. Well enacted, this could be worth anything up to three lengths to your crew in the race.

Once the Umpire has risen majestically in the bows of the launch, silence is the golden rule. Your crew's attitude to the Umpire should be carefully studied. Suggest to them that they treat him as a rich uncle from whom they have expectations.

If the Umpire should happen to ask them any questions one man should be deputed to reply in a loud, clear voice: 'Yes, sir' or 'No, sir'.

This latter reply should be accompanied by raising the hand. Don't forget the Umpire may be deaf, so shout it out. Always call him 'sir'. He may pretend he doesn't like it, but your crew will be giving him the impression of being a nice lot of respectable, clean-living chaps. This is the only way to encourage the Umpire to like them.

If you have carefully followed all the foregoing instructions, you should, in an incredibly short space of time, be ready to take your place amongst the heaviest of rowing heavies. Your coaching efforts have, or most certainly should have, been crowned with success. Young oarsmen sing your praises, and even old oarsmen sportingly admit that you've got something. The rowing world in all its watery glory is at your feet.

Walk warily. You are now at your most vulnerable. The serpent, disguised as another 'heavy', is waiting for you. One evening he will catch you unawares. A large glass of port heavily laced with his lust-for-power potion, will be placed in your unsuspecting hands. As you sip, he will murmur quite casually: 'Can't think why they haven't made you a Steward of Henley, years ago.' 'You know we could do with someone like you on the A.R.A. Council.' Or: 'You could wake up that old Selection Board a bit; it needs a jolt.'

It is for you to make up your mind whether you aspire to these glittering symbols of authority. You have much to gain and quite a lot to lose. Should you accept, the young oarsmen will suspect you. You will no longer be one of them. The image you have so assiduously built up of being just a big, clean, wholesome boy at heart, will fade overnight. It is possible you may never be asked to coach a crew again. Meanwhile the older oarsmen will start whispering behind your back. As you try to join them at the bar, they will break off in the middle of a conversation. This is to underline that it's you they have been discussing, and that whatever they have said does not redound to your credit. Very much the reverse. You have suddenly become an outcast—a pariah. In one fell swoop you have thrown away the work of years.

A real old Megaphoney

My advice, in fact, is—stay as you are. In your unassailable position of coaching pre-eminence, who knows, you may find yourself flying off as coach of a first-class crew to some terribly important International Regatta with a glittering gold medal as good as in their pockets. The attainment of success in this role is worth more than all the other paltry baubles put together.

It now only remains for the author to wish you many happy coaching days in the rowing world. We've come a long way since you donned that cap, scarf and blazer, and were stood that first drink at the bar. You now appreciate how important were all those stop-watches that you hung rather self-consciously round your neck. That dented old megaphone and that battered, ancient bike were the essential adjuncts to a new and glorious personality which is *you*. Without these humble beginnings you never could have attained to the position of glittering and much-envied eminence you hold today. Have no doubts, the struggle has been more than worthwhile. Your reputation has been well and truly earned.

At last you are a pundit, a rowing 'heavy'—a real old Megaphoney.

Goon Away—Try Next Door

There was a young man from Cathay
On a slow boat to China one day
Was trapped near the tiller
By a sex-crazed gorilla
And China's a bloody long way

This piece of T. S. Eliotry was produced at a Goon Show rehearsal by the simple method of each person writing a line apiece. To many a puzzled listener no doubt the Goon Show appeared to have been written in the same way.

Actually, Spike Milligan would work all week writing the script, sometimes assisted by Larry Stephens or Eric Sykes, and Peter Sellers and I would only come into the picture on the Sunday afternoon before recording the show in the evening. Let us take a typical day. . . .

I roll up at the Camden Theatre in North London at about two-thirty, and my first thought is to wonder what conveyance Peter has arrived in. He was always changing his cars. One Sunday it might be a Goggomobile, and the next an Austin Princess. I believe at one time he was negotiating to buy a steam-roller.

As I enter the stage door, conveniently next door to a pub, I sing a burst of *Return to Sorrento*. There come cries of 'It's Singo, the approaching tenor, folks' from Sellers, who is playing the bongos in a prone position, accompanying Milligan's frenzied piano playing. 'Ah! The well-known danger to shipping has arrived. Ned of Wales is here.' Milligan announces my arrival with a NAAFI pianist's version of *We'll Keep a Welcome*. 'They'll never take you back, Ned.'

I reply with a raspberry. 'He's ad libbing again,' says Spike. 'Nurse, the screens—at once.' Bloodnock Sellers is now using the bongo drums as a pair of binoculars.

There follows a rapid exchange of Army jokes and the latest gags, mostly of scatalogical nature.

'All right lads, that's enough.' John Browell appears in the auditorium. He is the producer and it shows in the worry lines on his forehead. 'Let's have a look at the script.' With cries of 'Cobblers' and 'Ying ton Iddle I Po' we retire to a back room in the theatre where we are given scripts.

This was always the best time for us. It made everything worth-while—the frustration of tackling audiences in variety theatres where we were still finding it difficult to establish ourselves with a public accustomed to a less frenetic kind of comedy, or having to deal with managements who were completely against what we were trying to do—understandably perhaps, because we were not sure ourselves. Ours was a kind of anarchy in comedy. We were against the estab-lished form of presentation. At the time when we began the Goon Show in 1951, the profession was full of stand-up comics who came on and told a string of jokes and finished either with a song or a dance.

Our approach was different. We had spent the war years with lads of our own age in the Services and we had fresh ideas. We were all first generation show business—apart from Peter, whose family was connected with the Theatre. Perhaps I had better go back to when it all began.

Spike was born in Burma, and was the son of a Warrant Officer in the Indian Army.

When I first met him, he was Lance-Sergeant Milligan, Terence A., and one of the crew of a large 7·2 gun howitzer which had been installed in a gun-pit insecurely dug in the hard rock of a Tunisian plateau. His howitzer was being fired by a lanyard—a rope attached to the firing lever which was used when the gun crew were not quite sure of what might happen. It was night time, and the crew left the gun while the 'No. 1' of the gun, a sergeant, pulled the lanyard. The crew turned their backs to the gun as it fired, and when they turned round, it had disappeared.

At that time I was in an Artillery Regiment deployed near by, and I was sitting in a small wireless truck at the foot of a sizeable cliff. Suddenly there was a terrible noise as some monstrous object fell from the sky quite close to us. I immediately began looking in my German dictionary for suitable phrases for surrendering. If they were throwing things that big at us there was no alternative.

There was considerable confusion, and in the middle of it all the flap of the truck was pushed open and a young, helmeted idiot asked 'Anybody see a gun?' It was Milligan, and our paths were destined to cross many times.

I have fond memories of Spike dressed as a gypsy with black-dyed hessian trousers, brown plimsolls and a red bandana tied low on his brow, singing in all sincerity 'Down in the forest, playing his old guitar, lives an old dream man. . . .' This was in Italy after the war, when we were together in an Army show. In addition to being a comedian I also had to be a ballet dancer and ballad singer. I used to do an act which portrayed how different people shaved, later to get me into the Windmill Theatre, and later still to get me removed from the Grand Theatre, Bolton, where the owner told me as he paid me off on the Monday night, 'You'll not shave in my bloody time.'

When I was demobbed in 1946 I started at the Windmill Theatre, where I had the good fortune to meet Mike Bentine. He was half of an act called Sherwood and Forest, and played the drums while Tony Sherwood played piano. I first saw him when he and his partner did the dress rehearsal for the show which followed the one I was in. From the beginning we found we had the same sense of the ridiculous. We used to sit in the Lyons Corner House in Coventry Street and spend most of the night over a cup of coffee and beans on toast, sometimes pretending we were Russian. The game was up when we picked on a Hungarian waiter who spoke Russian.

When Spike eventually left the Army I introduced him to Mike Bentine at Allen's Club—a haven for Windmill performers. Here you could eat now and pay later, and sit and pour out your ambitions into the ears of other young comics like Jimmy Edwards, Frank Muir, Alfred Marks and Bill Kerr, who were simultaneously pouring out their ambitions. It's a wonder anybody heard anything. It was an exciting period when we were all keen to get on, but the rivalry was friendly and the comradeship of the Services was still warm.

Later at a broadcast for Pat Dixon, the professorial-looking man who had an ear for unusual comedy and was always on the look-out for young talent, I was introduced to Peter Sellers. Peter had recently got himself a broadcast by the simple expedient of ringing Pat Dixon and using the voice of another radio producer, telling him he was sending this new comic Peter Sellers along to see him. Minutes later he turned up at Dixon's office and was booked on the spot.

I was very impressed by Peter, by his friendliness and the uncanny way in which he became the person he was impersonating. Later, standing next to him on the Goon Show, I could never get over the way he would shrink himself for Bluebottle and then seconds later, puff himself out for Bloodnock. It was almost frightening to see it happen. Yet when he was called upon to do his own natural voice, he was always worried. 'I can't, lads,' he'd say. 'I don't know what I sound like.'

How the Goon Shows eventually got going is somewhat vague at this distance. By that time Spike and I were sharing a flat in Notting Hill Gate with two other fellow ex-Servicemen, Norman Vaughan and Johnny Mulgrew. Johnny played the bass in a comedy-musical act called Hall, Norman and Ladd, in which Spike was the guitarist. We all clubbed together to pay the rent and the hire of the radio set—although one day Norman Vaughan arrived back from a week's variety just in time to stop the hire firm from removing it. We had, however, taken the precaution of removing the valves.

This particular period returns today almost as in a kaleidoscope. I remember cooking spaghetti on a gas ring with the steam loosening the wallpaper; running outside and around the block wearing only a vest and underpants on a pouring wet November night, and nobody taking any notice; the hysteria which we generated among ourselves at our own jokes; Spike doing his impression of the last turkey in the shop; sitting with Spike and Norman in a café at Golders Green, and buttoning my war surplus duffel coat over my head for a gag, then five minutes later finding myself alone at the table facing an unamused waitress and the bill for the meal; going with Spike and Peter to watch Charlie Chaplin in *City Lights* and the three of us leaving the cinema in tears; drinking free brandy in Jimmy Grafton's pub in Victoria Street.

During this chaotic time, the Goon Show was written by Spike and Larry Stephens, and Pat Dixon persuaded the BBC to do a pilot show. It was called *Falling Leaves* and featured 'those crazy people, the Goons'.

I had to drive down from Blackpool, where I was in a Summer Show, to London for the recording on a Sunday. It meant driving through the night to be there in time for rehearsals. From then on I was known as 'He drives through the night'.

Pat Dixon produced the show, which even when listened to today is almost incoherent. To give the BBC due credit, they decided to take a chance on it, and so in 1951, with Dennis Main Wilson producing, it all began.

Meanwhile, back at the Camden Theatre. . . . We have finished rolling about at the script, and John Browell is wondering how he is going to control us. Wallace Greenslade is with us now, having finished his news reading for the day. He comes in beaming and ruddy-complexioned, with the lingering scent of an after-lunch Worthington on his breath.

'Sing us the news, Wal.' Spike has decided to stand on his head. Wally replies with a good-natured naval phrase. 'Hello, Sailor,' lisps Peter, looking up archly from under the piano, where he has retired for a short kip.

Spike now leaves for a chat with the effects boys. He is particularly anxious to get the effect of someone being hit in the face with a sockful of custard. They try several effects but Milligan is a perfectionist, he knows what he wants. He goes up to the canteen in the top of the theatre. 'Make me an egg custard, love,' he asks the very nice Scottish lady who runs the place. 'Of course, dear,' she says. Half an hour later he returns and asks for his custard. It is given to him by the Scottish lady who has prepared it especially, using the then rare shell eggs.

'Thanks, love,' he says, and removes his sock. Before her astonished gaze he promptly pours the egg custard into it.

Back downstairs again he arranges to have a mike set up. He bashes the sockful of custard against a piece of hardboard. 'Let's hear that back.' They play the sound effect back to him. 'Doesn't sound like a sockful of custard,' he says. 'We'll have to try something else.'

The musicians arrive, preceded by Wally Stott who looks too frail to pick up his baton. Ray Ellington enters with Max Geldray. 'Good job you've got a long nose, Max,' says Milligan. 'It keeps the rain off your tie.'

'Ploogie,' replies Max morosely.

'Hello dere, Gladys.' Ray Ellington is using his Southern Negro voice today. The son of an American Negro and a Russian Jewess, Ray is having difficulty reaching a decision about whether to have his son barmitzva'd or baptized in the Anglican Church. 'Have a word with my brother,' I say. 'He's in that business.' It's my most useful verbal contribution of the day. Ray agrees to talk to the Reverend Fred Secombe.

We do a run-through with effects and orchestra. We have a little difficulty with the effects again. 'It's the chickens, followed by the 1812 Overture bit, and *then* the Wembley Cup Final.'

'OK Spike, we'll sort it out later.' John Browell's soothing voice comes over the speaker from the control-room. Spike snorts.

The run-through over, Spike sits in with Ray and some of the band boys. Spike plays his trumpet, eyes closed and cheeks puffed out like those of a cherubim representing a trade wind on a sixteenth-century map. Peter has taken over the drums and is giving a creditable performance. I stand tapping my feet, wishing secretly that I had taken those piano lessons I was offered as a child: then I remember that we had no piano at home anyway. I go to the side away from the noise and sing a snatch of *La Bohème*. I feel a bit better, and stroll back on stage.

The queue has started forming outside and we head for the pub next door. Inside are the orchestra, friends of ours and Goon addicts, all of them would-be Bluebottles and Eccles and Neddies. 'Hello, my Capitain,' says one to Peter. He smiles politely, trying not to wince. Spike is complaining about his sock, still wet from the custard. We order drinks—brandies. I have a double. 'He'll be the first one to go, Mate,' says Spike to Peter. 'I don't want to be there when it happens; he'd rupture the lot of us trying to move him.' I blow a raspberry. 'Very nice, dear,' says the barmaid. 'Now do it with your face,' says a Goon fan with a delicate sense of humour!

'All back, lads.' John Browell herds us back into the theatre. We take a bottle of brandy and a pint of milk for the musical interludes, when we nip backstage. It also explains why sometimes the last part of the Show is the most frenetic.

The audience is already in and we start the warm-up. I sing *Falling in Love with Love,* accompanied by Wally Stott and the orchestra, and behind me Spike and Peter are clowning outrageously. Spike's trousers fall to his ankles. I sing on, hoping he has not forgotten his underpants.

Wally Greenslade steps forward and asks for silence. The green light goes on. 'This is the BBC Home Service. Tiddly pong.'

F/X BURST OF STEAM AND CASTANETS

GRITPYPE THYNNE: Moriarty, men of the Royal Labour Exchange, good news. I have had talks with the Prime Minister and he has granted us a further extension of unemployment.

ORCHESTRA AND GRAMS: CHEERS

We're off, and the audience laughter spurs us on to ad libs which will eventually have to be edited out.

When the Show comes to an end, with Eccles saying: 'Well, dat's dat!' the audience leaves—some of them bewildered, the *aficionados* gleefully repeating the Bluebottle–Eccles exchanges, or the familiar catchphrase: 'And there's more where that came from.'

We sign autographs at the stage door and say our good-nights. 'See you next week, lads.' Next Sunday is already something to look foward to. Peter gives Spike a lift back to Highgate in his new American car. The electric windows go up and down as they move off. 'Ned of Wales is a pouf,' shouts Milligan as they round the corner. I blow a raspberry. 'And there's more where that came from.'. . . I wish there were.

Magpie: 'How about preserving our wild life together in the Mediterranean Fleet'

(The frigate H.M.S. Magpie was the first command of Lieutenant-Commander H.R.H. the Duke of Edinburgh, R.N., in August 1950)

JOHN WINTON

Have Polaris, Will Travel

For me, it's not just the policemen who are looking younger, it's the submarine captains, too. It comes as a shock to see the young men I used to know now becoming respectable, and highly respected, pillars of the naval establishment. A few days I spent at sea in the British nuclear-powered Polaris submarine HMS *Renown* made me feel about ninety years old, and to be called 'Sir' by the First Lieutenant—a Lieutenant-Commander—made me feel not just old but positively antediluvian.

Antediluvian is right. In the decade or so since I left it there has been a flood of changes in the submarine world. It is as though every aspect of the submarine life and technology I used to know has now been raised to a much higher power.

For instance, the Navigating Officer used simply to point at the coffee stain on the chart and tell the Captain, 'We're somewhere about there, sir'. Not so any more: *Renown* has a miraculous table of gyros known as a Ship's Inertial Navigation System (SINS) which can fix her position on the earth's surface to within a few yards. Ship's course, speed, tides, ocean currents, magnetic variations, make no difference to SINS.

The First Lieutenant used to trim the boat by the seat of his pants and a few simple calculations. Every dive was likely to be something of a venture into the unknown. The First Lieutenant in *Renown* still works out the trim, but the depth-keeping, steering and planing can all be done automatically, untouched by human hand.

In the old days, the Coxswain was the boat's medicine man, and dispensed from the POs' mess his own empirical brand of diagnosis. Above the waist—aspirin. Below the waist—the Number Nine depth charge, an explosive laxative capable of moving the bowels of the earth. Now, they have a qualified doctor on board, and a properly-equipped sickbay.

Submarine food always used to have a certain spectacular un-predictability; quality and quantity depended upon the progress of the Chef's sex-life and the accuracy of the Coxswain's arithmetic. We seemed to subsist on a staple diet of 'bangers, beans and babies' heads' (babies' heads: an especially glutinous variety of steak and kidney pudding) often with a rib-sticking Cabinet pudding, known as 'figgy duff' or 'zizz pud', for afters. And there was always that favourite brand of tinned, skinned tomatoes known as 'train smash'.

Actually they still do have 'train smash' in *Renown*, but it looked much less macerated than of old, and it was just one item from a very good menu. The food in *Renown* was excellent, with a choice of main courses and frequent salads, served cafeteria-style in a dining-hall—a vast compartment by old submarine standards. Polaris submarines carry Supply Officers, the first time officers of this branch have gone to sea in submarines—yet another innovation.

That *smell* has gone, that characteristically pervasive submarine attar of diesel oil, rubber boots and boiled veg., underlaid with something more sinister, as though there had been a recent human sacrifice somewhere down in the bilges. Compared with that, *Renown* smells like a rather superior clinic.

They don't even wear the same clothes at sea any more. Where are all those exotic 'steaming rigs', striped football shirts, leather jackets, Davy Crockett hats and woolly caps? All gone, apparently for ever. They wear uniform now, blue shirts and trousers, with smart gilt lapel badges.

No more 'hot bunking'—where a man climbed into the bunk vacated by his relief. Every man has his own bunk, with ventilation louvre and reading light. Never more the great glad cry of 'One all round!'; smoking is virtually unrestricted. They've never heard of the old ritual of Ditching Gash, when bins of rubbish were hauled up the conning tower and ditched over the side from the bridge. *Renown*'s garbage is chopped up, packed in special weighted containers and fired overboard through a garbage ejector—a fitting like a miniature torpedo tube.

No need to do your dhobeying in a bucket. They have a laundry. No more rationing of fresh water on a long patrol. They have hot showers and distilling capacity to spare. Above all, no more jealous hoarding of every amp in the main battery. The reactor has enough power to supply a small town.

But *surely*, I thought, looking around me, it can't *all* be changed? What about the blokes? Well, at first sight, they are a typical submarine company: typically cheerful, and cynical, and competent—the very best people in the world to serve with. Huge though she is, *Renown* still has an unmistakable small ship atmosphere. There are still some tattooed forearms to be seen. Wilsons are still called 'Tug'. They can still coin apt nicknames and phrases, and they still have that special submarine brand of black humour.

They have changed, though. For one thing, there are very few ordinary bods about—the plain hewers of wood and drawers of water. One of the most common remarks heard in *Renown* was 'too many Chiefs and not enough Injuns'. Of a total ship's complement of about 150, more than half are chief petty officers or petty officers. The Chiefs' Mess in *Renown*—though, again, a huge compartment by old submarine standards—is seriously overcrowded. A Polaris submarine crew requires a quite unusually high proportion of men with sophisticated skills—nuclear engineering, computers, electronics, fire control systems—who are normally senior ratings.

The Polaris programme has made extraordinary demands on the Navy's manpower. Each submarine has two complete crews, designated Port and Starboard, who relieve each other on a three-monthly cycle. The 'On' crew carries out maintenance, pre-patrol training, and the deterrent patrol of sixty days. Meanwhile, the 'Off' crew go on leave, attend courses, and generally support the boat from shore.

Besides the crews, there are many men coming up in the training 'pipe-line'. Many of *Renown*'s ship's company have come straight from general service, some even from the Fleet Air Arm, with no intervening apprenticeship period in orthodox submarines. By no means all were volunteers for submarines. The wonder is that they take to the life so quickly; though some of them are serving in their first submarine (some of the junior rates in their first *ship*) they all look as though they have been doing it for years.

The wardroom has the same mixture of old- and new-type submariners. *Renown* has thirteen officers, half of them with University degrees, and normally another three or four additional officers borne for training or understudying the men they are going to relieve—some duties take a whole patrol to turn over.

The Captain, who is a full Commander, has been through the traditional mill of the submarine service, starting years ago as a junior 'fourth hand' and working his way up through third hand, first lieutenant and finally to command. He might also have had experience in a fleet nuclear submarine or as first lieutenant of a Polaris. With the comparatively junior rank of Commander, he has awesome responsibilities which hardly bear thinking about. At the same time he must lead his crew through the long tedium of their patrol—yet keep them on their toes. In this sense, he is like a coach training a team to run a steady successful marathon and yet be ready to sprint a hundred yards in even time at any moment in the race.

His First Lieutenant, a Lieutenant-Commander, is also a submarine captain in his own right, having passed the Periscope Course (the 'Perisher', as it is popularly called) and commanded his own submarine. The other executive officers, the Torpedo and Sonar, Navigating and Communications Officers, and the Senior Technical

Officer and his assistants, will also probably, but not necessarily, be submariners of long standing; such is the Polaris programme's rapacious appetite for men that some of the junior engineer and electrical officers may well be new to submarines. The Supply Officer and the Medical Officer are also likely to be newcomers. In *Renown*'s Polaris Department—popularly supposed to be nicknamed 'the Polaroids', although I never actually heard anyone in *Renown* use the word—the Polaris Systems Officer and his assistant were electrical officers, both new to submarines, and neither was a volunteer. However, now that they were there, they felt they 'would rather like to stay'.

At sea, *Renown* is a totally enclosed and private world, hot and rather noisy, and abounding in buzzers and bells, dials and gauges and indicators. Submarines always were happy hunting grounds for the instrument-makers, but the instrumentation in *Renown* is like wallpaper in a house. There are instruments everywhere, some mounted in neat display consoles, worthy of an executive suite, but others gathered in great amusement arcades of colours and glass and levers, looking as though they were just waiting for some mad twenty-first century theatre organist to sit down and play them.

Polaris sailors work an average 70-hour week and many of them spend most of their working lives just looking at instruments. Design attention has been paid to ergonomics, but watchkeepers still complain that they find some of the displays tiring.

Renown is a creature of the deep and with a length of 425 feet and an underwater displacement of nearly 8,000 tons—the size of a pre-war cruiser—she is clearly not built for periscope depth acrobatics. A submarine's role, traditionally, was to detect and identify a target, and then close and attack it. In Polaris, this concept is completely reversed. If a target is detected, no matter how tempting, *Renown*'s duty is to evade. Only when the missiles have been successfully launched can *Renown* take up the 'hunter-killer' role for which she is fitted with long-range sonar equipment and six torpedo tubes.

The popular press and public's notion of the Polaris captain running amok—'the madman with his finger on the button'—is simply not possible. No one man can launch a missile on his own. The active co-operation, and the physical presence, of several others are needed. The firing system is so encompassed about with precautions, key combinations, cross-checks, inter-locks and verifications that the order to fire must be proved to be authentic beyond any possible doubt. Furthermore, every senior member of the firing team must be convinced of its authenticity. Officers and senior ratings have discretion to refuse to play their necessary parts if they are not so convinced. However, a man cannot refuse unreasonably or whimsically; every member, even the Captain himself, can be over-ridden.

In other words, the system ensures that the missiles cannot be fired unless the country really means it, and if the country really means it then the missiles will be fired.

Renown carries sixteen A3 Polaris missiles with an operational range of nearly 3,000 miles. The 'sharp end'—the re-entry body, nuclear warhead, fusing and arming devices—is British-designed and built, but the rest of the missile, and the stowage, launching and fire control equipment are all American, supplied under the 'Nassau Agreement' between Harold Macmillan and John F. Kennedy.

The missiles are stowed in colossal vertical tubes, 33 feet long and seven feet in diameter, which reach down through the three deck levels of the Missile Compartment like great white columns. The compartment is supposed to be called 'Sherwood Forest' but, again, I never heard anyone in *Renown* call it that; usually, it was just the Missile Compartment, or perhaps the 'rocket shop'.

To be effective, a deterrent must be reliable and credible. Polaris is fantastically reliable and is kept so by constant practice drills and by treating each missile as though it were an 'Old Master' painting, cosseting it, keeping it warm and dry and comfortable, at a steady desirable temperature, pressure and humidity.

The ship can be ready to fire in a few minutes—as, of course, she must be. Information on the ship's position is fed to the missiles from SINS until the last moment before firing. The targets' positions are pre-programmed and fed into the fire control system on prepared tape; many tapes are carried on board, each relating to different targets. The fire control system incorporates eleven separate computers, and there is another in each missile. Once away, the missile's own guidance package governs the flight path.

The missiles can be fired from the surface but are normally fired when submerged. A gas/steam generator launches the missile and boosts it to the surface where the rocket first stage ignites automatically. On board, a launch is entirely unspectacular: a hissing noise, a very slight trembling of the deck underfoot. And that is all.

What do the ship's company think about that weapon on board? The question has hoary whiskers on it, having been asked ten thousand times before. A patient, long-suffering look comes over a Polaris sailor's face when it is asked yet again. Actually, there is no clear-cut answer. Broad generalizations about a Polaris crew's feelings can be dangerously misleading.

'Drop-outs' on moral grounds are very rare, but that does not mean that the great majority are insensitive.

There are, of course, some doubters who suppress their misgivings and say 'Anyway, it'll never happen'. There are those who are 'all for it'. And there are some who clearly have never thought about it at all: to them it is, in a quite literal sense, unthinkable.

But most have given the subject a great deal of thought and now console themselves with the absolute certainty that under no conceivable circumstances would Britain ever start a nuclear war. Polaris is therefore a 'second strike' weapon, used as morally justified retaliation. With that certainty to support them, the ship's company are free to get on with the job they are paid to do, to address themselves to its undoubted professional challenges, and to achieve a high degree of personal involvement. The Polaris Systems Officer says, 'During a practice missile firing I get so absolutely absorbed in what I'm doing. I'm so pleased to see all those green lights coming up just as they should, quite honestly I don't think any further than that.'

When *Renown*'s two crews each fired a practice missile on the Cape Kennedy range in July 1969, the predominant emotions on board were exultation and triumph, tempered with a certain relief. When, after a lengthy count-down, the missile went off successfully it was a deeply satisfying moment for all on board: 'Everybody was grinning, and talking too much; it was just like being intoxicated.'

But practice launch drills, which can be and are ordered at any time, are only brief flurries of excitement in a patrol, when the ship's pulse seems to slow right down, and the hours pass in a suspended state rather like a controlled hibernation. All the normal parameters of submarine existence—speed, depth, course, even time itself—no longer have the same meaning or relevance. The routine eats time and a patrol passes strangely quickly, in a way which the crew almost resent: 'It's two months out of your life, cut out just like that. It's gone. When you get back and meet somebody, you forget it's weeks since you last saw them. It hasn't been weeks to you.' Although time of day means nothing, the watches change, meals are served, the lights are dimmed and raised again, as though obeying some atavistic memory of a solar day. As one wag said, 'We're like battery hens.'

The Navy has paid much attention to the physical and mental well-being of Polaris crews on patrol. It was thought that men would have time and inclination for study, but in practice this has not happened. A few ambitious men study for GCE 'O' levels or take correspondence courses, but most spend their leisure time reading, sleeping, playing cards, crib or uckers (coarse submarine ludo). Some do embroidery, rug-making, marquetry or tapestry work, or model making. For the energetic there is weight-lifting, rowing and cycling machines, and table tennis. Ship's contests, quizzes, bridge tournaments, darts competitions, are all organized. There is a film-show every night. Each man gets a daily issue of canned beer. The Chiefs also have keg beer on tap in their mess. *Renown* has a ship's newspaper, the *Hi-Ho Journal*, with all the news that's fit to print, contributions from all departments, and Andy Capp cartoons, supplied *before* national publication, by courtesy of the *Daily Mirror*.

Personality clashes on board are inevitable, but rare—'the ship's big enough to get out of each other's way'. Towards the end of a patrol, according to the Doctor, a few may get symptoms of a mild form of 'twitch'—'they may go off their food a bit, and get vague feelings that they're not doing their jobs as well'. But in general, British Polaris experience confirms the American—'You only get psychological problems on board when you get a psychologist on board'.

Although they do have a tendency to be overweight, Polaris crews are generally healthy and the Doctor expects to treat only minor ailments: cuts, abrasions, stomach upsets, headaches, constipation, rashes. If needed, a portable operating table can be set up in the Chiefs' Mess. This would be clean but not sterile and the policy for Polaris submarines is to avoid surgery if at all possible; a rumbling appendix, for example, would be treated with antibiotics for as long as possible. In the event of a death on board, the body would be brought back; the authorities would certainly require a full post-mortem. (If the doctors want another symptom to mull over, I can tell them that my eyesight, not very good anyway, deteriorated rapidly and noticeably while I was on board, to the point where I was worried about it. It took a couple of days to recover.)

The Doctor's main concern is the monitoring and control of air pollution. A Polaris submarine is a unique environment: totally sealed off, for very long periods, with an artificially controlled atmosphere. Oxygen is made from water by electrolysis. Impurities such as carbon monoxide, carbon dioxide and hydrogen, are burned or chemically 'scrubbed' out.

Oddly, the most obstinate pollutant is the coolant gas used in the ship's refrigerators. There is no way of removing it except by ventilating and although it is basically non-toxic itself, it gives off the lethal gas phosgene when at high temperature (for example in contact with a lighted cigarette). Although the quantities are minute, they are very carefully watched.

Radiation is *not* a health hazard, although the levels are constantly monitored. When they are developed, the sensitive film badges everyone on board wears only show how little radiation there is rather than how much; in fact, a man would get more radiation from cosmic rays standing on the submarine's casing in the open air than he would down below in the submarine.

Samples from the reactor coolant liquid are tested daily, in a delicate process known colloquially as 'Drinka Pinta Gamma'. Alarm clocks and wristwatches with luminous hands, or indeed any fitting with luminous paint, are firmly banned on board. Their emissions are tiny but they do accumulate over a long period until they trigger the boat's hypersensitive radiation alarms. This is irritating and distracting, and could be dangerous.

The principal power source (there is, of course, a battery for emergency use) is the British-built pressurized water reactor which drives the single shaft through steam turbines. To fit a reactor and propulsion machinery inside a submarine at all is a marvellous technical achievement, but it is still disappointing to find in *Renown*'s machinery spaces habitability conditions no better than those of small surface warships of twenty years ago.

Renown's machinery compartments are very hot, very humid, very difficult to keep clean, and large portions of them are virtually inaccessible for repairs or maintenance. There must be some residual puritanism in the British national character, which believes that to be comfortable is also to be sinful; or perhaps we all secretly believe that air conditioning is somehow cissy and unnecessary. Whereas American nuclear submarines have ample air conditioning capacity, the British system is barely adequate, particularly in the after spaces.

Renown's Starboard Crew are lucky to have an artificer who has a way with air conditioning machinery and can 'tweak' it to optimum performance. But even when he has done his best, most of the machinery spaces aft are, as the watchkeepers down there describe them, 'do-it-yourself sauna baths'.

It is disappointing, too, to see by the apparently random routing of pipe systems that British ship-builders have seemingly not forsaken the competitive, 'Olympic' method of ship-building—'the fastest dockyard matie won, you see. If he was quick, he got there first and got a clear run with his bit of pipe. All the slower dockyard maties then had to bend their pipes around his. And it didn't matter what size the pipes were.'

On patrol, a Polaris submarine can receive messages but cannot transmit. Therefore, before sailing, every man decides what action he wants taken in the event of family emergency, such as his wife or child's illness or a parent's death. Many opt not to be told. There is nothing they can do, and the knowledge might distress them. (The recall of a Polaris submarine from patrol is a decision for the Defence Secretary.)

However, they are not entirely cut off. There are the 'Family-grams'—twenty-word messages from families, transmitted periodic-ally to the submarine when signal traffic permits. They are discreetly handled, by as few people as possible. The need for brevity sometimes lends wives an almost epigrammatic wit; nearing the end of one patrol one *Renown* wife signalled: 'Put away your toys boys nearly time to go to bed.'

Polaris crews will never get a traditional 'run ashore' in a foreign port, but the three-month changeover cycle between the crews is inviolate and the sailors can therefore plan their private lives—dates of holidays, weddings, house removals, and so on—with a degree of confidence unusual in the submarine service. Nevertheless sub-marines, and particularly Polaris submarines, have notorious repu-tations as marriage breakers. The figures are, of course, impossible to check reliably but the proportion of men in the Polaris pro-gramme with broken or troubled marriages was put as high as one in five.

Certainly the establishment of a huge Polaris base has created social problems ashore—and not just from the nuclear disarmament demonstrators who still make their migratory appearances at certain times of the year. The Clyde Submarine Base is on the Gareloch, at Faslane in Dunbartonshire. The nearest town of any size is Helens-burgh. The population of the whole area has nearly doubled in ten years. Whole hillsides, fields when I was last there, are now married quarter estates. (For one of them the sailors have coined the perfect name—Moon City.) The neighbourhood's educational and medical facilities are under strain. Despite good intentions on both sides, there has so far been little social mixing between the sailors and their families and the solid Scottish bourgeoisie of Helensburgh.

Originally, there were to have been five Polaris submarines which, allowing for maintenance periods and refits, would have guaranteed at least two submarines on patrol continuously. The fifth boat was cancelled when the Socialist Government took office in 1964, leaving a maximum potential of 1·7 boats on patrol (whatever '1·7 boats' may mean in strategic terms).

The names of the four in commission—*Resolution, Repulse, Renown* and *Revenge*—reflect the Polaris submarine's present capital ship status. *Renown* is the tenth ship of her name in the Royal Navy, and her battle honours stretch from the Battle of the Gabbard in 1653 to the bombardment of Sabang in 1944. Most of the honours—Norway, Atlantic, Cape Spartivento, Mediterranean, Bismarck, Malta Convoys, Arctic, North Africa and Sabang—were won by the ninth *Renown*, the battle-cruiser.

Nobody wants any battle honours for the tenth *Renown*. If the missiles are ever used, then the deterrent will have failed to deter and the £350,000,000 so far officially spent on the Polaris programme might just as well have been torn up note by note and scattered on the sea.

However, it could still be said that the Polaris submarines and the men who serve in them will have bought us all a little time—time indeed for the occasional lucky Ancient Submariner like me to have had a fascinating and humbling experience. There were moments in *Renown* when I felt like Orville Wright having a ride in Concorde. When I got home my wife was spring cleaning and had one of my old uniform jackets out of the wardrobe. 'Funny,' she said. 'I can't smell the moth-balls.'

But I could.

On the day arranged for the Coronation of King Edward VII in June 1902, Lancashire were playing Surrey at Old Trafford. But the Coronation ceremony could not happen; King Edward was stricken by, and operated on for, appendicitis. So popular was he with the nation at large that appendicitis became, among that section of the aristocracy which could afford to have it, fashionable. But the general national holiday to honour the Coronation was not cancelled, and in golden sunshine, sunshine so lavish and Edwardian that it spread to Manchester and Old Trafford, cricket and every other form of English enjoyment proceeded and prospered.

As I look back on 1902, life then might appear, compared to life and the world today, to have existed on another planet. For consider: there was no radio, no television, no aircraft, very few motor-cars (that's what we called them in 1902, private possessions of the rich), no public telephones (they were also perquisites of the wealthy), no electric trams. The streets clattered with the sound of horses' hooves as the horses pulled hansom cabs and four-wheelers. On that glorious June day I walked from Timperley to Old Trafford, a schoolboy of twelve. County matches in those older times began Mondays and Thursdays; and as I journeyed on foot to Old Trafford that Friday morning I knew that at close of play the evening before, J. T. Tyldesley had been not out. Somehow I got on the wrong side of the canal which travels (or did travel) from Timperley towards Old Trafford; I did not know how to get off the pathway of the canal, so I ran on and on in panic that Tyldesley might get out and I not there, so on I ran, stopping only when I got a 'stitch' in my side and had to bend down and press a knee against the pain. Some men in a barge cheered me as I ran.

I received full consolation for my sweaty toil along the canal when I arrived at Old Trafford. The crowd was vast, all men in billycock hats, except far away on the pavilion, where, even at Old Trafford, you could see members adorned in tall shining 'toppers'. No girls or women mingled in the general multitude—they were exclusively confined to the elegant Ladies' Pavilion, all, and not many in numbers present, wives or relations of members. I paid sixpence to enter Old Trafford on this Coronation Day of 1902 (where did I get it from?); and I crawled through the crowd's serried ranks and got a place on the grass. And I saw Tyldesley cut Tom Richardson for four after four, crash against the pavilion rails until white powder, dried paint from the rails, snowed the adjacent turf. Tom Richardson, I still believe, was the greatest of all fast bowlers, tall, strong, swarthy, leonine, a black moustache and hair. He bowled from a twenty yards or so run, long strides, culminating in a superb leap upwards. In four consecutive seasons, he took 1,005 wickets, bowling most overs with an old ball, half on the ton-rolled wickets of Kennington Oval.

Tyldesley's innings, on King Edward VII's postponed Coronation Day of 1902, was truly Coronation cricket, brilliant and audacious. Cricketers of recent birth may conjure up an idea of Tyldesley's batting by imagining a combination of, say, Denis Compton and Bill Edrich. Tom Richardson bowled him, clean bowled him, for 165, this deathless day in my memory. And this same day, Sydney Barnes bowled for Lancashire, when Surrey's second innings began. Barnes the Master of all bowlers. He was an aloof saturnine figure. We Lancashire boys never took him to heart as we took Tyldesley, Spooner, Brearley. Barnes was not genuine Lancashire; he was a sort of 'mercenary'. We liked to see him get Lancashire's opponents out, but there it was; he wasn't a Lancastrian lad. He certainly dealt destruction out to Surrey on 26 June 1902; he routed Abel, Hayward, Brockwell and others. And as each wicket fell the crowd stood to stretch themselves, shouting 'Up, Up, Up!' Then, when the next batsman arrived at the wicket, the crowd shouted 'Down, Down, Down!' and laughed at their own humour. But, believe it or not, Barnes was mastered, as the sun burgeoned on Coronation Day (revealing the dust in Coronation Street). V. F. S. Crawford, backed-up by a stubborn Surrey amateur called Captain H. S. Bush, temporarily saved Surrey's day. Crawford actually drove a ball from Barnes for six. And in 1902, a six meant that the ball had not just been hit into the crowd. A six then was from a ball removed from the *premises*, out of the enclosure. Only three times in the triumphant career of S. F. Barnes was he hit for six in first-class cricket—on this occasion I am now recalling, when V. F. S. Crawford took the liberty; and nine years later, by V. F. S. Crawford's brother, J. N. Crawford. And J. N. smote Barnes for six in another hemisphere, notably in Brisbane, Australia, playing for 'an Australian XI' (J. N. Crawford, a great Surrey player, emigrated to Australia, after some sort of disagreement with the Surrey C.C.C. Committee). And in a Test match in 1912, at Lord's, Barnes was also hit for six by Charles Macartney, one of Australia's most trenchant batsmen ever.

As Lancashire were winning on this June afternoon at Old

Trafford, in a legendary past, I could enjoy Crawford. Most times, though, I hated to see *any* batsman not Lancastrian get runs against Lancashire. Heaven forgive me, but I used to pray that Ranjitsinhji would be bowled out first ball! Once, at the age of twelve, this identical year of King Edward's Coronation, I got into a dilemma about Victor Trumper, the Australian Beau Brummel. For in 1902, Victor was at his most youthfully masterful and fascinating. I made a hero of him. But, of course, I wanted Australia beaten, yet at the same time, I wanted a score from Victor. One night, saying my prayers, I was visited by inspiration. (Never since have I been so marvellously inspired.) 'Please, God,' I prayed, 'make Victor Trumper score a century tomorrow against England—out of 150 Australia all out.'

As Tyldesley's batsmanship matched the Coronation sunshine, I saw D. L. A. Jephson bowling 'lobs', underarm. Imagine a 'lob' bowler these days. Would not Boycott, Illingworth, Edrich and the rest laugh at a 'lob' bowler? As a matter of fact, D. L. A. Jephson could spin out batsmen as clever (to say the least) as Boycott and company. There was another 'lob' bowler of the 1900s, named Simpson-Hayward, who playing for England against South Africa at Johannesburg, in January 1910, took six wickets for 43, and among his victims were Aubrey Faulkner, A. D. Nourse, J. W. Zulch, J. H. Sinclair, all top-class batsmen, Faulkner as accomplished as any of our present epoch.

I went home to Timperley that evening of 26 June 1902, tired, hungry, happy. Again I ran along the Bridgewater Canal; but I was not conscious of canal now, right bank or wrong. And the barges were of burnished gold in my boy's eyes; barges of Coronation Day, on which I had looked at Coronation cricket. . . .

MARY STEWART

The Loch

It must be fully fifteen years since we first saw the loch.

It lay in a high fold of the hills to the west of the Great Glen, and to get to it you drove up a pretty loch-side by a narrow road winding through birch woods. Down on the left the water flashed and glittered through the tree-trunks, and to the right the wooded slopes rose steeply, hung with woodsorrel and wind-flowers and the young green of bracken. Greyhen picked shyly around among the blaeberry tumps, and deer stood staring in the shade of the silver birches. At the head of the loch the woods gave way to open sunshine—water-meadow with knots of oak and pine—then in a mile or two the road twisted sharp right to shake itself clear of the last trees and run steeply up between slopes of scree and heather. Over the brow, and there was the long, high glen, filled with the three-mile stretch of remote and quiet water.

It was really two lochs in one, the eastern and western stretches joined by two brief, brawling streams where a pair of grey stone arches carried the road across the water. From the west the river flowed in a flat and placid meander through reed beds from which came the occasional whistle of a feeding bird. At the other end of the loch could be seen, remotely, small islands floating on the water, cloudy with trees.

We drove down the curling road, across the bridges, and up the far slope of the hill. Below us the long loch looked placid, still, lifeless except at the western end where the rich reed beds lay and, not far from them, a large mounded island. Just offshore from this a bird was swimming; we thought it might be a diver, a bird which we had then seen only rarely. We parked the car, and scrambled down over the rough, boggy heather to the shingle at the loch's edge opposite the island.

We had thought, from the safe and insulated distance of the car, that the water was almost deserted. But down here on the shore we found that the glen was alive and ringing with birds. Right at our feet in the heather was a hatched duck's nest, and a few moments later the wigeon launched herself, with her gruff alarm call, from the bank below us, and seven coffee-cream balls of fluff went bobbing in her wake. The air was loud with larks. Somewhere above us a raven barked, and a heron flapped slowly up out of the reeds at the river's mouth. Swifts scythed and screamed among the insect swarms above the water, and the surface was ringed by rising fish. A sandpiper flew out from the shore. From across the water came the ceaseless soft chatter and whirr of dunlin. But all these sounds were abruptly lost under the sudden, excited clamour as a feeding greenshank shot up into the air, to be joined by another, and then another, till the whole glen seemed ringing with the rich, piercing call, and from the far hillside came an echo, and then the flash of other wings.

The diver surfaced a hundred yards away. A black-throat, with the brilliant black-and-white barring of the back, the glossy snakelike head and dramatically streaked neck—the most conspicuous of birds, you would have thought, till you saw how it settled low in the water, merging its barred back invisibly with the run and ripple of light and shadow as the breeze ran down the loch's length, and the diver vanished. . . .

It had vanished near the mounded island. These birds nest at the water's edge, and to reach the nest they dive close in to shore, then creep up the bank to settle—still miraculously invisible—on the two huge, blotched olive-green eggs. The island looked a long way away, but the water was calm, the day hot and still, we had swimming things with us, and what better place could we spend our day than here. . . ?

We swam across, to discover that it was no island after all, but a peninsula, a near-island like a round hill, linked to the far mainland by a low, narrow neck of land. To each side of this narrow isthmus was a shallow, muddy bay dotted with bars of grassy shingle—too small to be called islands—and reedy inlets starred with water flowers and noisy with dunlin. The peninsula itself looked very well worth exploring. There were stretches of dry heather, alternating with boggy ground studded with moss hags at least two feet high; there were rocky banks, pools, little cliffs hung with long heather and a species of mountain willow; and at the centre of the peninsula, like a crater in a volcano, lay a small lochan, with clear, still water and muddy verges.

There is a limit to the amount of exploring one can do in bare feet and swimsuits, and we found no trace of the diver, but our first, brief survey determined us to come back. Though it was a long way from the road, the place could be reached by land. We could come properly clothed, and bring the camera.

We came the following spring, and left the car at the bridges. There was a sheltered bank under the parapet where melancholy thistle grew, and the water rushed by at one's feet, making a small artificial storm which rattled the sedge and blew through the heather-bells. We boiled a kettle and drank Nescafé, while a dipper fled up and down stream in front of us, and a pair of grey wagtails fed their young among the stones of the bridge. Then we set out along the south shore of the loch, towards our peninsula.

It was terrible going. It had been a dry season, I remember, but still the ground was deeply boggy, and one had to make wide detours round the worst patches. Within the first fifty yards we were soaked to the knees, and no longer troubled to leap clear of the burns that threaded what was a full mile of some of the worst going I have ever encountered. It took over an hour. Beside us rose the hillside, steep, stony, with clumps of rowan clinging to the tumble of granite screes. Ridges of stone thrust out into ground treacherous with bog; there were long tracts of deep heather that dragged at the feet; there were hundreds of yards of soft, tussocky ground where each step was like wading through cottonwool soaked with treacle. Then came a stretch of muddy land seamed with high strawlike tussocks. These presented their own problems; if you trod on them, they collapsed with ankle-twisting suddenness; if you plodded between them, you sank to the ankles in mud. But where these muddy runnels had dried they were printed with countless, criss-crossing tracks of waders, and the pitted holes dug by their feeding beaks. And over these, everywhere along the runnels, went the big, stealthy prints of a wildcat's feet.

At last we reached the peninsula. It was hot, and there was no shade here, not even the sparse shade of a rowan. We sat down on a boulder whose stone was warm to the touch, and opened our picnic lunch.

I still remember that first day, and all that it brought. The smells of damp ground drying rapidly in the heat; bog myrtle and peat and the rich mud. The incessant calling of birds—a pair of sandpipers dipping and chattering on the stones at the water's edge, larksong rising and falling like jets of clear water, a cuckoo's breathy shout somewhere up the hillside. There were dunlin everywhere, running along in the shallows, busily quartering the shore for food. A golden eagle stood out from the mountain crest like a ship from land, and sailed down three miles of high blue air in the time it took us to turn our heads from left to right to watch it. Half a mile away, easy to see in the clear afternoon, a family of hoodies hunted low over the heather. There was no sign of the diver; nothing on the water but a mallard with half-grown young, and the wheeling shadows of the swifts. And no faintest echo of the sound we were listening for; the greenshank, it seemed, were not there.

We finished our sandwiches, then sat where we were, content to rest in the sun, and listen and watch, while gradually round us the life of the loch settled back to normal. Apart from the social noises of the birds, the glen was very quiet. The air was still, but the patches of bog-cotton quivered in the rising heat, and a few yards from where we sat the lichen stirred and wavered on a tall moss-hag that looked for all the world like a broken tree-stump.

It was an afternoon for sleep, but we had come a long way to see the place. We moved at last, and got to our feet. Two steps forward and it happened. Straight up from the apparently empty ground, just beside the mossy hag, a sitting greenshank rose with a winnow of wings and a long, startled call. It fled high down the loch in swerving, flashing flight, its alarm-call clanging like a bell. But we hardly noticed it. We were both on our knees beside the nest.

It is rarely indeed that one finds a greenshank's nest. I have seen one, since that day, with its full complement of four eggs, and it is a beautiful sight. But nothing ever equals one's first greenshank, and this we would never have found but for the strange circumstance that the bird was sitting on a single egg. Usually a greenshank completes the clutch of four before she sits, laying an egg every two days, and trusting to the perfect colour-camouflage to conceal the nest from the eyes of predators. This egg was the same blue-green colour as the lichen round it, and smudged with spots like shadow. It lay in an open cup furnished with the same lichen, and with bits of dried sphagnum moss and leaves of heath. Without the bird's movement, I am sure we would both have walked straight by, unseeing.

Far down the loch, still, we could hear the greenshank calling. Perhaps if we went quickly, she would come back soon. Or perhaps the camouflage would be enough to conceal the egg from those arch-enemies, the hoodies; the moss-hag which marked the nest (these birds usually put their nest beside a 'marker' of some kind) threw a concealing shadow clear across the place. The crows had disappeared. We left the nest, and for the rest of the afternoon gave it a wide berth. We did not see the bird return before we started the long trek back to the car.

After that, year by year, we visited the loch, and every year showed us something new. I remember how cold it was one spring, the ground sodden, the struggle to the peninsula worse than ever. But that year a nesting dunlin got off right at my feet, and there cuddled together in the nest—a sight one hardly ever sees—all four newly hatched chicks, kept, I suppose, by the cold from leaving the shelter of their mother's feathers. Each chick was barely an inch long, a tiny ball of dusky, gold-tipped fluff, dark-eyed, dark-billed, and totally unafraid.

As I looked at them it began to rain, and in a moment, it seemed the large cold rain turned to hailstones, big and hard; this was the Maytime storm, the *teuchat* storm that kills young birds, and batters eggs into fragments. And here, exposed to it by my presence, were the four tiny chicks. If I hurried away the mother might come back in time to shelter them, but she might wait too long. There was no sign of her. I did the only possible thing; I crouched there in the beating hail and arched my cupped hands over the nestlings. The soft down brushed my fingers. They settled, unafraid, cheeping like chickens in the warmth. The storm seemed to go on for ever, but it was probably less than ten minutes before the hail cloud drifted by, the sun came out, and the whitened grasses streamed, glittering, as the hailstones melted. As we walked away we saw the dunlin come back quietly, running between the tussocks, and settle herself on the young, fluffing out her breast.

Two or three years later we noticed, disquietingly, that someone had been out to the islands at the east end of the loch, and cut down the trees. The dead boughs had been left where they fell, in ugly, decaying piles. And then for the first time we heard the rumour that we did not want to believe: that the high glen, and our peninsula with it, was due to be drowned. 'They' were building a dam. 'They' had already devastated the bigger glen, the head of the contracting firm (who was staying in our hotel) saying blandly in reply to our anxious questions that 'more people will drive along a glen to look at a dam than will ever drive along it to look at the trees. If it's beauty and amenity you're talking about, then a dam's much better to look at than a wild glen.' So the birch woods of the lower glen had gone, and the old winding road with the fern and the wild flowers, and all along the edge of the loch was a raw, dreadful patch of scoured mud and shingle like a never-healing scar.

And now the high loch, our own loch, was to go too. That year we saw dunlin in plenty, and at least three pairs of greenshank feeding young, and found a merganser's nest (eight creamy eggs in a pillow of flecked grey down), and heard the wildcat grumbling to itself in its stony cairn.

The following year we were comforted. Nothing had happened. A new road was to be built, said our friends at the hotel, that was all. It was to go past the eastern end of our loch, high up, and the little road over the bridges would gradually crumble into disrepair. Oh yes, they told us, the dam had already been built, but then 'They' had found that the water was not needed after all, so now the scheme would not be completed; the glen was safe. It was a pity about the trees, but if that was all . . .

We toiled to the peninsula. A greenshank whistled; a startled sandpiper went *twee-wee-wee* across the water; the dunlin clustered in the shallows. Larks sang in the tranquil air. It was the same; they were not going to destroy it; it was as it had always been, remote, exciting, familiar.

Then from overhead came a strange call. We looked up, alert and puzzled. A bird was circling, high up, obviously disturbed by our presence. A wader, certainly. But what? A greenshank? Too small. A redshank, no. A sandpiper? Nothing like the same note. We watched it, puzzled, then it flew down behind a hillock and vanished, and after a while we walked on. My husband clambered down to the shore, while I trudged—idly enough—to look at the little mud-bound lochan. And halfway across the tussocky heather, straight up in front of me got the strange bird, scared and noisy, and its mate flushed with it from the mudbanks of the lochan. The pair of them flew in a noisy, agitated circle for a few minutes, then landed with a flutter of wings a few yards away and settled down to watch me. The nest lay a yard from my feet, a deep cup in the dry heather.

It was some years now since we had lugged the camera across that dreadful terrain. We had always feared we would regret it, and this time, more than any other I think in my life, I did regret it, bitterly. The scooped hollow lined with grass and heather was a typical wader's nest, but the eggs were unlike any we had seen before. We examined them carefully. There were four of them, beautifully arranged with their narrow ends in. Warm buff, thickly splashed at the broad end with smears and scribbles of purple-brown; matt surface, warm in the warm cup. No, not a greenshank; not a sandpiper; nothing that we knew. We moved carefully back a few paces, and sat down and looked at the birds. They stood quite still, silent now, and looked back at us. They were well within camera range. After some minutes of thinking how well they were within camera range, I remembered that I could draw. It was then that we found that neither of us had a pencil. In the end I drew the birds on the back of an old envelope, with a series of burnt matchsticks. They stood still, watchful but apparently unalarmed, and the sun shone down, comfortingly warm on the eggs. It was a rough drawing, but careful and accurate enough, and as soon as it was finished, we left them.

And told nobody. Perhaps we should have reported our find, recorded it, but the dilemma over this kind of thing is always the same: one wonders if the over-assiduous 'watchers' and ringers and photographers with their hides do as much damage by disturbing the shy, rare birds, as the people who wantonly destroy them. Our pleasure in wild creatures is a private thing, and in their turn the creatures have a right to privacy and peace. So we said nothing. Later, we were to find what our rare bird was, and that it was rare indeed: it had been recorded only once as nesting in Britain, and that more than a hundred years ago. Perhaps after all we had a duty to record it: next year we would go back, we decided, and if it was again happily and successfully there, we would photograph and record it properly.

The end was as inevitable as a play's ending, and in its own way appropriate. We drove up the following year, with camera and sketching pad and a telescopic lens. The new road was finished, and we went up that way—'It's a better surface, and we'll get there quicker,' we said. We drove smoothly up the broad road between the gashes of raw clay and the hacked stumps of birches. 'The land will soon green over,' we said. 'They can't really spoil it for long. Half a generation, and people won't know what they've been robbed of.'

And now here was the crest of the hill, and a beautiful new drive-in viewpoint, where you could get out of your car to gaze right up the glen, up the full length of the loch, up towards the mound of the peninsula and the rich feeding grounds of the river's mouth, and the tiny shepherd's hut, and the far blue hills where the eagle hung and the wildcat had its lair.

You could gaze; but now there was nothing to see. No bridges, no hut, no peninsula. Not even a river's mouth. Nothing but a flat sheet of floodwater, filling the glen and lapping the foot of the wildcat's cairn. Where the reedy river mouth had been, and the muddy runnels herringboned with the birds' tracks and pitted with the small, busy digging beaks . . . nothing. There was no sound but the lap of water in the wind, and the intermittent noise of cars along the new road as the people drove to look at the new dam.

'Oh, well, since the dam was there, they thought they might as well flood it,' we were told that night in the hotel. 'But do you know, they still say that the water wasn't really needed at all.'

We never went back.

JOHN BETJEMAN

A Pity about the Abbey

I was sitting in a Committee about six years ago while a smooth architect was explaining the pros and cons of some scheme. I was hardly listening to his language sprinkled with technical architectural terms like plot ratio, judicious infilling, high rise, low rise, density, viability. 'On the other hand . . .' I heard him saying, and tried to follow what there was on the one hand, and gave up and heard him say 'on the other hand . . .', and if this was meant to be contradicting what he had said before, then I could not understand that either. I did not have to bother to understand what was being said even if the architect understood it himself. This was because a Senior Civil Servant was chairman of the committee and it is the business of well-trained civil servants such as he was, to listen to both sides of a matter (even if to me there is only one side to it), and come out with a balanced judgement.

During my reverie I thought of the destruction of things we cherish that could be brought about by taking this 'on the one hand' 'on the other hand' attitude. For instance a committee cannot design a new building and a new building is not just the building itself, but its neighbours and its siting.

As everybody knows, the permanent Civil Service is an incorruptible thing which advises the different administrations elected to Parliament. The Civil Service has a shrewd idea of how far, in a two- or three-party system, a Government is likely to go. It has alternative suggestions, suited to the different parties. If there were more than a two- or three-party system or less, the Civil Service might either cease to exist or be in charge of us all. People who were by nature secretaries and advisers might become dictators. That would never do. They should be our servants, not our masters. But who are we? Goodness knows.

All I know is that as this verbiage was going on on behalf of some new building which was to replace an older one the idea formed in my head which might make a short story.

There is, as everyone knows, a hierarchy in the permanent Civil Service. The top is the Treasury and below it come lesser but influential Departments of State such as the Foreign Office, the Ministry of Health, the Ministry of Labour, the Ministry for Transport Industries, the Ministry of Works, the Ministry of Housing and Local Government (these last two now amalgamated and called the Department of Environment, but you may be sure are just as jealous of each other as ever), the Ministry of Education, the Air Ministry and so on right down to Weights and Measures, if that has a Ministry to itself.

Then there are the Clubs to which senior civil servants belong. Young aspirants join the United Universities Club and possibly go via the Oxford and Cambridge Club or the Reform Club to the Athenæum, which is the Mecca of senior civil servants, as it is of doctors, bishops and scholars.

By the time I had finished thinking of all this, the next matter on the agenda had arrived. Long experience of committees has shown me how they can be run by a really skilful civil servant. If there is some very important matter which may not get through without a debate and you yourself are anxious to put it through smoothly and quickly, then you can either put it on right at the beginning of the agenda, if you know potential opponents are likely to be late for the meeting, or you put it on at the end of a long agenda when people are very tired. In order to achieve this tiredness in the meeting you make unimportant matters very important and have them discussed at length. Another technique I have noticed a good committee man can employ against opponents is to put forward his argument in an even voice, and then when the opponent chips in with an objection, to go on talking much louder, so that the objection is not heard. Another technique is totally to ignore the objector either by turning to another subject altogether and treating him as though he does not exist or by passing him off with a light smile and someone not to be taken seriously. Of course there is always the standby that this is a very long agenda and we cannot spend any more time on the subject.

It then occurred to me that I might write a short story about how some iniquitous thing could be pushed through a committee by a cunning committee operator. I imagined a situation in which it would be possible, on perfectly reasonable grounds and 'in the public interest', to order the destruction of Westminster Abbey. The person in favour of the destruction in the first place would be, of course, a developer. He would lay his plans carefully by buying up property in the neighbourhood of the Abbey. The Ministry for Transport Industries, always one of the most dangerous ministries because of its enslavement to the motor-car and lorry, would have a scheme for relieving traffic in the centre of London. This would mean driving a road through the Abbey. There would be a certain amount of opposition of course from the Ministry of Works and from various amenity societies and from the Dean and Chapter. The great thing to do in a matter like this is to keep the projected plan out of the newspapers, because once the public heard about it, there might be such serious opposition that even the developer and the Minister and the architects and engineers in charge might take fright.

When all the plans are laid and the various officials and ministries are squared, the matter is put forward by a skilful chairman as a *fait accompli*. A full dress committee is held and every appearance of free speech is encouraged. The Ministry concerned with ancient buildings weeps crocodile tears and much lip-service is paid to our historic past, our essential amenities, something worthy of this great capital city to take the place of what is being destroyed. In fact I could almost hear the government spokesman architect saying all the different things there were to consider about the Abbey. There he was placed in the difficult position of either having to destroy the Houses of Parliament, which would be unthinkable, or not being able to provide sufficient accommodation for civil servants near the Houses of Parliament, which would be equally unthinkable, or holding up all the north/south and east/west through traffic which the Ministry of Transport would insist has to pass through the heart of London. Once the scheme was through the committee stage, then the plan would be released to the Press.

That was to be the plot of my story. I outlined it to my Literary Agent, the late Jean Leroy, and she suggested it should be a film in a series produced by Harry Moore of the BBC. She also introduced me to Stewart Farrar, an experienced scriptwriter, who could bring a human element into this rather cynical and pessimistic story. A love affair was needed. I did not envisage any of the civil servants divulging important matters of state like a proposal to destroy Westminster Abbey. Stewart Farrar asked me who were the sort of people likely to oppose the destruction of the Abbey. I said I thought it would be voluntary societies, such as the amenity societies that have grown up in the country since the war. They consist largely of young people as the desire to destroy is a complaint of middle age. There are also the older voluntary societies like the Society for the Protection of Ancient Buildings, which was founded by William Morris and the London Society. He said, would it be possible to have a glamorous girl connected with one of the amenity societies and could she entice a junior civil servant into divulging the plan to destroy the Abbey? I said such a thing could happen but it was highly improbable. Stewart Farrar cleverly created a bewitching lady from an amenity society, to whom even the most senior civil servants were susceptible. We had two contrasting junior civil servants, the more likeable of whom fell in love with the amenity lady, and resigned from his Ministry out of protest against what his Ministry proposed to do.

Of course the solution to the plot was quite an easy compromise. One had to invent a face-saver for each person bent on destroying the Abbey. The Ministry of Transport was to think it wiser to press for a traffic roundabout south of the river instead of on the site of the Abbey itself. An impartial authority might suggest a compromise if it was found impossible to avoid removing the Abbey. This was to retain Henry VII's chapel and leave it on a traffic island.

The situation was saved by the plot leaking out to the newspapers, and all the senior civil servants changed front. The sad thing is that as we went on writing, Stewart Farrar and I realized that such a thing *could* come about. In fact in a minor way it is happening all over the country today, where the developers have wormed their way into small country towns and cut out their hearts and substituted glass office blocks with chain stores on their ground floors. Indeed within the last year I heard an official of a local authority say about some old building that he was 'afraid that this was another case of' 'Pity about the Abbey'. One must always remember that there is a deep-rooted hatred in some people of anything that is beautiful or reminiscent of the past. I should think there are millions of people who would not really mind Westminster Abbey being destroyed, provided the traffic ran faster. A London taxi driver said to me he could see no purpose in protecting any old buildings at all. I replied obliquely in the Civil Service manner by asking him whether he preferred new wine to vintage. He didn't like wine at all but preferred beer.

We made the permanent civil servants the villains of our plot. This is unfair because in truth you are often more likely to be helped in a civilized cause by the senior civil servants in Whitehall than by local authority officials in the Town Hall. Civil servants are a necessary brake on political ambition, and politicians are essential to stand between the electors and what should be a public service. Long may politicians continue to protect us. The greatest blessing of all is that we have an hereditary monarchy to stand between us and over-ambition. With the Duke of Edinburgh it has been possible to deal with matters that are above party politics, such as Conservation. Should the Abbey really be threatened, it is safe while there is a monarchy. This is because it is a Royal Peculiar, though it would be impossible to show so delightful and abstract an historical fact in terms of television.

JOHN CHAMIER

Royal Yachts

By 'Royal Yachts' I for one mean Royal *Boats*, and the Royal racing boats at that. The Ships of State like the *Victoria and Albert* (there were three of them—did you know that?) and today's *Britannia* qualify merely for this passing nod rather than the 24-carat genuflection. I should also, I think, keep the subject 'at home' or we would be all at sea with, for instance, Plutarch. This correspondent of the *Roman Times*, you will recall, gave a blow-by-blow description of an exceedingly glamorous series of cruises undertaken by Antony and Cleopatra—dateline Alexandria 42–30 BC. On the authority of club member Enobarbus, Cleo's yacht had a counter of beaten gold and sails of purple simply *drenched* in Joy, de Patou, my dear. Good stuff but not, I fear, what interests me in Royal yachting—which is a pity, because nowadays we're far too ready, even in Royal Yachts, to accept a 'half dollar' line in gold-leaf and, for the most part, plain-jane white, unscented Terylene. Sometimes one wonders where all the oomph has gone. With which wistful glance over the port shoulder. . . .

For 1,600 years after Cleo had given Antony a floating eyeful south and east of Egypt Point (on the Isle of Wight) the high seas were dangerous places. Wars and piracy, legalized or under free enterprise, surged around the world like the waters of the Seven Seas themselves. But by then, protected by shoals and sandbanks, tricky currents and tides, seafogs and hard work, the Dutch were by way of establishing a comfortable prosperity based on fish. They became the first truly maritime nation in Europe and, by simple evolution, used their sea skills for the softer joys of recreation on their sheltered inland waters.

In some obscure way—since the rivalry between England and Holland was intensifying all the time to climax in battles off Lowestoft, the North Foreland, Sole Bay, the Medway, and in the name of De Ruyter—the Dutch East India Company presented Charles II with a 'jacht'. Royal yachting in Britain, I guess, started here.

As bright and breezy as 1646, Charles Stuart occupied some of the enforced leisure of his exile with 'practical study of the art of sailing' in the Scillies, the group of islands to the south-west of Cornwall. Later, in Jersey, 'he frequently took the helm during local sailing trips', and on 8 June 1646 he took over a boat built to his own ideas by French shipwrights in St Malo, which may be an historic reason for that harbour's continued popularity with British yachtsmen. Later still he reached Holland and was able to give free rein to his maritime interest. When he returned to his throne as Charles II there were things called Regattas (a word borrowed from the Venetians) against the Duke of York and other personages on London's river, and during his lifetime he cannot have owned fewer than twenty-eight boats.

Good King Charles's golden days faded into turmoil and six or seven decades passed before sailing as a sport came to be fact and not a court diversion. True, the scene was studded with Lords, Dukes, Marquises, and some pretty eminent Colonels and Misters, but Royalty came back to yachting in 1817 when the Prince Regent became a member of The Yacht Club—which thus became the Royal Yacht Club. By 1826 the Royal Yacht Squadron, as the Club had become, was organizing racing. In 1827 King George IV signified approval by presenting a cup to mark the occasion. The Kings' Cups gave way to the Queen's Cups when Queen Victoria succeeded William IV, 'Sailor Bill', to the throne. The establishment of yachting as a competitive sport owed a lot to Royal intervention and support.

Considerable as this was there was more, much more to come. In 1893, under the Rule

$$\frac{\text{Length} \times \text{Sail Area}}{6,000} = \text{Rating}$$

Edward, Prince of Wales, Queen Victoria's eldest son, ordered *Britannia* from Gordon Lennox Watson. She shaped up to 151 Rating, and achieved a career which can only be called legendary. Although that career pleads eloquently for virtues of the Rule which fostered her, *Britannia* was by no means judged to be a *'non pareil'*. In her early days she was especially criticized by the serried ranks of punditry for setting a vogue for over-beamed boats which drew too much water and which were of insufficient displacement. Designs of her era were soon being castigated by critics describing them as 'costly to build, costly to operate, with neither headroom nor space below decks, and which would have broken up at the first occasion if they hadn't been so well constructed'. In view of *Britannia*'s long career we may perhaps say that, when considering boats of her size or thereabouts, the critics were talking out of their hats—though to do them justice they did spotlight the excellence of construction!

Books or parts thereof have been written about *Britannia*, long articles devoted to her. Too much cannot be expected of this short, sharp trot amongst Royal Racing Yachting but there are a few favourite tales which give the saga a third dimension.

For instance, there is a splendid Beken photograph in *Beken of Cowes, 1897–1914*, taken in the days when she was rigged as a jackyard tops'l cutter. It took something to get that main and the jackyarder set. The shot shows twenty-five hands heaving away— my hearties ho! And each hand was one of Britain's hardy sons— not just one of those things which come in handy with a beer tankard. There is one at the mainmast cap; another in the ratlines near the futtocks, guiding and directing; twelve on the foredeck on the tail of the halyard; three urging them on, and *eight* on the fall of the halyard putting their weight on it, hanging on by their hands, knees, ankles, and—Booms-a-daisy? That part of the story goes this way. The Prince of Wales was leaning over the main companionway house smoking a cigar—in the classic phrase 'as was his wont'—and watching the crew hustling that mainsail aloft. Through mistiming or misjudgement the inanimate weight overcame the weight of the crew, and the weight of a boom approximately 100 feet long 'falling on the Prince's head and shoulders, knocked him unconscious'.

Britannia was 123 feet overall, 88 feet on the water-line. She had a beam of 23·3 feet and a draft of 15 feet. She was 221 tons Thames Measurement. Her original sail plan encompassed approximately 10,000 square feet: Twelve Metres, today's Queens of the Ocean Wave, are pushed to muster 2,000 square feet! The height of her mast was some 110 feet, and it is said that it was stepped root end aloft. The late John Scott Hughes of *The Times* is quoted as saying that *Britannia* cost about £10,000 to build.

In her first season she scored 33 firsts out of 43 starts—and £2,200 in prize money—20 per cent of her building cost. In 1895 on her passage out to the Mediterranean she logged on an occasion 26 sea miles in two hours. In the same year she won 32 prizes in 39 starts and notched £3,000 in cash and a lockerful of cups and trophies. For a different style of tale look to 1893 and a famous triple collision in the Dover–Boulogne cross-Channel Race when *Vendetta*, a small boat of 76 tons, crossed the startline first in a smart north-easterly but collided with *Valkyrie II*, losing her topmast. Like any motorway pile-up *Britannia* was then in collision with *Valkyrie*, her bowsprit fouling the latter's rigging. In the mêlée the Royal Yacht took *Vendetta*'s bowsprit with her, and her mainsail, pressing against the 'small' yacht's mast, split from boom to gaff. It was *Valkyrie*'s crew who finally succeeded in cutting away *Britannia*'s bowsprit to free this log-jam of fine ships. There was a famine of bowsprits this day.

Never a dull moment! *Britannia* was altered, modified, rigged and rerigged, and yet she still carried her bat in innings after innings.

In 1901 Queen Victoria died and the Prince of Wales ascended the throne as King Edward VII. *Britannia* was sold to Sir Richard

Williams-Bulkeley who cut her down and used her mostly for cruising. The new King soon regretted parting with his boat and he bought her back. *Britannia*'s complete record to the end of 1927— remember the first World War intervened—was 405 starts, 188 first flags and 69 second and third prizes. And there was still a decade to go before she was 'buried' at sea in 1936 off St Catherine's Point, Isle of Wight, in waters over which she had raced for nearly half a century.

Years were to pass before Royal Ownership again appeared in regatta programmes. The contrast in size was shattering. Her Majesty the Queen's and HRH the Prince Philip, Duke of Edinburgh's Dragon class yacht *Bluebottle* was 29·2 feet overall, 18·7 feet on the waterline, had a beam of 6·4 feet, drew 3·45 feet and set 236 square feet of sail. She was just 4 tons Thames Measurement.

The Dragon class, a design of Norwegian Johan Anker, was founded in 1928 and first introduced to the British Isles by Clyde yachtsmen. In 1938 a modernized rig was prepared. The war interfered with its adoption, which did not take place until November 1945. *Bluebottle* was built by Camper & Nicholson at Gosport in 1948. This was the year of the first post-war Olympics which, so far as yachting was concerned, were staged in Torbay. *Bluebottle*—the name caused both grins and shudders at the time—was a wedding present from the members of Cowes's Island Sailing Club to Princess Elizabeth (as she then was) and the Duke of Edinburgh. The Business of State obviously precluded 'Himself' answering the starting guns every weekend—Cowes Week was usually on his sailing menu but otherwise his yachting fare was fairly slender commons. Nevertheless the Royal Boat, operating under a system of Navy sailing masters with two-year terms of appointment, was notably successful. She was maintained in topflight condition and captured the public's imagination. The story goes that somewhere an earnest society columnist recorded breathlessly on one occasion that '*Bluebottle* was extensively modernized this winter, including being fitted with a new hull'. She raced at regattas round the British Isles and made several visits across the Channel and to Scandinavia. In 1954 she went to Canada, as Nicholas Monsarrat recalls elsewhere in this book.

The apex of *Bluebottle*'s career was 1956—eight years after her launch. With Graham Mann at her helm she represented the country at the 16th Olympiad at Melbourne—and hoisted a Bronze Medal. There's no doubt that this was a handsome effort.

In the end *Bluebottle* was honourably retired to the Britannia Royal Naval College at Dartmouth in April 1962. An eminently intelligent and satisfactory solution to the problem of what to do with a wedding present (when it has to be done) without causing any offence anywhere to anyone.

Alongside *Bluebottle*, so to speak, there was the Flying Fifteen *Coweslip*, which was presented to Prince Philip by the townsfolk of Cowes in 1949. In 1962 she was rebuilt. She too was—and is—a vastly successful boat and in her life has run up a prize list as long as your arm and longer—much longer. Uffa Fox thought up the idea of the presentation and looked after *Coweslip* at his own quay in Cowes. Prince Philip sailed both the Dragon and *Coweslip* during his visits to Cowes in Cowes Week. Of late his children have also sailed *Coweslip*, usually with a friend of Uffa's, Geoff Budden, as mentor, since Uffa has been obliged to take life easier.

The Flying Fifteen has always been a great design in spite of denigratory comments from people who don't know enough and others who should know better. It is without doubt the perfect in-between—between, say, the 14-foot dinghy and the small keel boat. The keel boat mob don't care for the Fifteen because it's too small and handles rather like a dinghy. The dinghy squad don't like it because it handles rather like a keel boat. But I never found anyone who understood the boat and who had learned to sail this 'mini-yacht' who didn't have a great affection for it as well as a respect for its sailing ability. Prince Philip is certainly among the enlightened in both these sectors.

Finally—or only finally as far as this deadline is concerned—there is just one more Royal Racing Boat to come sailing into this picture. But that's not accurate either because she has already sailed out of it again. *Bloodhound* was bought in March 1962 and sold in October 1969. Her racing days on the high seas were already behind her—her generation was riding high in the four or five years before the second World War. With *Bloodhound* at that time you named *Latifa*, *Zeearend*, *Stiarna*, *Maid of Malham*, *Ortac*, *Elizabeth McCaw*, *Aile Noire*, *Trenchemer*, *Bamba*, *Rose*, *Ilex*—the names sound like those of a pack of hounds, and so they were. They all finished up front in the 1937 Fastnet, and *Bloodhound* herself won the 1939 Fastnet.

Rather like *Britannia*, *Bloodhound* came back to do battle after a shattering war. Their new crews served both vessels well (the parallel is particularly drawn). However, by the time she came into Royal ownership—and that takes the story onwards one step—the rules as well as the years had done their work. For lack of exceptional circumstances she was unlikely to beat the opposition's brains out on the offshore racetracks. But *Bloodhound*'s new role was an imaginative and a constructive one—as one might have expected from her owners.

Bloodhound gave Royal Sailing Time to Royal Cowes Week. She also gave copy for the papal bulls of yachting correspondents, the itchy bitchy graffiti of the press diarists, and the prying, gimlet eyes of the Press and television cameras. Nevertheless the roles of boat and crew were executed with *sang-froid*, aplomb—and the occasional rich turn of Navy-learnt phrase. Both gave as immense pleasure to 'yachties' afloat as they did to the sunburnt open-necks and floral blouses ashore. It is my personal and earnest prayer that, during this phase of her life, *Bloodhound*'s owners got at least a sniff of a rub-off of the pleasure that others had in just 'having *them* around'.

This, however, is the least of it. Apart from Royal use, *Bloodhound* with her permanent crew did an astonishing job. Team after team of club yachtsmen put up to 'have a go' in *Bloodhound*. So, in offshore racing and cruising, many clubs and their members were introduced to wider seascapes than their fleets of one-design dinghies could offer in the ordinary course of the club's programme for a given year. They are all to be fairly and squarely enshrined in the pages of *Bloodhound*'s Visitors' Book. The same of course cannot be said for the Imperial Poona Yacht Club of which Himself is Maharajah and his Consort and senior partner is referred to in reverential terms on the occasion of the Loyal Toast as the Queen Empress. No indeed—the IPYC is especially squarely enshrined, and this hardy band of armchair Sinbads have on several occasions added to *gloire britannique* 'in forays to Normandy in *Bloodhound*'.

Bloodhound, built by Camper & Nicholson at Gosport in 1936, had two near sisters from the same builders, *Foxhound* and *Stiarna*. They were single-stickers while she was a classic yawl. Her original sailplan was drawn out by the American firm of Sparkman & Stephens. In later years it was redesigned by Illingworth and Primrose. All three were strangely enough International 12 Metres—though naturally enough they demonstrated the deep-sea expression of the rule rather than the more usual regatta racing application. Both *Bloodhound* and *Foxhound* were to the order of the redoubtable Isaac Bell, an MFH of the Galway Blazers, who decided that the best way of evaluating the respective virtues of the yawl and the cutter rig was to build two boats. Of these, 'Blooders' was the second and reflected the performance of the *seed-boat* of modern ocean racers, *Dorade*. *Dorade* came up with numerous triumphs, including a Fastnet win overall in both 1931 and 1933. In 1936 she was first home in the California–Honolulu, notching the 2,240 mile slide at over 200 miles per day!

Bloodhound's principal statistics were LOA 63·2 feet, LWL 45 feet, beam 12·5 feet, draft 9·08 feet, sail area 1,595 square feet. She was 34 tons Thames Measurement—a biggish boat for these days but a pigmy alongside such real Giants of Sail as her Royal predecessor, *Britannia*. And this perhaps explains the comparative paucity of interest shown in her by the yachting press when she came into being—that and the fact that ocean racing had yet to come into its own, for in 1936 Sir Thomas Sopwith's *Endeavour* and *Endeavour II* were racing with the great J class, and the run up to the Olympic Regattas at Kiel and later the Olympics themselves were taking up a lot of the scribblers' time and vision. The United States won the British–America Cup outright in the 6-Metre class on the Clyde, Stewart Morris was queuing up for his fifth Prince of Wales Cup— and there was erected a new general store in Piccadilly called Simpson's. In competition for the public eye the Bermuda Race mustered 43 starters (a figure to be counted a disaster in these days). Even more derisory was the 7-strong field for the Morgan Cup—I quote: 'In a hard race *Latifa* finished first, but *Bloodhound* won on time by rather under five minutes. A fine performance, as she had scarcely sailed at all previous to the race.' But *Bloodhound* went on winning from then on—for instance she took the Channel Race that year from 15 starters in a fresh breeze affair. The incontrovertible measure of *Bloodhound*'s success is the number of owners she has had in thirty-five years. Up to being sold out of Royal ownership the total was the startlingly low figure of *three*! She was a well-loved ship—and there we'll leave it. For the time being we've come to the end of a chapter.

I'm sorry if you wanted to know more about the *Mary*, the first English Royal Yacht, presented to Charles II by the Dutch at his Restoration; or the *Cleveland*, named after the notorious Duchess of Cleveland, formerly Lady Castlemaine; or *Fubbs*, the King's pet name for the Duchess of Portsmouth. If they were fast ladies they weren't really racing boats—though they had their pride, of course.

Racing a yacht under canvas—like jumping horses, flying gliders, ski-ing skis, bobbing bobs and chasing pretty women—is a deeply personal affair. We're lucky in Britain to have a deep-rooted sporting instinct—and equally men and women who have come to wear crowns and yet still retain their nation's taste for the heady salt of the chase.

ROBIN KNOX-JOHNSTON

A Shocking Affair at Vizagapatam

'Did you go outside the Harbour yesterday?' the Chief Officer asked me accusingly.

'Yes, sir,' I replied, conscious from his tone that I would have to play my request to go sailing today rather carefully.

'Don't you know that there are sharks out there? Suppose you had capsized?'

This was difficult. To state the fact that there were unlikely to be any sharks for miles would only count as impertinence. No Apprentice should ever give the impression that he knows more than the Burra Sahib. And to say that there were more likely to be sharks in the Harbour than in the open sea, obviously untrue anyway, might stop small-boat sailing from the ship altogether. It would pay to be youthful and over-enthusiastic, admit I had taken unnecessary risks yesterday and then try for today.

'I'm terribly sorry, sir. I'm afraid that I hadn't thought of a capsize. There wasn't very much wind out there.' Now there was a master stroke. I stood patiently for five minutes listening to a stern lecture on the dangers of underestimating the weather in this part of the world, of the signs of trouble that only experience such as that of the Burra Sahib could teach me, of the folly of taking an unseaworthy boat out to sea, of taking as crew the other two Apprentices, and of the lack of lifesaving facilities on the Indian Coast. This completed, the Chief Officer gave me a stern look and I felt that I ought to say something to show how his remarks had affected me.

'In view of what you say, sir, I think we should stay within the Harbour from now on.'

'Who said there was going to be any more sailing?' Blast! I'd failed. He'd seen through me all the time. I decided to remain silent, looking glum, but not sulky.

'Go on, then. But not outside the Harbour, and by that I mean the entrance channel as well.'

'Aye, aye, sir.' Reprieved. 'May we go up the creeks?'

'Anywhere!' Exasperated. 'But not outside the Harbour, and be back by six.' He turned back to his desk. I left hurriedly before he changed his mind and went to round up the other two, whose enthusiasm for sailing owed more to the fact that I was the senior Apprentice than any keenness on their parts.

The *Chakdara*, a 7,500-ton cargo vessel, was loading tobacco in Vizagapatam, a port on the east coast of India. We had been there a week and had another week to go at the rate the cargo was arriving from the interior. I was twenty years old and working my passage home to sit for my Second Mate's Certificate. As such, the Chief Officer had decided that it was high time I started to gain real experience, and I was currently understudying the Second Officer on night work, from 6 p.m. until 6 a.m. This left the daytime free, and as it was impossible to sleep after 11 a.m. it left me on the loose for seven hours a day, and I spent the time sailing. The fact that I had managed to 'obtain' the other two Apprentices as crew was due entirely to an impertinent offer from me to get them up to the standard necessary to pass a 'Lifeboatman's Certificate'. The Chief Officer had been so amused that he had agreed.

I ran back to the half deck and called Peter and Mick and we went aft to the poop where the dinghy, *Chakdarijie*, was stowed on chocks on the sun deck. She wasn't much of a dinghy. She had started life as the ship's gig, but as the ship carried a motor lifeboat, she had been used mainly for painting the ship's side. Ten years of misuse in this role had left its scars, but the wood was basically sound and, where it wasn't, the inch or so of paint that had fallen into her acted as a very waterproof skin. At some stage an enthusiast had constructed a bolt-on keel, made up spars and rigging and laboriously stitched up a suit of sails. None of these accessories was in very good shape, but they were better than nothing. At least we could *sail*—and we always took a pair of lifeboat oars with us just in case.

The method of launching was simple. We tapped a derrick, hoisted the dinghy three feet in the air, bolted on the keel and then swung the derrick round until the boat was plumbed over the ship's side. Mick usually handled the winch, while Peter as the First Tripper (which meant he was on his first voyage at sea and therefore most expendable) was detailed off to go down with boat. I acted as Foreman. *Chakdarijie* was lowered into the water and Peter let go the slings, and then hung on to a lifeline while Mick and I swarmed down to join him. At that age we scorned ladders.

I had already explained the Imperial Edict against sailing outside the Harbour, and suggested we go and explore the creeks. To a Junior Apprentice such a suggestion from a man about to take his Second Mate's Certificate was akin to a commandment from Mount Sinai. Peter wasn't even consulted. We got out the oars and rowed across the Harbour. To reach the creeks we had to pass beneath two low bridges and after the second one we stepped the mast and hoisted the sail.

The creeks covered a large area of saltmarshes behind the main port. At one time there had been a plan to connect a nearby oil refinery with the Harbour by means of a canal, but the idea had been dropped, although not before a great deal of digging had been done which left a main channel from which many interesting creeks branched out. The only inhabitants of the area, apart from the wildlife, were a few fishermen who used the age-old method of swinging a circular net, with weights attached to the rim, round their heads and letting it go with a skilful flick that caused the net to spread out and sink to the bottom trapping any fish caught beneath it. The fisherman then bent down, gathered whatever he had trapped, retrieved his net and then waded a few yards before trying again.

For two hours we tacked up and down between the salt brush, startling wildfowl and mud-hoppers at every turn before we finally ran aground. I ordered Peter overside to push us off, warning him about leeches and water snakes at the same time. He went white beneath his tan, but jumped into the mud and gave us a shove. We immediately paid off down the creek to clear the shallows, but this left Peter floundering on the bank behind us and losing the race, so we ran into the mud again to allow him to rejoin us. This time when he had pushed us clear he hung on and climbed back into the boat as we took off for home. To assist our passage we hoisted a topsail, a stolen sheet bent onto the boathook which pulled very well, although the thwart through which the mast passed creaked ominously.

We sailed quickly back towards the second bridge to which I intended making fast whilst we unstepped the mast. As we approached it, Peter, who was forward standing by to make the painter fast, suddenly gave a little jump and said he had felt an electric shock. I told him that it was probably an electric eel that had bumped into our keel, and Mick gave me a grin. The next moment there was a terrific flash and Peter was thrown about three feet into the air. Mick admitted later that he immediately thought an electric eel *was* responsible, especially as he saw what he thought was a brown, snake-like object, rushing through the water from us towards the bank. I put the helm over and told Mick to sail us into the bank while I jumped forward to grab Peter. He was lying across the forward thwart in a heap and I bent to heave him up, receiving a shock myself as my back came against the rigging. My immediate concern had been to get him clear of the water in the bottom of the boat as I suspected that the keel had cut an underwater power cable. On looking up though, I discovered that the two cables that ran alongside the bridge had been reduced to one and it dawned on me that the forestay must have earthed the missing cable. Poor Peter in the bow, holding on to the forestay with his feet in the bilges, had acted as a conductor. He was conscious, but complained that he had no feeling in his legs, which were quite badly burned. I remember thinking 'Oh my God, he's paralysed' as I held him up against the mast whilst Mick put the boat into the bank.

The obvious thing to do was to get Peter to a hospital, and the nearest place I could think of for that was the Indian Navy base about three-quarters of a mile away. Mick held Peter whilst I jumped overside into two feet of mud. Having found a footing I took Peter on my back and carried him ashore. By the time we reached firm ground we had toppled over twice, which did not help our appearance. I carried Peter up to the road and started across the bridge towards the Naval Base, telling Mick to row the dinghy back to the ship. Halfway across, a bus passed us, and I think more out of curiosity than anything the driver stopped and asked where we were going. We explained in our halting Hindi that we wanted a doctor and without more ado the driver helped me to get Peter aboard and, ignoring his other, chattering passengers, drove us straight to the Naval Base and deposited us at the guardroom. A rather disdainful CPO, a Sikh who obviously felt that his guardroom was no place for two filthy mud-covered young Englishmen, asked what we wanted and at first refused to help us. However, news of our arrival had sped quite quickly and a sub-lieutenant soon arrived and escorted us across a huge parade ground to the sickbay. I heartily cursed my country-man who built that parade ground as I carried Peter across it; the Indians declined to assist as it would have meant dirtying their clean white uniforms.

After a short pause in the sickbay, a doctor rushed in, apologizing for the lack of lights and air conditioning. 'We have just had a power cut.'

Peter looked up and because the realization was only just dawning on me I failed to warn him and he managed: 'Oh, Knox, that must be the . . .' before my hand closed firmly over his mouth.

We returned later to the *Chakdara* in an ambulance, Peter half hidden by burn dressings. Needless to say that was the last time we went sailing in Vizagapatam. Peter recovered fully within a couple of weeks, much to my relief, but about four months later was involved in another accident which put him out of action for three months. This time he fell down a hold. I think he must have been accident prone.

'He Remains an Englishman'

To anyone fortunate enough to have played cricket in every country associated with the first-class game the inevitable question is 'Which overseas tour have you enjoyed the most?' The answer has rarely satisfied the questioner or really convinced me, but after carefully weighing the pros and cons of the three major contenders, Australia, South Africa and the West Indies, I invariably come down in favour of the Caribbean Islands, since it was in Barbados that I was first privileged to wear an MCC touring blazer.

Embarkation day was 23 December 1947, the port was Liverpool and the weather filthy. A 4,500-ton empty banana boat with cabin accommodation for fifteen (if three shared a cabin) may have been fine for a summer Mediterranean cruise, but certainly not when lashed by 90 mph gales in the Atlantic. It therefore came as no surprise when we finally anchored off Bridgetown Harbour, Barbados, a couple of days late. As a result practice was limited to a few hours before taking on the might of the Barbados XI.

Our first Test side in that 1947 tour, even fully fit, in constant match practice and accustomed to the vastly different conditions, would have been hard pressed to contain a West Indies Test side, but to attempt to do so without Messrs Len Hutton, Cyril Washbrook, Bill Edrich, Denis Compton and Alec Bedser, all unavailable, appeared to give us as much chance as an unseeded player winning Wimbledon. This thought was further enhanced with only a cursory glance at the West Indies selection. Heading the squad arriving at Bridgetown for 21 January 1948 was the great George Headley, quickly followed by Weekes, Worrell and Walcott, not to mention Stollmeyer, Gomez and Christiani. Their only problem was who to leave out.

Cricketers as a rule are the most superstitious breed of all sportsmen and therein lay the one glimmer of hope. It was an acknowledged fact that MCC had never yet won a series in the West Indies since Test Matches out there had been given official status, but perhaps it was not quite so well known that despite this, England had never been defeated in a Test Match in Barbados.

I have no wish to dwell on the statistics of this Test Match, or to emphasize the fact that an obliging leak in the wicket covers made a very naïve England off-spinner the happiest and probably the most fortunate cricketer in the West Indies, but simply to state the position as the last day's play began.

England had been given the monumental task of scoring 395 to win in the fourth innings and overnight had lost two wickets for 60 runs. With Denis Brookes out of the game nursing a broken finger and two more wickets falling cheaply, England's score after less than an hour's play stood at 86 for 4, with Jack Robertson and Winston Place batting bravely on against a side scenting a kill. The hopelessness of the situation was endorsed by the sight of J. C. Laker and J. H. Wardle padded up with five hours' play still remaining.

In subsequent years both Johnny Wardle and myself used the Spinners' Prayer Mat to good effect, but our chances of a Dispensation were always a sight rosier at Bradford's Park Avenue and Manchester's Old Trafford than on a warm sunny day in the West Indies. A couple of maiden overs followed. Then from nowhere at all it seemed, two or three enormous raindrops fell on my forearm. Leaping to my feet and searching the hidden sky behind the Challenor Stand I realized our prayers were being answered. Moving swiftly and surely in the direction of the Kensington Oval was an enormous, dirty black cloud! As though guided by help from above its progress halted immediately overhead and the rains came. It doesn't rain too often in a West Indian cricket season but when it does there are no half measures. There was no question again that day of inspecting the wicket. The biggest problem would have been to find it, for within twenty minutes the wicket was awash and the whole square was a lake. England had retained their proud un-beaten record in Barbados.

Several hours later I emerged from the pavilion to a car, waiting outside a completely empty and deserted cricket ground. Deserted, that is, with one exception. Leaning against the car was a Barbadian boy, I suppose some thirteen or fourteen years old. His ragged and torn shirt was still saturated, his shoes were covered in mud, but worst of all were the great tears streaming down his face. I asked him what was wrong—could I help him, did he want a lift into town? For fully a minute no reply was forthcoming. The tears streamed down and I was left staring at a boy's face I shall never forget. Then finally, with a huge sigh and an honest wiping away of tears with the back of a jet-black hand, he very slowly replied:

'Oh, Massa Laker; de God sure is an Englishman.'

GERALD DURRELL

The King versus Corfu

I would love to have been fortunate enough to have been born in the island of Corfu. In a world that is rapidly becoming destroyed and becoming increasingly full of extremely dull-witted human beings, it is a great comfort to know that there still exist places like this. It is, of course, justly famous for its beauty and was historically of great importance. It is quite possible, for example, that Shakespeare chose it as his setting for *The Tempest* and, at the opposite end of the scale (since he had very little to commend him as a writer) Napoleon considered it vital to his arrogant and pompous schemes in the Mediterranean.

But there has been one aspect of Corfu that has never really been investigated or documented with the scientific seriousness that it deserves. That is, that it contains a population of *Homo sapiens* who are without doubt the most charming and the most illogical people that exist anywhere in the world.

The Corfiots, with immense good nature and the best possible intentions, always seem to create a situation that is hilariously ludicrous to everybody except a Corfiot. As an example of the sort of thing I mean, they once received for the one and only cinema that existed there at that time two Laurel and Hardy films. Typically, they only had half of each. Rather than disappoint their public, the manager and the projectionist decided that the simplest way around the problem was to join the two films together. The result was that the opening sequences showed Laurel and Hardy in a house on the outskirts of Hollywood looking for a gas leak in the cellar with a lighted candle. Inevitably, there was a gigantic explosion. The next scene showed Laurel and Hardy marching through the desert in the Foreign Legion. The interesting part about this is that very few of the Corfiots who saw it thought that there was anything at all peculiar about the film.

If you live in an atmosphere of kindly illogicality you either go mad or end up accepting everything as normal, rather like Alice when she went through the Looking Glass. I remember once, with my brother, meeting a Corfiot friend sitting in the sunshine on the Platia sipping his ouzo pensively and coughing with monotonous regularity. We asked him how he was, as we had not seen him for some time. He said he was all right but, slapping his chest, that he was smoking too much and this was having a detrimental effect on his lungs. We suggested in a tentative fashion that perhaps he should give up smoking.

'I can't,' he wheezed, 'I'm an addict. But I've just thought of the right method of curing it. I am going to go to my doctor and tell *him* to tell *me* that if I don't give up smoking I shall die. And the shock will make me give it up.' The interesting point is that he was serious.

Naturally, this strange attitude of mind creates situations that are almost beyond belief and I think the occasion when the Corfiots really came into their own was when the King of Greece, King George II, returned in November 1935 after the overthrow of the Republican government.

Unfortunately for the King, the first port at which he was going to set foot on Greek soil happened to be Corfu. Naturally, the Corfiots, wildly excited, were determined to show the rest of Greece that they could do things in a style which could not be emulated even by the arrogant and superior Athenians.

Meetings were held, arms were waved, arguments almost bordering on murder took place all over the island while they decided on the best method of greeting His Majesty. Eventually several splinter groups formed, each determined to carry out its own particular project.

One of these was led by Nicolas Panayiotopoulos. He was the only man in Corfu rich enough to possess what one could, for want of a better term, describe as a yacht. As he had added so much superstructure to it in a wild endeavour to make it look like the *Titanic*, everybody used to lay bets in the town when he set off in it as to whether he would survive or not. It had a list to starboard that would have made even the Ancient Mariner think twice. Nicolas's particular plan for greeting the King was that he was going to have printed some six thousand small paper Greek flags. He was then, as soon as the King's ship was sighted, going to rush out into the Bay of Corfu and distribute these on the surface so that the King would arrive, as it were, on a carpet of Greek flags.

After several experiments it was discovered that the small paper flags sank almost immediately. After numerous conferences, however, they discovered the way around this was to have a cross of thin wood to support each flag so that it would float.

While this mammoth operation was being undertaken, other schemes were afoot. The Governor of the Venetian fort which overlooked the harbour where the King was to arrive had discovered four incredibly decrepit cannons, *circa* 1880. He felt it was only right and proper that these should be fired as a salute. Being, however, a stickler for protocol, he said that this must be fired at the *exact* moment that the King's foot landed on Greek soil. This posed certain problems. The fort was some considerable distance away from the harbour and so how were the people standing by the cannons going to know when the King set foot on Greek soil? After considerable argument (when ideas like waving flags, flashing torches and similar devices had been rejected), the Commandant came up with the brilliant idea that an earnest and trusty lieutenant should be sent down to the docks armed with a large ·45 revolver. He would be instructed to keep a very close watch on the King's movements so that a second or so before the King stepped off the gangplank onto Greek soil he would fire the revolver in the air, the people in the fort would hear the sound of the shot and immediately fire the cannons, thus synchronizing with the King's First Footsteps on Greek Soil.

So all was set for the great day and everybody was agog. And in Corfu people get twice as agog as people in other parts of the world do. Nicolas Panayiotopoulos's boat was furbished and ready, listing even more heavily to starboard owing to the pile of flags, and he had stationed a man at a suitable vantage point, armed with a telescope, so that he could keep watch and the moment the King's ship appeared round the headland and entered the Bay of Corfu he would alert the yacht, which would then zoom out and prepare the carpet of Greek flags.

To anyone knowing Corfu it will not come as a surprise to know that the signal was given and Nicolas Panayiotopoulos rushed out with his boat and started throwing flags in all directions, but it was unfortunate that the man with the telescope was not nautically minded and it was, in fact, not the King's ship but a rather grubby little tanker.

This did not at first appear to be a major catastrophe since the flags were all floating on the water and any minute the King was due to arrive. The whole thing looked very impressive and Nicolas Panayiotopoulos was rather proud. He felt that he, of all Corfiots, had made the best gesture. They waited patiently, the lieutenant standing on the docks with his revolver, the cannons on the fort primed and ready, and Nicolas Panayiotopoulos gazing with pride at his sea of Greek flags.

They waited a fairly long time and it was then that Nicolas Panayiotopoulos noticed something that he had not taken into consideration. The glue with which the flags were stuck to the little crosses disintegrated under the influence of sea water. As he watched, horrified, one paper flag after another separated itself from its little wooden support and sank into the depths of the bay. At that moment the King's ship arrived so he was greeted not, as Nicolas

Panayiotopoulos had hoped, by a great meadow of Greek flags but a vast area of little floating graveyard crosses, which are, of course, in Greece considered extremely bad luck.

The ship ploughed its way through what must have looked like a sort of marine war cemetery and arrived in the harbour. The trusty lieutenant, who by now was sweating slightly and beginning to wish that he hadn't volunteered for this duty, watched with extreme care. What worried him, being of a meticulous nature, was the fact that he had to fire his signal before the King actually left the gang-plank to allow time for the cannons to be fired. He shifted up close to the end of the gangplank and as the King appeared he fixed his eyes avidly upon His Majesty's feet.

The excitement was intense. It was, in fact, a very emotional moment. Slowly and with great dignity, the King came down the gangplank. The crowd, most unusual for a crowd of Greeks, was silent, waiting for His Majesty to set foot on Corfiot soil. The lieutenant was watching His Majesty's feet with immense attention, making mental calculations as to the synchronization of this whole magnificent piece of organization. Steadily and regally, the King approached, and then, as he got to within some three feet of the end of the gangplank, the lieutenant fired off five shots in rapid succession, with the result that not only the King but everybody around— whom nobody had thought to inform—was under the impression that he was being assassinated. Immediate uproar broke out, but this was drowned by the tremendous roar from the cannons on the fortress.

Once it was discovered, after a certain amount of altercation, that the lieutenant had not in fact been trying to assassinate the King, all the Corfiots treated the matter with great joviality. How the King himself felt, as far as I can ascertain, is not on record.

The patron saint of Corfu is St Spyridion, whose mummified body is preserved with immense reverence in the church in the centre of the town. He is considered by Corfiots to be almost more important than God and so naturally the King's first duty was to pay his respects to the Saint. He entered his car, smiling and waving to the excited and enchanted Corfiots. It was then discovered that the front door of the car did not close, so they had to drive off in a rather haphazard fashion with the chauffeur holding the door closed with one hand while driving with the other. Strangely enough, they got to the church, driving through streets lined with excited and emotional Corfiots, without actually hitting anything. The King, with the Archbishop, disappeared into the church to pay rightful homage to the Saint.

The driver of the King's car, knowing from past experience how long and tedious these things were apt to be, did what any sensible Corfiot would do in the circumstances—he left the car and went round the corner for a quick ouzo. Either because the King had been slightly shattered by his reception or for some other reason, the driver had miscalculated, with the result that the King, with all the church dignitaries, suddenly reappeared from the interior of St Spyridion's Church and discovered that the King's car was driverless.

However, Corfiots take this sort of thing in their stride. Everybody immediately accused everybody else of having made the mistake, and three hundred people were sent rushing in different directions to try and ascertain the whereabouts of the driver. He was eventually found, the King was once more installed in the car, and they drove off to the enchanting Villa Mon Repos where, presumably, His Majesty had a well-earned rest.

But the Corfiots had not finished. They were determined that they would leave no stone unturned to make His Majesty's return to Greece a memorable one. In the evening on the Esplanade they had a march past of all the local bands, all playing different tunes, so the cacophony of sound was something that had to be heard to be believed.

And then, as the final touch to the whole procedure, they had a display by the Boy Scouts. They did any number of things that Boy Scouts are taught to do with great efficiency, and the Corfiots were proud of them. Their final act, however, was of a somewhat warlike nature, which one doesn't normally associate with the Boy Scout movement. On the dusty earth of the Platia they proceeded to build a pontoon bridge over an imaginary stream. The idea was to show how swiftly and efficiently they could do this and, indeed, they did it so swiftly and efficiently that everybody was entranced. After the applause died down, the Scout Master, flushed with success, said that they would now demonstrate how, in times of stress, one could demolish the bridge so that any (presumably anti-Scout) enemies following would thus be thwarted.

The original intention had been that two or three innocuous little fire crackers should be detonated under the bridge. But, of course, the Scouts were Corfiot Scouts and several of them had decided that the job should be done properly. The considerable crowd had been so entranced by their efficiency in laying the bridge that they had moved closer and closer. The Scout Master now gave the signal for the demolition of the bridge. What he did not know was that several members of his troop had obtained (quite easily, since the dynamiting of fish was a common practice in Corfu) several sticks of dynamite. The bridge went up with the most impressive roar, throwing bits of itself into the air and landing on various members of the crowd.

The front ranks of the crowd were in fact knocked backwards by the blast.

Fortunately, nobody was killed or hurt. But the front ranks of the crowd, who had received the full blast of three or four charges of dynamite, got to their feet, brushing themselves and their wives down, and said that it was a most remarkable display and so realistic. None of them thought to ask the question why were Boy Scouts allowed to let off large quantities of dynamite in the middle of the town. But then this is Corfu.

Of course, it will change, as everywhere else in the world is changing. But it has a certain quality about it which I hope will make it last for a long time. It is summed up rather neatly by the following incident.

A friend of mine, one Dr Theodore Stephanides, used to frequently make what he called 'excursions' into the countryside in order to observe the natural history. He would always take the same route so that he passed by the local lunatic asylum where, in enchanting grounds, the less fractious patients were allowed to wander. There was one particular man with whom he struck up a friendship and so whenever he went on one of his walks he would take him a bag of peppermints and pass these through the tall iron railings that guarded the gardens.

One day, the lunatic said to him, 'They say I am a lunatic.'

Theodore Stephanides, being of a very precise and scientific turn of mind, said, 'Yes, that is what they say.'

'Well,' said the lunatic, popping a peppermint into his mouth, 'this is a nice garden, isn't it?'

'Yes,' said Theodore gravely.

'And I've got a nice bed to sleep in,' said the lunatic.

'Yes,' said Theodore.

'They feed me and they look after me very well,' said the lunatic.

'Yes,' said Theodore.

'And I don't have to pay any taxes and I don't have to do any work,' said the lunatic.

'That is quite right,' said Theodore.

'Well, tell me,' said the lunatic, in a spirit of gentle inquiry, 'who is mad—me or you all out there?'

In the present state of the world, the fact that there are still places left which produce this gay brand of lunacy gives one a certain amount of hope for the future.

NATHANIEL GUBBINS

Till Death do NOT *Us Part*

Dear Bride and Bridegroom,

While doctors are becoming increasingly interested in geriatrics and prolonging life beyond its normal span a scientist in America has stated that in the not too distant future it may be possible to extend active life to beyond 200 years.

So, before you take your final marriage vows read the following warning that longevity may not always be a blessing unless divorce becomes as easy as buying a new dog licence.

> When life is prolonged by our medical seers
> Until marriages last for 200 years
> And even the doctors are bored unto tears
>   Will the last hundred years be the worst?
>
> The first hundred years should be jolly and gay
> With honeymoons lasting a year and a day
> Or even until you are toothless and grey
>   Will the last hundred years be the worst?
>
> In the last hundred years till you come to the end
> Will you both be so happy that both can pretend
> That both still are lovers—or both round the bend
>   Will the last hundred years be the worst?
>
> In the last hundred years will you know who you are?
> Or the name of that man who is still at the bar?
> Your husband—remember his loud 'Har, Har, Har!'
> At jokes so unfunny for two hundred years,
>   Will the last hundred years be the worst?

Test Match

The England second innings was over and the fifth Test Match against Australia was in its final phase. Australia to bat in the fourth innings, the rubber all-square at two wins each and Bradman's team set 193 to win.

The Yorkshireman laughed at the Australian.

'Tha'll have to pull summat out of bag, Bluey,' he said, easing his shoulders in the burning sun.

'Fingleton and Brown'll do it, sport. Maybe won't lose a wickut.' The Australian flicked away a persistent mosquito.

'Don't come it, Bluey. Tha' said the'sel' Melbourne wicket would be tricky last day.'

'Fat lot you know about Melbourne, Dusty.'

The man from Sowerby Bridge grinned in reply as he shuffled the double pack of cards. He fumbled the bulk, his fingers shaking involuntarily over the small wooden crate.

'Right, Dusty,' said the man from Ballarat. 'Deal plenny o' runs.'

Dusty dealt. Two hands of six cards each—the crate was too small for eight-ball overs—lay face up in front of Bluey.

'Not bad, not bad,' said the Australian. He studied each set closely. 'This lot's Brown as he's takin' first strike, and the other's Fingleton. Right, sport, open the bowlin'.'

'I'm givin' Voce first over,' said Dusty. From the top of the deck left in his hand, he turned over the seven of hearts.

'I gotta seven o' clubs,' said Bluey. 'One run. Bill Brown's off the mark.'

He licked the pencil stub greedily and entered the run on the neatly ruled writing pad beside him.

Dusty dealt the second card. A King. . . .

'Bowled him!' he yelled.

In consternation, Bluey consulted Fingleton's six cards.

'Not a bloody ace or king to beat it. What d'yer know about that?' He entered Fingleton's duck '*b. Voce* . . .' on the score-sheet.

'OK. One for one. Stan McCabe now. Deal him a fresh six, mate, but shuffle 'em first—and shuffle 'em good.'

Voce bowled his remaining four cards to McCabe. There was a boundary as the Australian matched identically the bowler's four of spades. Bluey applauded the stroke.

'Bowes's bowlin' next over,' said Dusty. 'Fra' Yorkshire, remember, and he did well, first innin's.'

'He'll only bowl as well as we'll let him,' said Bluey. 'Deal 'em, Dusty. One for Brown, McCabe four.'

Each batsman's quota of cards was made up to face the new over from Bowes. A spade ace, delivered second ball, had Brown caught.

'How wuzzie!' yelled Dusty. 'A black ace . . . he's caught behind. . . !'

'He never touched it,' snarled Bluey as he entered '*ct. Ames b. Bowes* . . . *1*' against Brown's name. 'Not a black card in his hand to play that soddin' ace. Hell, we're doin' bad.'

Hassett was dealt fresh cards but Bowes continued in devastating form, trapping him leg before with the queen of clubs.

'Unfrien'ly cow!' Dusty banged his fist on the fatal card before marking the score. 'Ah well, Bradman now. Deal him somethin' worth havin', for Pete's sake.'

Dusty dealt out six cards—and there was an ace and a king in the great man's batting hand. Enough to combat anything Voce could hurl at him. The Don registered eight runs before the over ended.

'That's me boy,' chuckled Bluey. 'No more panic. . . .'

But Voce struck again. A red ace. . . .

'Caught,' said Dusty crisply. 'Got him! McCabe, that is.'

'This is as crazy as a two-bob watch,' muttered Bluey. 'Caught. Who by?'

Dusty cut the cards . . . a two. He consulted the England batting order.

'Young Washbrook,' he said. 'In't covers.'

McCabe's dismissal was duly recorded. But it was a long time before England struck again. First Bradman, then Barnes passed their fifties . . . even changing the attack to Perks and Verity found the cards still falling heavily in favour of the batsmen. Every ace or court card played by Dusty for England met some equivalent denomination from Bluey's Australians to frustrate the bowlers. Extras, evolved from a complicated division of cards between eight and ten, began to mount up. The pack's jokers appeared several times in their roles of 'no balls' which allowed the batsmen to use their highest cards to score from and still retain them to use again. Bluey and Dusty had devised the rules of this card-cricket right down to 'retired hurts'. Red cards against black, odds and evens, pairs and permutations, divisions and subtractions, all the science of the game had been distilled by two lonely men from two packs of sweat-stained, dog-eared playing cards.

Then Verity did the hat-trick . . . Barnes, Barnett and Waite.

'Hell's teeth!' snorted Bluey as Dusty capered in delight. 'Forty-five to win and only three wickuts left. But the Don's still there, cobber, he's still there.'

Gasping from his excitement, Dusty dealt the cards again, providing Bradman with six fresh ones and O'Reilly with his first set.

The runs crept up . . . until Hardstaff caught O'Reilly. Thirty-three to win and Bradman not out ninety. Fleetwood-Smith had yet to score. Bluey knew now that the odds were against him. By the intricate rules of their invention, the same mathematical protections for established batsmen were not allowed tail-enders. Subtle alterations were enforced to make it difficult for them to keep aces and court cards from taking their wickets . . . as in the true game their limited batting ability had to be taken into account. Now Bluey had to rely on the strength of Bradman and playing his cards carefully to enable him to farm the bowling.

Bradman passed his hundred but Verity's bowling still kept him in check.

'There's a single there,' observed the Yorkshireman drily.

'No takers,' said Bluey. 'I'm leavin' Braddles with the battin'. He's still got a good hand. Fleetwood-Smith's got nothin' but a long name.'

Eighteen runs were still needed when Fleetwood-Smith was stumped by the jack of hearts. Had it been the diamond jack he would have been run out.

'Aw, hell! No chance!' Gloomily Bluey pushed the dismissed batsman's cards over to Dusty to shuffle back into the pack. 'McCormick, now . . . last man in. Make a name for yourself, Mac.'

But the cards did not go his way. Bradman nudged seven more hard-fought runs and played a maiden, leaving McCormick to face Voce, his six cards looking a sorry, valueless lot. Dusty laid down a king . . . the Australian had nothing to offer in reply. McCormick was bowled.

'We've won!' yelled the Yorkshireman triumphantly. 'We've won bloody rubber!'

Bluey sank his head in hands dejectedly.

'You had the luck o' the devil,' he said drawing a line under the final total. 'Eleven stinkin' runs. I should have played Badcock, I knew I should've, to strengthen the middle battin'. But Bradman did it agen, me ole cobber, hundrid and fourteen, not out. But other than him and Barnes, they batted like burks.'

'That was a great hat-trick o' Verity's,' said Dusty grinning. 'I had to play him in team—in his memory, like.'

'Turnin' point of the match, that was,' Bluey conceded. 'Good game o' crickut, though. Reckon?'

'Ah, I reckon,' agreed Dusty as he gathered up the cards.

They shook hands over the up-turned crate of Melbourne cricket ground.

'You have finished, yes?' asked the bespectacled little man in the peaked cap. 'Who wins today?'

'He wins, captain,' admitted Bluey, 'by eleven soddin' runs.'

'An' took the Ashes, lad, don't thee forget that.'

'They'll come back to Aussie next series. . . .'

'They won't, Bluey. 'Ee, we'll be playin' that in England, remember.'

The man in the cap made an impatient gesture with his malacca cane.

'To latrine work now,' he commanded. 'Rest period is over.'

'Ah, yes, we mustn't keep the gent waitin',' said Bluey, scratching the nape of his white-bristled neck. 'Time to get back to dunny duty.'

'Watch out for the mozzies,' warned Dusty.

'I've nothin' left to bite,' said Bluey, jerking up his sagging, torn shorts. Then, picking up a spade, he walked slowly towards a basha hut in the far corner of the compound as squirrel-tailed tree-rats bounced and scurried from his path. Above, in the motionless, heat-hazed trees, the monotonous call of the bul-bul bird seemed to increase in intensity: *'won't-be-long-now'* . . . *'won't-be-long-now'* . . . *'won't-be-long-now'*. . . .

'Be seein' you, Bluey,' called Dusty as he over-turned the crate and flung into it the two empty ammunition boxes which had served as their seats.

'Be seein' yer, Dusty. . . .' The Australian's reply was cracked in the distance.

Beyond him the voice of Tokyo Rose, amplified from the prison camp radio, was chiding the British in dulcet tones. Soon, she exhorted, the magnificent armies of the Rising Sun would be marching on Delhi. The Japanese captain watched Dusty pause as he stowed the crate on a veranda and answer Tokyo Rose. Idly, as if by instinct, he made one of those filthy British squirting noises with tongue protruding from lips and cheeks fully extended. Angrily the captain struck at the barbed wire with his cane. The midday sun was no time to reprimand that man now . . . but later he would suffer for that insult. Dysentery was depleting the British labour force and these two men had actually volunteered to try to make that evil-smelling latrine more hygienic. Certainly no Japanese could be allowed near it. The officer pulled at the cross-brace of his sword belt and shuddered fastidiously.

How he hated this mysterious game called 'critic' that so dominated these two particular prisoners. Ever since their move from Singapore they had absorbed all leisure time with cards called Bradman and Hutton. Even when working on the railway they had made two-handed motions with their picks, talking about using their front foot and 'getting over the top of it'. This, apparently, was also 'critic' . . . without cards. Yet that strange oblong net which had been found by a Japanese patrol on a New Guinea hill-top left by the Australians . . . official Tokyo reports said that, too, was 'critic'. To the British, maidens were 'critic', ashes were 'critic', stone walls were 'critic'—their whole damned system was 'critic'.

The little captain stamped into his slotted bamboo hut to deal with the problem of fast-diminishing rice supplies. Anything to get away from that foul latrine—and 'critic'.

Nonchalantly stuffing the pack of cards and the score pad into his ragged khaki shirt, Sergeant Dusty Rhodes followed Bluey into the fly-buzzing basha hut. It was untenanted, of course. As planned the Australian had already escaped. Now it was Dusty's turn to burrow under the filth.

'Funny,' he thought as he retched and sweated, 'if Bluey had taken that single, the way the cards fell after he'd have won!'

As he slithered into the slimy tunnel and kicked earth behind him he laughed. 'Tokyo bloody Rose. White Rose, here I come!'

He was still laughing when he crawled into the sunlight—and answered Bluey's low whistle.

Four months later a British patrol in log canoes crossed a hyacinth covered lake and entered the small village. Lieutenant Walters halted his grinning Gurkhas and stared in stunned amazement.

Two teak-brown, half-naked, bearded men squatted in the shade of a banyan tree playing cards. As he approached cautiously, flicking off his revolver's safety-catch, a young Burmese girl in a red and gold longyi swayed from the trailing creepers and touched his arm.

'Please be quiet,' she whispered, her finger on her lips. 'Fingleton is ninety-eight not out.'

'Pardon . . . ?'

'The cricket,' she said, pointing to Dusty and Bluey.

'I don't get it,' said Walters in bewilderment. 'Who are they?'

'Your soldiers. Escaped from a prison camp. They live with my sister and me now.'

The lieutenant smiled, pushing back his bush hat, releasing rivulets of sweat, while his sun-narrowed eyes roved over her firm contours.

239

'You mean they just sit there playing cards. . . ?'

She laughed, a sound reminding him longingly of ice tinkling into a glass.

'Oh, they will call for us soon,' she said. 'At close of play.'

SHEILA SCOTT

Yesterday's Islands Tomorrow

Zeus was grumbling and occasionally a lightning flash of rage from his eyes darted down and reflected in the vast ocean beneath me. The aircraft trembled. As though to find reassurance her wing tips flirted with the cobwebby strands of grey cloud strung out over the 5th Southern Parallel. Beside us, cathedrals of towering cumulo-nimbus threw out sombre, mysterious shadows. Below, sullen waves were born which grew to giants throwing white spittle up at us, only to dissolve, leaving a whirling dark pit where they had been.

Boom! went the empty steel cabin tank, and I looked back at the thing which had caused the noise inside the aircraft. It was the Tabua, the tooth of a sperm whale, banging against the metal. Only a few hours before it had been presented to us by Fijian Chiefs who had risen during the night to put it aboard to keep us safe and happy during future flights.

At dawn the sun had burst forth from the other side of earth and watched from just above the horizon the strange and time-honoured, hundreds-of-years-old ceremony that took place on the charcoal tarmac of a sophisticated airport. Hard, ugly concrete surrounded us and monstrous, shining, gleaming giant jets silently surveyed the little 'Te Wanikiba'—flying canoe—which was the local name for my Piper Comanche, *Myth Too*. The woven ceremonial mats contrasted with the tiny modern white aeroplane, and the daytime sulus of the Chiefs showed up the dull grey trousers of the Europeans. I sat barefooted and cross-legged in Fijian fashion before leaving these gentle but warrior people.

Today I was leaving the island where, for too short a time, I had probably found the greatest peace and happiness in a whole world of flights. Tears were in my eyes as the age-old ritual words were spoken—words I could not speak myself and yet there were no barriers between us—not even those of words. We were of different beliefs, different colour, and born at opposite ends of the earth, but I inexplicably understood what they meant.

Gently the Tabua was placed in my hands, and I felt the positive thought and the power of love and affection behind this, the highest honour that a Fijian could show anyone. They gave it to me with words, which in English would say that they felt I belonged to Fiji, and it would guard *Myth* and me across the great oceans until the day we happily returned.

This huge yellow tooth, with its necklace of woven grass, had played its part in life over many years as the symbol of great ceremonial occasions. Nowadays a genuine Tabua is used only to honour or install a great Chief, and is rarely allowed to leave Fiji. Over the decades this one, like its fellows, had probably been used to secure the hand of a lady, on other occasions as an atonement for a crime, or even to secure the death of another man, or to assuage the temper of a person of rank, as well as for great honour! Now it was to be used in a much more homely way—to keep a lone pilot company, and remind her of past happiness.

The night before, the Fijians had sung the Pacific song, Iso Lei, which tells of love, joy, and lingering memories; a token of sympathy, and great sadness at farewell. I too felt a great sadness because the people I had met were unique in my world and I dreaded returning to the Western, uncivilized way of living, of thugs, of strikes, of riots and religious and political wars, of inflation, of sophisticated superciliousness.

Now, high above the sea, the Tabua reminded me that I was still on the edge of the Pacific and there was much more to discover before I finally re-entered my cage a third of the globe away. Indeed, the clouds were lessening and the aircraft became a gliding bird instead of a frightened bucking animal. It was as though a curtain was lifted from the grim, gaunt, black and white sea which became a kaleidoscope of rich turquoise streaks, intermingled with royal blue ribbons and emerald depths melting together in a frothy white lacy collar, rolling up to the minute beach of the reef ahead. Deep down, the coral gave hints of orange, blue, and red in clear, ever-changing, translucent depths. The remaining clouds became tinged with lilac pink against the palest ethereal blue, colours which can only be truly seen from the air, for there are no such colours on earth or in the sea. It is a beauty which is completely satisfying, as a meal is to a starving man, and completely fills all one's emotions and physical needs. Almost too much so, and one can hardly draw breath with the wonder and yet tranquil delight.

Soon the specks of reefs and rocks that were at first just a brooch became a whole necklace, and I flew towards the chief atoll of the Gilbert group, Tarawa Atoll. Unbelievably these sixteen small atolls house 45,000 people and yet the Gilbert and Ellice isles cover a mere 369 square miles in two million square miles of Pacific Ocean! There were people here nearly two thousand years ago, although the first European did not discover them until the sixteenth century and it was the nineteenth century before we actually moved in. It is debatable whether we have necessarily been a good influence. Indeed, the men that really discovered the Gilberts for us were the tough captains of the convict ships returning from Australia—almost as violent in a different way as the near-cannibals they were discovering.

My delighted eyes looked down at sparkling, platinum gold beaches edged with lustrous coconut palms, like purple-green stars on ribbons of land and coral reef, protecting the still lagoon. There were flying fish and, alas, heart-shaped fishing traps, a single floating coconut husk, the fastest of canoes—a slim outrigger—with a red sail in the brilliant blue sea, cleaving its way through white froth, and blue-black patterned shadows of the clouds on white crests. Occasionally the sea was disturbed by the fin of a sail fish. But my mood abruptly changed as I saw rusting, twisted metal and concrete pillboxes. This was Betio, where civilization had once again reached out its hand in 1943 and 5,000 men died on Betio beach in a week.

Time to stop philosophizing and to find the landing strip. In places the long strips of coconut-tree lined land surrounding the lagoon were only 50 yards across. Surely there could be no room to land even an aircraft as small as *Myth*? A break in the line of tropical foliage and there it was—a coral runway appearing to lead straight out of the emerald green sea into the turquoise blue lagoon! As *Myth*'s wheels touched down, the palm trees suddenly towered above us on either side and beneath them a village of brown grass roofs and gay washing flashed by.

Wonderingly I taxied back to where I thought I had seen a truck, while the spray lifted by the breeze covered *Myth*'s windows with salt. Bright eyes in little brown Micronesian faces and bodies appeared beside the aircraft, dancing and chanting in the rainspots which made their skins gleam as though covered with brown sequins as they escorted us along the strip. The air was heavy and sultry and yet there was a feeling of fiesta.

The sign 'Bonriki International' came into sight and below was a single large grass-roofed, open-timbered hut. This was the entire airport complex! Customs, immigration, control tower, freight handling, booking hall—the lot! Dark-skinned refuellers dressed in bright cottons with crooked ringlets of flowers crowning their thick black curly hair took charge of *Myth*. Amid shouts of excitement or laughter they refreshed her tanks under the shelter of a large umbrella to protect the fuel from the usual brief but brisk midday tropical shower. A misty grey cloud swiftly dipped down to the sea's edge of the airfield and yet the sun was still glinting on the lagoon at the other end of the runway.

Only three or four Europeans waited there amongst the chattering and brightly assorted crowd of people: Derek and Vrai Cudmore of the British High Commission; Glyn Jones, chief greeter, news-hound, general dogsbody for the British; and Australian Peter Barker, hotelier, travel agent, taxi owner.

After many greetings and presentations of sweet-smelling leis I was instructed to be sure and eat all my bananas before going through Customs! A crazy beginning but they did not want me to waste them!

In the middle of the crowd stood a shining modern contraption—a Mini-Moke. It was one of the only two taxis on the island, and a source of great pride as it had only recently arrived. But, with its gay canopy, it somehow looked just right for the scene. We drove along roads made of reef mud which dries as hard as concrete. Fallen coconuts rolled out of the forest of palms, and hermit crabs scuttled across the road carrying their lodgings of shell on their backs. Occasionally I caught a glimpse of a woman knee high in mud tending her precious Babai (taro, the starchy staple food crop). Here a man's riches and honour are judged by the size of his taro crop, though he considers it woman's work to tend it! Every clan has its own closely guarded secret method of planting it, and the chief only passes the secret on to his eldest son on his deathbed.

Lizards, centipedes and dragonflies flashed and weaved between the knotted roots, and dogs and pigs slept unconcernedly in the middle of the road as we approached the village. Bare-footed and pretty raven-haired girls dressed in green and red straw mini-skirts topped with white and red singlets bound with human hair braid, wearing jewellery made of straw, shells, and brightly coloured flowers on their hair and arms, giggled and clapped as we drove by and called 'Tiakibi te anie' (woman that flies like a bird) to me.

Bare-bosomed older women breast-fed their babies as they leant against grass huts. Not all huts were thatched. Some were tumble-down tin shacks, but even these shabby remnants of the Western influence seemed picturesque to my delighted eyes. Every hut had its own patch of beach, and a Gilbertese outrigger, with odd, up-ended, colourful sails. It also had its own wild birds as well as more domestic animals. The villagers catch and train the birds to return to their own hut each night. I inquired what the strange half-timbered huts on stilts out to sea were. These turned out to be kainakotari (the loos) and you walk the plank to accomplish your mission.

The little eleven-roomed Otinai Hotel sprawled along the water-front, and my room opened out onto a conch shell covered beach edging the lagoon exactly as I had always imagined a Pacific atoll should. Though not luxurious, everything was there that I could need, even a shower (cold water only, of course, but who cared in a minimum temperature of 80°). For room service you merely gave a shout. A graceful girl brought in a beautiful flower arrangement made of real flowers, shells and straw which must have taken her all day to make, and lit an incense burner to keep the multitude of flies away.

She gave me the laundry list. Fivepence for panties and tenpence blouses and dresses, and returned within a couple of hours. Paradise island in more ways than one. Later I was to find the laundrymaid had a delightful disrespect for sexes and invariably the men ended up with pretty pink panties, while I was presented with Y-fronts! But it did not matter—everyone becomes part of one family at the Otinai, and wanders in and out of each other's rooms regardless of whether anyone is in bed or not. Life is completely natural and there are no embarrassments. Sometimes the new guest is a little bewildered when he arrives to find his single booking mixed with a single woman but, in spite of only eleven rooms, it all gets sorted out happily!

European food is sometimes a little short, but you will not starve on this island. The sea is rich in fish and the land in coconuts. Nothing is more delicious than raw fish soaked in coconut cream, onions and lime! An aircraft brings in mail and some supplies once a week, and visiting ferry pilots bring a dozen lettuces instead of more conventional presents for their hosts!

As the setting sun sent fingers of gold to dance on the darkening sea, and drifting clouds took on the colours of the dyes of a gorgeous grass skirt, the green-purple trees turned into long, thin, black shapes against a pale, starlit sky. I heard music and laughter. My refuellers, who had finished tending to *Myth Too*'s needs, had now arrived to serenade me! They squatted cross-legged on the beach nursing guitars, and sang delightfully naughty pidgin English songs. Soon the laundrymaid, the houseboy, the owner, the whole hotel joined in, and one of the most romantic parties of my life began. Hurricane lamps and steaks appeared from somewhere and between munching and songs, a great story-telling session began (mostly from Peter Barker, who came to visit years ago, found the rest of the world well lost, and stayed on to start this idyllic hotel). It was all there, just like the travel brochures which normally never turn out to represent the place they advertise. Why, even the moon came up in double bumper size!

They told of the olden times when the outriggers of the islanders sailed for hundreds of miles and weeks at a time, their food supplies being coconuts and their shelter coconut mats. Their tools and knives were made of coral and shell. They even shaved with shells! They navigated with 'shell charts' made of a lattice work of sticks with shells representing the islands, and plotted their 'position lines' by weaving a supple stick through the lattice work.

They spoke of sadder times, of the Japanese, American, and British occupations. They quaintly called each other names like 'Careless' and 'Kindly' and talked of 'Speedie', the son of a New Zealand coastwatcher who stayed behind to report Japanese movements when the islands were evacuated. When the Japanese landed they looked for all non-Gilbertese, and in spite of the villagers' attempts to hide their friends under straw and leaves, they found them—all but one—and shot them without trial. The Japanese executed reprisals on the villagers but still they would not give up their remaining friend. Eventually he gave himself up and the Japs marched him in triumph through the village to the beach to be shot. He did not look at the houses or the villagers lest they be recognized as his friends—except at one of the last houses. A woman who had just given birth sat there sheltering a newly-born babe in her arms. He looked straight at the babe without a flicker—and within minutes was shot. His last glance had been for his son—Speedie. The village believes he did not die in vain, for he has lived on in his son.

Later, when the Americans came in, the missionaries got worried and moralized and issued sweatshirts to the women to cover their bare breasts. Next day all the women obediently appeared wearing the sweatshirts—with two holes cut in them for their breasts. And maybe with reason, for a woman was once kept alive only for her child-bearing qualities and these were judged by her breasts! Modesty forbids naked thighs though.

Another told of Ocean Isle nearby, when all Europeans and part-Europeans were lined up on a cliff by the Japanese and shot so that the bodies fell into the sea. One man fainted and fell over into the waves and was washed up into a cave. The Japanese searched and could not find him. He survived there for a year on the fish in the rocks in the caves. At night he climbed to the surface to find coconuts to drink. One night he heard voices close by, but he was nearly blind from lack of light and could not see their hurricane lamps. The people saw a ghostly, stumbling figure with a white-bearded face and ran away to their American rescuers with tales of a banshee. The Americans investigated and saved him, but too late to save his sight.

There were stories of the 20-stone giant, despotic King Binoka of Abemama. He had his own trading empire and navy, and thirty-six plump concubines who used to dance naked in the pool. His tomb is still honoured and his trading stations still trade among the wrecks of the Blackbirders schooners.

Then there is Tabiteuea, the home of the beautiful dancing girls where the bones of Kourabi, the seven-foot giant, are kept with a basket of shells, and solemnly washed with due ceremony every five years!

We even talked about Outer Space and the first men on the moon. They told me how they listened on the radio and stayed up all night just as I had done, listening and living the great new adventures of Space. I believe they knew more about the astronauts than I did. They had watched our satellites take birth among the old stars for years.

They knew without being taught that the barriers on this tiny earth must come down because of the great discoveries out there. There is no room for political and religious strife and prejudice unless we are to starve or blow ourselves to pieces.

Next day I was invited to a feast in a local village. We left the Mini-Mokes at the edge of the forest, and stumbled through the undergrowth by the ethereal lights of the enormous South Sea moon and hurricane lamps towards the dimly lit mameaba, the meeting-house.

The roof is deliberately built low so that all must bow as they pass under it. The men remove their kaneu, their flower rings, as they enter, and the old men are offered the timber pillars to lean against. The young women of the village light the old ladies' pipes, and it is etiquette not to comment or talk loudly until the chief men ask you if you have anything to say.

The old are honoured in these islands, and the great courtesy reminded me of Fiji. Those gracious warrior Fijian peoples, always smiling. Why? Because they have learnt what we have forgotten. Everyone is plump and well nourished, but not from cannibalism. They may have only recently put this aside but, unlike our civilization, they have not turned man's baser instincts into further violence. There are no lonely, sick old people. Orphan children are given love and education freely. Why? Because the whole village community looks after its own—not just the feudal family. All races live happily together in Fiji.

All religions worship as they will, though the Gilbertese have not advanced as far as the Fijians, and missionaries and Western teachings abound and seem determined to convert them still. One can only hope not too narrowly.

Everyone has his own special place in the meeting house and we sat on palm mats around the open sides. The ceiling was intricately thatched with pandanus leaves and held up by old timber beams. The thick foliage around us formed a natural wall. The women of the village openly dressed tiny children and the young girls in all their finery ready for the ceremonial dancing, just as if it were for a grand opera at Covent Garden (but I was amused to see, incongruously hidden at the back, a child's plastic potty!).

Tonight there was no musical instrument, but it was as though there was a huge orchestra, and yet it was all done by clapping, stamping, chanting and singing. The children danced a perfect hula with tiny, twisting hips in their grass mini-skirts. The men acted out more masculine dances and wore mat-like skirts (lava lava) held up by human hair belts (the girls grow their hair long to be able to make belts for their favourite man). The girls danced the famous South Sea hand dances expressing love—and, in front of them all, lay a little black and white cat, like a little green-eyed princess surveying her courtiers.

After an evening of hospitality, I got up to thank and honour the chief man by giving him some twists of tobacco (the only gift these non-commercial people will accept). It is a great insult to give anything more, although they will spend hours making their guest a present.

Back in my tranquil room at the Otiana I saw many lights bobbing up and down out in the lagoon like dozens of fireflies. The inlets of the reefs allow the tides in and out even in the lagoon, and the fireflies were the other village walkers out to catch octopus!

Sitting through the night on my atoll I wondered, could it be that earth will be like the atoll? This atoll must once have been part of a turbulent volcano that blew itself up to subside below the waves, leaving the basic coral polyps to breed a new kind of earth. The skeletons of the polyps became rocks and reefs until, over thousands of years, the coral island emerged above the waves, growing big enough to catch a floating coconut, a seed, and for a migrant bird to alight on it. Particles of floating sand built up around it, killing off the plankton on which the coral polyps lived, and so the coral reef in the middle subsided, leaving the living coral on the outside in the cleaner water building up a sea wall and forming eventually a beautiful central lagoon. The coconut became the ancestor of many trees, and the insect it carried bred, as did the migrant bird. Fish hid in the shadowy caves. One day a human family sailing the high seas in a timber-hewn outrigger discovered this new island by accident and so a new civilization was born—but a much more beautiful one than the original angry volcano.

I sat quietly watching on a giant conch shell, leaning against the palm tree, looking out across the timeless silvery lagoon, remembering another but more sophisticated, rushing world. I did not need a light, for the whole sky was a 'Milky Way' and this reminded me of night flights over deserts and jungles and great cities and little homesteads far in an Outback. I remembered that but for a tiny aircraft I could never have seen these places, nor known the people who inhabit them.

'Why do it?' the smart young men around London town superciliously ask. My answer should be, 'Once you find the way it will be an obsession—but it will be a magnificent obsession', but alas, that was written by another and about another love. But what else explains flying so well?

For those of us who have been so bewitched and obsessed, it becomes like one of the greatest love affairs of our lives and nothing will ever be the same again. There will always be the relentless master pulling us back to his charms and lessons. Even his Zeus-like moods are an exciting drug, although he has to be treated with respect for us safely to circumvent or climb through his stormy passions to the glistening, heavenly sunlight or calm moonbeams beyond. The excitement, and yet the peace, that comes after such a battle can only be likened to earthly love, and yet it is so much more magnificent in reality.

How can what I have learned be expressed in mere words?

In the air, beauty is of greater impact and more concentrated than in any other sphere: colours are brighter, clearer, vivid and yet more delicate in a way it is impossible to describe. Every sense is acutely awake, even the sense of smell. Sensations are intensified and yet the body remains still, with feet and hands on the controls while the brain becomes crystal clear, receptive and active.

Fear is almost a cleanser in the air. One feels the physical stab momentarily and then comes a great calmness in spite of the shaking, fumbling hands and shivering knees. You think very lucidly and clearly, even though your thoughts are tinged with emotion. You are afraid, but you find a power inside yourself which you did not know you had, and you are able to conquer the animal, anguished panic.

It has taken flying and a small aircraft to show me the signs of a mighty overall power or pattern. Producing documentary films led the way for a famous actress friend. Another friend, a scientist, saw it in his physics. Others have glimpsed it on a mountain top. Some, a fortunate few, out in Space itself.

The solo long-distance flyer feels a freedom which can rarely be found in another sphere, and yet, although free, is made aware of an overall, magnificent influence which gives him a sense of humility at his inability to even imagine the vastness of this power, while lifting him beyond the barriers of earthbound thoughts to glimpse the future that is Space.

After crossing the Dateline, when today became yesterday, and within hours of leaving the South Pacific, there was to be more violence in my own life as a result of man-made troubles earlier in the year. The results should have killed me and yet each time we, *Myth* and I, survived by a miracle. We made more friends across the world than ever before and, although life on the Prime Meridian is as difficult and chaotic as ever, somehow it does not matter. There is great happiness even on the ground now, which sustains me. I do not even get cross very often any more. Could it be the influence of the age-old Tabua, or has flying a little aircraft called *Myth Too* begun to give me a clue to a better understanding of what life is all about, by showing me there can no longer be prejudice of any sort on this tiny Earth if we are to survive.

'It's a Guinness sponsored Test Match'

PETER SELLERS

A Party Political Speech by Max Schreiner

My Friends,

In the light of present-day developments let me say right away that I do not regard existing conditions lightly. On the contrary, I have always regarded them as subjects of the gravest responsibility and shall ever continue to do so. Indeed, I will even go further and state quite categorically that I am more than sensible of the definition of the precise issues which are at this very moment concerning us all—we must build but we must build surely. (*Hear, hear.*) Let me say just this—if any part of what I am saying is challenged then I am more than ready to meet such a challenge, for I have no doubt whatsoever that whatever I may have said in the past or what I am saying now, is the exact, literal and absolute truth as to the state of the case. (*Hear, hear.*) I put it to you that this is not the time for vague promises of better things to come, for if I were to convey to you a spirit of false optimism, then I should be neither fair to you nor true to myself. But does this mean, I hear you cry, that we can no longer look forward to the future that is to come?—certainly not. (*Heckler: 'What about the workers?'*) What about the workers indeed, sir. Grasp I beseech you with both hands the opportunities that are offered. Let us assume a bold front and go forward together. Let us carry the fight against ignorance to the four corners of the earth because it is a fight which concerns us all.

And now finally, my friends, let me say just this . . .

SETON GORDON

'The Kiss of the King's Hand'

When Charles II inspected his army at Torwood, near Stirling, early in the seventeenth century he saw no fewer than eighty pipers in a crowd, bare-headed, and 'John M'Gyurmen in the middle, covered. He asked what society that was? It was told his Majesty, "Sir, you are our King, and yonder old man is the Prince of Pipers." He called him by name, and coming to the King, kneeling, his Majesty reacht him his hand to kiss, and instantly he played an extemporarian part, "I got a kiss of the King's Hand", of which he and they all were vain.' A pipers' competition was suggested, but the idea was abandoned because none of the pipers would compete against 'the Earl of Sutherland's domestic'.

It can I think be inferred that 'John M'Gyurmen' is possibly the same man or of the same family as 'Donald Maccrummin, pyper', whose name was recently found in the Sutherland estate archives regarding the payment of a certain quantity of meal in the years 1624 and 1625.

Charles II does not appear, from this contemporary account in the Wardlaw Manuscript, to have been unduly impressed by the homage of the 'Prince of Pipers', so he probably had no piper of his own. But the Pibroch *Kiss of the King's Hand* is almost the only pipe tune mentioned in old writings in connection with royalty, until the time of Queen Victoria. Angus Mackay, who for some years was her piper, published a book of the Classical Pipe Music known as Pibroch, or Ceòl Mór, which in English is 'Great Music'. It is still, more than a century later, almost the 'Piper's Bible'. Queen Victoria knew quite a lot about pipe music and it was perhaps through her that her grandson, George V, inherited a love of the Great Music. When I judged the piping at the Braemar Gathering he used to send for me and ask me many questions. I soon found that his interest in piping was unusual.

At that time two distinguished pipers, Robert Brown and R. B. Nicol, were on the Balmoral Estate and the King used to give them great encouragement. There were afternoons when they were invited to Balmoral Castle, and were asked to play one Pibroch after another, the King sitting on the stairs and listening intently. I have sometimes wished that a great artist could have immortalized that scene.

Both these pipers were pupils of a very great player, the late Piper Major John MacDonald of Inverness. When the King invested him with the MBE at Buckingham Palace the investiture was held up for several minutes while the King and the king of pipers conversed—King George later appointed him his Honorary Piper. On the morning of one Braemar Gathering he sent his car to Braemar early, to bring John MacDonald to Balmoral Castle for a talk at 9.30 a.m. After they had conversed together for some time the King said to him: 'When are you judging the piping at Braemar today?' 'At 10.30, your Majesty,' replied John. The King looked at his watch: 'God bless my soul,' he said, 'here am I, *wasting your time!*' The royal car was summoned and the eight miles to Braemar were covered at record speed. Its urgent arrival created stir and excitement, for it was thought that the King himself was arriving, and clansmen and officials hurried to receive him. The King of Pipers stepped from the car!

At the Braemar Gathering the King used to talk to me about the playing of his son, the Prince of Wales, now the Duke of Windsor. At Oxford before the first war we had a piping class which met once a week, under the tuition of that great piper, Piper Major Willie Ross of the Scots Guards. He was stationed in London and used to travel to Oxford by train. The Prince of Wales was an enthusiastic pupil. I remember he was particularly anxious to learn *The Invercauld March*. The estate of the Farquharsons of Invercauld adjoins that of Balmoral. When the Prince became King, he used to play sometimes round the table after dinner at Balmoral. He composed a tune, *Mallorca*, which was for a time popular and indeed it is only recently that he stopped playing.

In those pre-war years at Oxford the yearly Caledonian Dinner was a memorable event, made still more outstanding by the presence of the Prince of Wales and his friend, Long Hay, a unique figure, in height seven feet one inch. There was then a strict university rule that undergraduates, whether living in college or in lodgings, must be in by a quarter of an hour after midnight. Anyone breaking this rule incurred severe penalties. University Proctors patrolled the High, and other streets, to see that the rule was enforced. I still remember the triumph with which, playing rousing pipe tunes, we pipers escorted the Prince from the Masonic Rooms in the High, where the dinner was held, to the door of Magdalen, his college. Bagpipe playing in the High long after midnight would normally have been considered an unpardonable offence, but we knew that even the sturdy Proctors had respect for the heir to the throne. We walked, and played, on one side of the street; they kept pace in grim silence on the other.

Incidentally, Long Hay, by then a major in the Black Watch and recovering from a wound, attended the first Oxford Caledonian Dinner held after the first war. He felt that the atmosphere was not sufficiently festive and convivial. He called, he told me, for twelve glasses of port. These being provided, he rose to his great height, solemnly drained each in turn, to the dismay of the sober diners, and then majestically stalked out of the room.

Our present Queen inherits some of her Grandfather's love of the pipes. She recently received, at a special audience at Balmoral Castle, one who is now the 'Grand old man of Piping', Angus Macpherson from Invershin in Sutherland. He received from her the MBE, and was impressed by the interest and knowledge she had of pipers and piping. He was able to tell the Queen that he had played to her great-grandfather Edward VII when, as Prince of Wales, he had visited Sutherland in Queen Victoria's lifetime. Prince Charles, our present Prince of Wales, inherits the royal tradition of interest in the Highland bagpipe and its background.

GRAHAM HILL

The Happy Hunter

About four or five years ago a friend of mine suggested I join him at his cottage one weekend for some shooting. Not having shot before I inquired as to what sort of equipment I would need. He said a gun and some cartridges. That sounded pretty simple so I went along to the gun shop nearest my office in London and said I wanted a gun and could they please sell me one. They said yes, with pleasure, and took me to a showcase and started handing me guns. Of course, I scarcely knew what a shot gun looked like, but nevertheless expressed delight at each one I was handed, took it to my shoulder and squinted down the barrels rather like a rifle, thereby immediately indicating to the salesman I hadn't got the foggiest idea about shooting. I subsequently discovered that you shoot with both eyes open, following the moving target with your head and relying upon the correct mounting of the gun to the shoulder to line up the barrels with the target. Anyway, after trying five or six guns, all of which looked the same to me, they suggested I first go along to their shooting ground, and meet up with their instructor, who would take my measurements with their 'Trygun'. This is a gun which the instructor can adjust in every respect to suit your build, until finally you arrive at the correct set of measurements—length of stock, cast-off, and so on, which enable you, supposedly, to hit the target every time you mount the gun and pull the trigger.

A couple of weeks later I returned to the gun shop with my measurements and the firm intention of buying a gun. Wanting the best, I had put £60 in my pocket and arrived at the shop to be told that my gun was ready. I inquired 'Which gun was that?' and they said, 'The one you expressed delight at.' This information took me somewhat aback, and as my memory is poor at the best of times, I said, 'Oh, really', not wishing to appear ungrateful. Then changing tack I asked how much my gun would cost, and they replied £600. It was not even a new gun, but some sixty years old, and obviously cost a damn sight more than when it was first sold. I just couldn't believe my ears, and looked round the shop to see if it was in fact me they were talking to. Upon seeing no one else it struck me that there would be no turning back without enormous loss of face, so, trying to appear as nonchalant as I could, I asked for some cartridges in the tone of voice that I hoped would convey that this

259

£600-a-time gun business was quite a normal occurrence to a chap of my standing. Anyway, there I was, stuck with this colossal investment and a few boxes of cartridges. It was then that the fever of this extravagance began to take hold and I felt it incumbent upon me to match the gun with some proper gear. I promptly bought a jacket, boots, socks, plus-twos, hat, gun belt, gun case, cartridge case and cleaning equipment, in a frenzy of spending. I walked out of the shop looking like a Christmas tree.

Then the big day arrived (it was only to be a walk around the hedgerows), and I turned up for the shoot looking like a tailor's dummy. Obviously this gleaming sartorial splendour demanded an explanation and so—rather ruefully—I explained the whole sad story to my friends and the gamekeeper. They all laughed like drains. Notwithstanding, all due deference was accorded my gun, and I soon noticed that whenever I had to cross a fence, everybody rushed to take the gun reverently from me and hand it back after I had crossed as though it were the Crown Jewels.

We spent the whole day walking, and standing in hides, and I must have fired off hundreds of cartridges at pigeons, pheasant, rabbits, field mice, in fact anything that moved. I never hit a thing. It had been a costly day for me but obviously afforded my friends and the gamekeeper an immense amount of enjoyment. At the end of the day I must have looked quite the opposite of the 'Return of the Happy Hunter', and I had become pretty disenchanted with the whole business.

The following day I had to go to a track in Norfolk to test my BRM racing car. Within twenty seconds of leaving the pits I clobbered a pheasant. There just ain't no justice.

JAMES GLEESON

Never Put a Nightingale in Berkeley Square

I did once and in consequence I nearly got the sack from a very good job. I also very nearly went to jail.

It was the time of the Coronation of our present Queen. Committees were formed everywhere to organize local celebrations and decorate the streets, and because I am by nature the nervous type and much put upon and usually incoherent, I was appointed the Secretary of the Berkeley Square Coronation Committee. We used to meet in Clubs around the Square where the rest of the Committee, who were all rich and successful businessmen, worked out ways of extracting money from the residents of the area. I made copious and indecipherable notes; they collected a vast sum of money and were delighted with everything except my minutes, which used to puzzle and bore them.

They were very honest men and they devoted a great deal of time to thinking up ways of spending the money. They bought flags and bunting to hang on the trees. But there was still a lot of money left so they bought streamers. This still left a good balance in the bank, so they bought some more bunting and flags. Eventually one very intelligent member of the Committee pointed out that there was a likelihood that everybody in the Square would be knee-deep in flags and bunting and that the Committee should think of something different.

The deep silence that followed this remark was my undoing. Normally none of them would have heard me or if they did they would have ignored me, but I spluttered 'Nightingale'. It was, I suppose, rather obvious and not very brilliant, but my Committee had been hitherto deeply engrossed in more mundane ways of spending the money.

My contribution electrified them. Every eye was upon me and I was petrified. Members of the Committee who had never before noticed that I was present now gazed at me in admiration. The Chairman blinked and shook his head: 'Go on,' he said.

Somehow I blurted out in monosyllables that Eric Maschwitz had once written a song about a nightingale in Berkeley Square, that we ought to get hold of a nightingale and stick him in the Square and that if he did not blooming-well sing we could install a loudspeaker and play some recording of one by Ludwig Koch or somebody.

They were kind to me then and congratulated me and helped me clarify the idea and approved it and told me to get on with it!

I found a chap who wore a flat cap and used to keep nightingales. I don't know why he kept nightingales because he did not like them much and he said there was not much money in them. He was very glad to meet me because he could get rid of one of the wretched birds for a period and get paid for it. He told me how to fodder it and keep it reasonably happy. We had a small aviary built in the square and he popped the bird inside. Reporters and photographers came from Fleet Street to take pictures of him and he was on the BBC. We had a very successful press.

Nightingales are a bit disappointing. Or it might just have been our nightingale. He was a rather dejected looking chap who could easily be mistaken for a sparrow. He drooped listlessly about the cage and was not a bit interested in Berkeley Square. Even Eric Maschwitz was unimpressed. It was probably the first time he had ever seen one, which was probably just as well. Otherwise he might never have written a great song.

One thing of which the Committee and Eric and I were certain was that it was not our bird who had sung in Berkeley Square! He never even twittered. We stood around the cage and whistled at him. We encouraged him and offered him tit-bits. One of the Committee members jabbered at him in Japanese because when he was a PoW he had seen a Japanese guard make a bird sing by talking to him. Not our bird.

We hurriedly erected loudspeakers around the Square and the BBC gave us a splendid recording of a nightingale singing. At dusk the square was full of the wonderful sound and we went away happy because we had done a good job and had added to the gaiety of the London Coronation celebrations.

I answered the telephone in the office the following morning. It was the Chairman of the Committee. 'It will have to stop,' he said. 'They are kicking up hell!' He said that scores of infuriated local residents were queuing up to abuse him and were threatening legal action. His telephone never stopped ringing. None of them could sleep. They had tried to cut the loudspeaker wires. The nightingale song had driven them mad. They hated nightingales. They had subscribed to the fund and look what it had done for them!

The Press got hold of the story and they said I had gone too far. *I!* I had to carry the can because the other members of the Committee were respectable tycoons and it would not do them any good to be accused of driving their neighbours mad with a ridiculous recording machine. We cut out the nightingale singing in the Square except for a couple of hours at dusk, and then much more softly. We relaxed.

I was told that an Inspector from the RSPCA wished to see me. There was nothing strange or alarming about that. The advertising agency I worked for handled the publicity for that organization and it amounted to many thousands of pounds a year. They were good friends of ours. There was, however, nothing friendly about the Inspector who came into my office. He refused my offer of a chair and curtly refused a cup of tea and a cigarette. He exuded an icy aura—I began to feel chilled.

He took out a black notebook and in a flat monotone asked me if I was the Secretary of the Berkeley Square Coronation Committee. I said yes I was. He told me that it was his duty to inform me that I had broken a sub-section of some Act or other by caging a nightingale; that by so doing I had become liable to a heavy fine or imprisonment and that the longer the crime lasted the greater would become my penalty. He wrote down my name and the address where I worked—the address of the agency which profited by spending so many thousands of pounds of the RSPCA's publicity allocation.

Ruin stared me in the face. My heartless but very attractive Australian secretary who also had a morbid sense of humour started to hum 'And a nightingale sang in Berkeley Square'. The Inspector was a kind of a policeman and having pointed out the offence he had then to write down what the accused said. He wrote down 'Unintelligible gibberish'.

The Press heard about this as well and they wrote it up. The Chairman of my Company sent for me and explained in a tense way that I had probably lost the Company several thousands of pounds a year. The Chairman of the Berkeley Square Coronation Committee sadly shook his head and muttered: 'Secretaries should be seen and not heard.'

Succour came from an unexpected quarter. The man in the flat cap said it was all bloody nonsense. He knew all about the Act, he said, and I was as innocent as a new-born babe. All I had to tell the Inspector was that the nightingale had been born in captivity. 'And', he added, 'if the Inspector doesn't bloody well believe you, tell him to bloody well prove it.'

I did—and he couldn't. But whenever I listen to a nightingale now, I have a suspicion that what I am hearing is more like a good old-fashioned belly-laugh than a song.

C. GORDON GLOVER

This Distinctly Fishy Business

I love to read of fish and of fishermen. The wiliness of fish, the guile of the angler, the fierceness of the fights between great game-fish and great game-fishermen; the peace which seemeth to pass all understanding and which attends quiet, patient men by sluggish watersides, drowsing away long summer days with their bottoms cushioned by meadow-flowers and grasses and their nostrils filled with the fragrance of such things, and that 'sweet and rotten, unforgettable, unforgotten river-smell'. I like to read of bearded bravos cast in the mould of Hemingway, lashed to their seats in tropical waters, their great rods almost double-bending in battle with some Goliath of a sail-fish or tarpon thrashing for freedom in the cobalt seas far astern, creaming the waters into furies of foam, then diving deep, to be glimpsed as a vast turning white belly in the magnification of his sun-shot element.

I react with awe to men with double-ended tweed hats frilled with flies, standing wader-deep in the spume of Irish and Scottish salmon rivers, or tramping through the warm summer rain to where, in the peat-brown depths of Pettigrew's Pool, curded with foam from the fall, the 'big fellow' is known to have been lurking these many days. I like to see in glass cases about the walls of water-side taverns, the varnished flanks of giant chub and bream, pike, perch and carp, with the details of their capture set out upon the glass.

Bream. 9 lbs 3 oz, taken by Colonel Bartholomew Rusper, June 24, 1901

What manner of man was Colonel Rusper, long gone to join his bream? What rejoicings were there in the tavern when, on that evening long ago, he returned from the waterside with his great bream and placed it upon the scales before the envious eyes of the rest of his party? Colonel Rusper is the one second from the left of the faded sepia photograph—one of many—alongside the mantel-shelf. Six whiskered figures in Norfolk jackets and knickerbockers, posed outside the stone portico of this select little fishing hotel. Rusper is tall and has a daunting black moustache. Heaven help the bream, one feels, with Rusper on his tail. A great fisherman, Colonel Rusper, for here he is, again and again and again in these bar-room photographs, year after year. Even in the 1914–18 war

265

he is there. A staff colonel in Whitehall, probably, faithful each summer to his high-point of the year. The colonel ages before our eyes. He becomes more bent. The dashing black moustache turns grey, turns white. 1901, eh? Why wasn't he fighting the Boers in South Africa? Was he really a colonel at all?

Suddenly, in 1924, the colonel is no longer there. He is not among 'Major Pilkington's Party' on that sunny June morning. It was Major Pilkington who 'took' the '4 lb. 7 oz. Trout' whose glassy eyes goggle for ever in the hall. Colonel Rusper comes no more to these deep Derbyshire waters where lapwing and curlew used to call to him, and dippers bob from stone to stone in the shallow reaches, and the mayflies dance, and the summer air smells of sheep, and moss, and young bracken.

A hook mightier than the colonel's has fallen before his white whiskers, and he has been reeled aloft—we hope—to Paradise.

All about the watersides where the colonel fished there seem to drift the shades of Izaak Walton and his great fishing friend, Charles Cotton, and whenever I am thereabouts I like to think of these genial, gentle men, carefree by the singing waters of the Dove, the Derwent and the Manifold three hundred years ago. Each is remembered in a Derbyshire pub, and to them is raised, I fancy, a small Memorial Temple.

Walton fished many rivers, even the Lea whose valley today, a strange complex of flooded gravel-pits and multiple plant and glass-houses, must have greatly changed from the times of the Compleat Angler. Is it the image of Walton, I wonder, who is the figure in a small and serene aquatint which I possess and which I picked up for a shilling or two in a London print shop some years ago?

It is called 'Want's Inn, Broxbourn'. In what might be deemed a private sitting-room of the inn there part-reclines at manifest ease a grey-haired man in a red coat and sandy breeches. He is seated in a high-backed armchair and would appear to be tying a fly. His cloak and top hat (yes, top hat) are thrown across a side-table where he clearly cast them on return from a long and happy day. The walls of the room are lined with cases of fine fish. The gentleman's rod, creel, gaff and landing net lie beside him on the boarded floor. A pewter jug, tankard and tobacco box stand upon the polished round tripod table beside the fisherman. If it is wintertime, as suggested by the rich glow of the fire in its metal grate, perhaps he is not tying a fly at all, though he is concentrated upon something small between his hands. Before the fire there sits, as his only companion, a fat black cat.

I greatly love this image of tired content. It breathes the peace and self-sufficiency of a happy man—a fisherman, home from his hunting. To gaze upon him is to escape from the stress and the shindy of this today's world, and to breathe, 'Ah, but could I be like him!'

And this sentiment I feel towards all fishermen, that happy breed of men.

Why, then, after all this idyllic vapouring, am I not of their company? It is not for the want of trying, but more likely because of the lack of that patience, concentration and perseverance which abide in the hearts of all true anglers. It is a defect of temperament, the failure to find relaxation in what always seems to be an exercise in extreme nervous tension, croak the moorhen ever so beguilingly, and brood the tall heron ever so dramatically. *He* is not at ease nor truly relaxed, nor the other waterfowl who haunts the slinking or the rushing rivers. When I have several times tried to 'take up fishing' I seem but to exchange one workaday world for another.

Boyhood, however, was very different. There *was* no 'workaday world', and tensions there were none by that deserted Thamesside boat-house which was a private paradise to me, and to me alone. For some reason the boatbuilders had forsaken this site for a larger place of business half a mile downstream where they hired punts, canoes, skiffs, launches and even those sybaritic, deep-cushioned boatbuilders' masterpieces, 'electric canoes'. How sweetly they purred, as well they might at a fiver a day!

But 'my' boathouse with bleared and broken windows, full of summertime nesting swallows, was the storage-place of three old launches, paintwork peeling, brasswork green with verdigris, cabin-cushions nests for mice. And from the crumbling concrete of its waterside apron I fished, and fished, and fished, alone with a bamboo rod, bread pellets, maggots and pink garden worms. I caught trifling things like finger-length dace, little roach and the small fry which swam in thick shoals over the sunlit, gravelled shallows, and under the spidery oars of the water-skaters. It seemed eternal summer there—a world of watervoles plopping from the far banksides, of moorhens and dabchicks about the midstream eyot, of swallows and of sand-martins, and of little slippery fish upon the hook, smelling of reeds and the river. Time passed timelessly, its punctuations the electric quiver of fish taking bait, the odd punt passing, the call of 'Ferry-Ho-o-o-o' from the Buckingham to the Berkshire bank where the old punt ferry lay, wide-beamed and heavy for the ferryman marching from end to end of his craft, great pole between his big red hands. Sometimes, around the bend in the river, with a 'toot' upon her whistle, would appear the pleasure-steamer *Empress of India*, wooden-hulled, fat, brown and varnished, after-deck awnings flapping in the breeze, a deck-piano playing, crates of bottled beer in her stern. And the gentlemen in straw-boaters, and the ladies in fruit-hats.

How I loved the *Empress* snouting upstream, cleaving the river into green bow-waves, leaving the waves of her wake to rock the waterfowl and slap against my concrete platform. I loved the *Empress* and I loved fishing.

My Grandfather in whose house I lived for three long-ago years was a taciturn, remote Scotsman and a fisherman of high class. He fished the Thames waters with fly, and fly only, and dace, I believe, were all who would rise to his fly. He was a game-fisherman, nourished on Scottish waters. He was very faintly interested in me and my fishing, but not interested enough to teach me any error of my ways, to show me how to cast a fly. For which I was grateful. I would not have cared for Grandfather, with his white hair and shrubby white moustache, to break into my waterside dreams, to burst the frail bubble of the magic of my boathouse.

We went once to Devonshire, my Mother, Grandmother, Grandfather and I, while my Father was sweltering in His Majesty's Service upon the doleful banks of the Tigris. My Grandfather could not fish with fly in the sea, but he fished just the same, using lancet for bait against my juicy lugworms. Dourly he brought a four-foot conger eel on board, but that was all. For my part I hooked three pollock, a fat little bass and a John Dory. We ate my fish, but not my Grandfather's conger-eel.

'I'll take you after trout tomorrow, boy,' said my Grandfather. We drove in a hired pony and trap to the banks of a busy little trout stream, Grandfather with his whippy rod and metal case of flies, I with my old bamboo and a tinful of small worms. We did not talk. After his oddly warm gesture my Grandfather clearly wished little of me, and desired, like all true fishermen, to be alone.

'You can stay here by the bridge,' he said, 'while I go and cast upstream. Stay where you are, and I will meet you at five o'clock.'

By the stone bridge I stayed with my bamboo rod and my tin of worms. I pulled eight little brown trout from the waters and talked with a dipper. I laid my catch upon bracken fronds and awaited my Grandfather. He returned with an empty creel.

'Any fool,' he said, 'can catch trout with worm.'

I sat silent in my triumph, none the less, and we all had trout for supper. 'They should have been put back,' said my Grandfather, as he poked the little tender mouthfuls under the curtain of his moustache.

It was many years later when I caught another trout—a North-umbrian one 'taken' on the River Coquet. I had met a genial old boy in the bar of a small-town pub. He discovered to his horror as we talked that I was not really a fisherman. Everyone within two miles of either bank of the Coquet is a fisherman. 'I'll take you out for a day by the waterside,' he said, 'and I'll fix you up with tackle.'

It was, indeed, a memorable day. The sun shone (too brightly, of course!), the curlews called, and we had knapsacks full of beer and sandwiches and a half bottle of whisky if it turned cold! It was a day to remember, and a moment to remember when, clumsily casting the only fly I have ever cast in my life, I hooked a four-ounce trout. The sheer bliss of it, underlined by the quiet good company of my friend-for-a-day and possibly even more exhilarated by the liberal drams of whisky with which we toasted my great fish!

I bore my catch triumphantly into the bar of the hotel where my wife and I were staying nearby, and to the Proprietor I said grandly, 'This,' I said, 'I would like for my breakfast tomorrow.'

The good man eyed my fish. 'You mean *with* your breakfast, sir!'

He told me of a London businessman who, staying in Southern Scotland, had paid £150 or so for a fortnight's sport with Tweed salmon. He caught not a fish until the last day when he laid upon the bar of his hotel a decent twelve-pound salmon. 'That fish,' he said, 'has cost me £150.'

'It's a good job, sir,' said the barlady, 'that you didn't catch another.'

I have had other spasmodic forays after fish—casting a red rag to the mackerel in Western Ireland and deliriously hauling them aboard one after the other. Great! A brief and lackadaisical spell with a borrowed rod from the deck of a hired cruiser upon the River Ouse—not a fish in a week, but the disturbing spectacle of a small eel snaking across the grass—yes, the *grass*—of a waterside inn and disappearing down a burrow. And there was a summer in my own rural district where two friends and I decided, under the guidance of a dedicated angler, to 'take up fishing'. We were far too frivolous about it, since we deemed it a good reason for having a nice uninhibited lunch in a small-town hotel, and proceeding thence to the apple orchard by the waterside of which a friend of our expert's had graciously bidden us to make free. We would take with us for summery teatime under the apple trees two bottles of Chablis.

It was magnificent, but it was not fishing.

It was instruction in the use of an instrument called a 'de-gorger' which made me realize that I would never, never make a real fisherman. This is, as everyone of course knows, a device for extracting from nearby the stomach of a fish the hook which it has swallowed. Need I say more?

Fishing, I realized, at that slimy, slippery and near-surgical moment, was not for the faint-hearted. And then came, a few days later, what I might describe as the *coup-de-grâce* upon all my latent feelings that I *ought* to be a fisherman.

A well-intentioned neighbour, responding to what he divined as a healthy new interest of mine, lent me a slim volume entitled *Character in Fish*.

It appeared, in a blinding moment of truth, that these slippery fry at whom I had been casting writhing and agonized maggots impaled upon hooks, were not the finny fools I had thought them. An element of witless wiliness I had been prepared to accept, but *not* the other qualities which the author revealed.

Fish, it seemed, were not only wily, but wise. They possessed conscious courage. They were capable, to varying degrees, of permissive passion. They enjoyed the exercise of deliberate play. They were good sportsmen. Their behaviour in the contrived circumstances of sundry apparatus designed for observation, showed them to be possessed of a marked sense of humour.

This was too much. To destroy a perch while he was enjoying a spasm of uncontrollable laughter at the latest sally of a witty pike was wholly unthinkable.

But I still, from the bottom of my heart, wish that I were one of that happy band of brothers whose souls are uplifted in the whole distinctly fishy business.

The Pond

P.S.

The mother duck swam across the pond surrounded by eleven newly hatched ducklings. In the window overlooking the water a two-year-old child laughed with joy. 'Babies Mallards,' she cried. The tiny balls of brown fluff foraged busily along the shore of the pond within a few feet of the window—held invisibly together by family ties and the soft quacking of their mother, who kept watch over them without having the slightest idea how many there should be.

The pond was a hundred yards long and fifty yards wide, specially dug at the same time as the house was built, so as to be in front of the great picture window. The pond was home for the Mallard family, and for hundreds of other waterbirds, some confined to it by enforced flightlessness, others free to come and go as they pleased, some like the Ross's Geese and Barheads and Mandarins native of faraway places, others like the Mallards and Pintails and Shovelers natives of England and joined in winter time by hundreds of their wild brethren.

The girl was eight years old when the very important visitor came to stay. Floodlights were installed so that the pond and its ducks could be seen after dinner. The bright whites of the Pintails' and Shovelers' breasts, and of the Ross's Geese shone golden in the glow. The lights had come to stay.

In February 1964 when the girl was eleven years old, the first wild Bewick's Swans, coming from far away breeding grounds in the Siberian Arctic, were persuaded by four tame Bewick's Swans to land on the pond. Twenty-four of them spent a month there, coming daily to the wheat that was put down for them in the shallow water in front of the window. Then they flew off to the north-east towards their summer home on the tundras of the Yamal Peninsula and the Kara Sea.

In the following winter they came back to the well-remembered feeding pond, and were themselves remembered by the watchers in the window, who had found in the previous winter that the yellow and black bill patterns of Bewick's Swans are infinitely variable and much more obviously different on each individual than fingerprints. The discovery had led to the naming of the individual swans—Pink and Rebecca, the Owl and the Pussy Cat, Lancelot and Victoria, the Major and Ethel . . . and when darkness fell, the swans fed on along the foreshore under the window, shining brilliantly in the floodlights. The plumage of all the birds looked wonderful against the dark water, but the white plumage of the white birds was most beautiful. As they swam the bright reflections of their ripples moved endlessly up their necks in flickering parallel lines. The duckling pond had become Swan Lake.

Not all of the original twenty-four swans came back the following winter but those that did brought their families and encouraged other passing families to come down and join them. By the end of the season seventy-two swans had been recorded by the watchers in the window. Already the girl knew them best. One pair she named herself—Leo and Stella—and they were, from then on, her favourite swans. On Christmas Eve 1966, although many swans were already assembled on Swan Lake, some now for the third winter, Leo and Stella had failed to turn up. There was talk about Christmas presents and the girl said the only one she wanted was the arrival of her special swans. Next morning, miraculously, they were there, and they have come each winter since.

The number of swans increased dramatically every year, their presence being recorded daily on a chart in a kind of 'roll-call'. Their heads were drawn and photographed, their behaviour noted, and from time to time odd individuals were caught, usually by flying into a tree behind the floodlights and making minor crash-landings in the garden or the small side pens. Thus a slowly increasing number could be weighed, measured, ringed and released again on Swan Lake. The birds seemed to care little about such indignities and rarely if ever flew away on release.

The study of the swans became the full-time occupation of a scientist, for the girl was often away at school, although she had special dispensation to watch and record the swans each weekend. At Christmas 1968 her Christmas present was a conversation piece in oils of her second favourite swan family—Peasant and Gypsy and their cygnet—painted specially for her.

Peasant and Gypsy

That winter 439 different Bewick's Swans visited Swan Lake and in the following year the number was 570, although the highest number on any one day was 404, and for most of January and February there were more than 350 together with three Whooper Swans and about sixty of the non-migratory Mute Swans. Also on Swan Lake daily was a great crowd of ducks, perhaps three hundred each of Shovelers and Pintails and a leavening of Tufted Ducks and Pochards. On one morning of frost there were, including gulls and

273

coots, not less than three thousand birds all within seventy yards of the great windows.

In the earlier part of the winter most of the swans stay on the pond but by the turn of the year most of them are going to the Severn Estuary to roost, flighting out in the late dusk, lit gloriously by the floodlights that were installed for the very important visitor, whose son came to see them in the spring of 1970.

That spring some of the swans left early on the first stages of their 2,600 mile flight to their Arctic breeding grounds. The girl, now seventeen, got a grant from her school to follow them as far as Holland. She arrived there on 22 March, and visited the known haunts of Bewick's in a car driven by a Dutch friend. The swans were mostly concentrated along the flooded meadows beside the River Yssel, and the first swan she recognized was Karroo (a son of Sahara and Gobi). He was a long way off and she could not be quite certain that day. Next day Gypsy swam into the field of her telescope and a moment later she found Peasant—her familiar special pair here 350 miles from Swan Lake. It was a moment for exultation.

Two days later she found Raquello. She knew he had a tall white plastic leg ring with large black figures that could easily be read through the telescope. The distinguished Dutch professor who had come to see how she was getting on was himself asked to read the number, which provided the proof that all good scientists need that the recognition system really worked.

The fifth old friend was a swan ringed originally as a cygnet (and therefore unnamed). He carried a metal ring of an earlier type and was too far away for the number to be read, though by a process of elimination he was almost certainly a son of Pepper and Amber.

On her last day in Holland the girl picked out Booster (a son of Boosey and Hawkes). Booster, she knew, also carried a metal ring, and being a male, it would be on his right leg in accordance with standard practice. But now he sat sleepily in the water, and in due course tucked his head back into his scapulars and slept. For more than half an hour the girl's eye was glued to her telescope, until at last the swan awoke. As he swam his right leg appeared briefly and it had no ring on it. In a flash she remembered that he had been ringed by mistake on the left leg, and as he turned, there sure enough was his ring.

The girl returned to her home beside the now empty Swan Lake in Gloucestershire, while the swans headed on north-east perhaps by way of Denmark, the Swedish islands, Matsalu Bay in the Esthonian Soviet Socialist Republic and away to the Siberian Arctic. By late October 1970 the first of them were back in England. On 7 November Bewick's Swans were pouring into Swan Lake—fifty-three came during the day, which constitutes a heavy 'swanfall'. It being Saturday the girl came post-haste sixty miles from school. At tea-time she was sitting at the binoculars in the studio when a pair of swans with two cygnets planed down out of the eastern sky on to the lake and water-skied to a halt. They were Peasant and Gypsy and their family, less than five months old, who had flown with them the 2,600 miles from the breeding grounds. They swam fearlessly up to the window to start feeding within less than ten yards of the girl who was watching them.

NICHOLAS MONSARRAT

Heard of Him, Never Met Him

Gentlemen, the toast is Prince Philip,
Duke of Edinburgh,
Which makes a nice switch,
Because usually Prince Philip, Duke of Edinburgh,
Is the toast;
And the things they do to that 50-year-old battered slice of bread—
Everything from buttering it up,
Or smothering it in ham,
Or smearing it with the rancid oil of envy,
To carving it into bite-sized pieces
For the spiteful to chew on—
Would make any self-respecting club sandwich
Resign from the club.
Yet it is an honour and a privilege to propose this toast
Because I am a King's man
And a Queen's man
And the Duke's man,
Believing that people behave better under a monarchy
Than under any presidential yoke
Or some hard-boiled egg of a dictator,
And that those who believe so
Should say so; and that,
Borrowing from another duke, another forthright battler,
The Duke of Wellington,
They should publish and be damned,
In a good cause.

I have never met him,
And I sure won't meet him now—
This contribution
Will earn me no royalty.
But I have *nearly* met him seven times altogether,
And they are all worth recording
For a variety of reasons
Which have nothing to do with history
And everything to do with loyalty,
And respect, and admiration, and allegiance—

All the old-fashioned words
Good for a giggle on TV,
Bad for a modish reputation,
True for all time.

*   *   *

THE FIRST TIME was long ago and far away
In the hoary old year of 1947,
When he was not yet in the public domain,
And Princess Elizabeth, the predestined bride
(I shall be coming to her later)
Was then at the marvellous age of twenty-one
And (for public consumption anyway)
Still foot-loose and fancy-free.
But there were rumours among the knowing and the pseudo-knowing
Of a young man waiting somewhere in the wings;
And when she,
And her father the King,
And her mother the Queen,
And her sister, who still had the sweetly-pretty label
Of Princess Margaret Rose,
Arrived at Cape Town on the Royal Tour of South Africa,
There was just a chance that this sailor-suitor would come out of the
    wings
And into this rare and splendid sunshine.
I *might* have met him then,
Being, for my sins (what sins? In those days I had hardly begun!)
Head of the British Information Service in South Africa
And co-opted also as a Royal Tour commentator.
But he wasn't there on that day,
And it was my loss, and his loss too
Because he missed a truly glittering occasion
When the battleship *Vanguard*
(The biggest afloat, and, for a change, *ours*)
Came out of the morning mist of Table Bay
Like a great grey friendly ghost
And nudged alongside the quay—
All the towering 43,000 tons of her—
As gently as a pram into a crèche
Without cracking an egg;
And the flags flew, and the guns saluted, and the crowds roared,
And against the enormous stone curtain of Table Mountain
And out from this great bristling ark of a ship,
The family came ashore.

Perhaps, on second thoughts, it was just as well he wasn't there.
It might have been
Rather too daunting an encounter
With one's future in-laws.

*   *   *

THE SECOND TIME I never met him was 1952,
And that's still long ago and far away,
But that time turned into a time of immortality,
Or rather, of mortality taking its toll, and
Brusquely, cruelly, finally, and beyond any argument
Thrusting the torch upon new players, new mortals,
A new generation of the Lord's anointed
Or of sacrificial goats,
Whichever way you choose to look at it.
The Edinburghs (as total London snobs called them,
Pretending a familiarity they would never dare put to the test)
The Edinburghs were holidaying in Kenya,
Literally up a tree, if the number one suite of the Tree Tops Hotel,
Which is perched on an enormous fig-tree in the Aberdare Forest
In Kikuyu country,
May be so designated.
After that strange tree-sojourn, it was thought
That they might finish off their tour in South Africa,
Where we were ready for them,
And my little British Information machine was ready for them also.

At dusk, beneath that ancient, patriarchal fig-tree,
The animals came down to drink at the water-hole:
Elephant and hippopotamus, gentle gazelle and ungentle lion,
Striped zebra, armoured rhinoceros, odious hyena,
All taking time off from strife
To slake their evening thirst,
While round them the expectant forest
Waited to give them cover again,
And the hotel flood-lights (which they took to be another moon)
Pin-pointed this royal gathering.
It must have been a marvellous setting
And the prince and princess must have been very happy there,
Very excited, very moved,
Watching the beasts come down to drink
Within the truce-lines in the heart of the Old Chief's country.
But in far-away London, on that same night,
Death himself came down to drink.

He drank the tired King,
And the news broke into their watching, or their sleeping,
In what must have been the strangest place in the world to receive
News of a King's death, and especially a father's death.
That was the end of that.
All we saw of them in South Africa
Was on the news-reels a week later
(No television in South Africa then, nor now either):
A sad, moving, tremendous moment when the new Queen of England
(It was difficult to get used to that word
After fifty-two years of kingship)
Appeared in the open doorway of the plane
Which had brought her from Kikuyu country
To a country now her own.
Behind her was a supporting star, in all the senses,
This same man I never met;
And he, like all the world, attended this lonely moment of majesty
As she came down the draped steps
Towards the clustered black top hats and funeral penguin suits of her
    Cabinet
And into history.

*   *   *

THE THIRD TIME was the nearest miss of all
And the most exciting of all,
Because it was almost my own occasion
And this time I *would* meet the Prince, by explicit royal command.
I had written a book,
And out of it they had made a film
Which was to have its première at the Leicester Square Theatre
On March the twenty-sixth, 1953,
In aid of a good solid sailors' charity,
And attended by the entire Board of Admiralty,
And a shining cluster of Sea Lords,
And Earl Mountbatten, and King Hussein,
And me,
And the supporting star again, the Duke of Edinburgh,
Whom we would meet afterwards.
In fact, a memorable night, for memorable reasons,
Was in immediate prospect.
But on the very eve, when all was poised,
And I couldn't have been more excited
If I had been starring in the film myself,
Death drank again:

Old Queen Mary died, full of years, full of that family love
Which a nation also knows, and feels.
Promptly the lights went out, as they had to,
And court mourning descended. Said *The Times*:
'The Duke of Edinburgh has cancelled all his engagements',
And among all his engagements was us.
Collapse of author,
Robbed of the handshake and all that went with it;
And sad also for a special reason—
I was damned sure he would have enjoyed the film
Because he knew all about the cruel sea himself,
At first hand.

* * *

THE FOURTH NEAR-MISS was another Royal Tour:
Canada, this time, a country of magical variety and attraction,
A country I liked so much
That I had just resigned from my British Information job
To stay on there and enjoy it the more.
If I had still been in the service
I would at least have been on deck
When the customary duke-baiting started,
And the reporters flocked round,
Hoping he would say something wrong
(He did: He criticized Canada's fatuous drinking laws)
Hoping he would do something wrong
(He did: He sprinkled them with a little water from a hose,
By happy accident, and enjoyed it)
While the photographers called out:
'Hey, dook! This way!'
And looked round for laughs,
And the good old Canadian general public
Which does not give a continental four-letter frolic for the monarchy
Except on the ignoble three-tier system
Of the snobbery, or the show, or the chance of juicy fiasco,
Waited for the ignoble fun.
But as it turned out, he did very well without me.
They had picked on the wrong man.
Eventually the crude French wilted
And the rude press gave up,
And the man in the street
Turned to his neighbour, and said:
'You know, this guy's *all right*!'

* * *

NICHOLAS MONSARRAT

THE FIFTH TIME was Canada again,
Canada under a gorgeous summer sun,
Canada at the lake-side,
Canada, and the promise of some blissful sailing
In the Duke of Edinburgh's Cup for Dragon Yachts, 1958.
I had one of these elegant toys,
And the Duke himself had another, called *Bluebottle*,
And *Bluebottle* was shipped out to have a crack at the trophy
On our own home water of Lake St Louis, at Montreal,
With HRH at the helm,
And a whole flock of dragons from all over
Fiercely seizing their chance to breathe fire down each other's necks.
I was all set to race;
I even had a joke ready, in case we won
And I had to make a speech:
'The presence of His Royal Highness
'Has certainly given these proceedings
'An extra fillip.'
(Well, it's not too bad
For after dinner.)
But perhaps it was just as well that suddenly I had to sprint down to
    New York
For one of those absurd television turmoils
Which hold out prospects of dollars by the literal million
And then whip them away again.
One moment they just *love* your idea,
And they're going to make a pilot film immediately—
'You *gotta* be here!
'We're all juiced up!
'This thing is sensational!'
But when you arrive, it's 'Sorry, the front office
'Has gone sour on it.'
One minute the man says:
'They're jumping up and down at CBS!'
And the next, he can't even remember your name.
But still I went down, at an hour's notice, on this fruitless, futile effort,
And so missed the race,
And the Duke,
And the splendid trophy,
And that terrific joke to crown it,
And all for less than nothing.
My crew, to say the least, did not win either;
So all I have to show for that one
Is a silver bottle-opener inscribed:

'Duke of Edinburgh's Cup, Royal St Lawrence Yacht Club, 1958.'
When I came back, my crew said:
'You missed a good man.'
I knew that already, damn it.

*   *   *

CHAPTER SIX was set on this same Lake St Louis,
When the Queen and Prince Philip
Were due to sail up river in the royal yacht *Britannia*,
To open the St Lawrence Seaway—
That 2,000-mile masterpiece of maritime engineering
Which could now carry salt-water sailors, for the first time,
Into the very heart of a continent.
The whole yacht club fleet of two hundred boats, big and small,
Dressed over all with every stitch of bunting we could buy,
Was turned out to greet them;
And I, now possessed of the fastest Chris-Craft cruiser on the lake
(And also the desperate shame of being a chauffeur,
Instead of a true sailor)
Was designated as 'POLICE LAUNCH',
With unlimited powers to order all my friends out of the fairway,
And a splendidly accoutred RCMP corporal
To back me up.
Britannia came out of the Montreal mist
Like *Vanguard* before her,
But this time the ship was a true yacht,
Blue and shapely as a magpie in flight,
Slicing her way up-stream like *Bluebottle* herself
On a noble scale.
We circled, and dipped our ensign, and then took station
A few yards off her starboard bow
(There was a cruiser and lots of destroyers hanging about,
But we were the *Police*, the civil power, the guardians.)
And when we looked up,
There, thirty feet above us on the upper bridge,
Was Prince Philip himself,
With his personal escort, who happened to be an old friend,
Minister of Transport George Hees,
The man in charge of the whole Seaway project.
We looked at the Prince
And the Prince looked at us;
We looked at George Hees
And George Hees looked away quickly
(I suppose there *were* a few bottles lying about,

And the smart Mountie corporal
Must have been lost among the half-dozen of my rackety friends
Who had been allowed to join the party.)
I shouted 'Good morning, George!'
And George continued talking to the Prince
(No doubt about the pollution of the St Lawrence River),
And when he was not doing that,
Staring straight to the front,
A very figure-head of aloof if borrowed majesty.
Well, we weren't going to have that sort of thing
From old George Hees,
Who was a drinking pal before he became a Cabinet Minister,
So I said: 'All together now!—One, two, three!—
'GOOD MORNING, GEORGE!'
In a shout which rang across the lake
And made even the police corporal jump;
Whereupon Prince Philip smiled,
And walked to the other wing of the bridge,
While George Hees looked down, and gave us a wave—
The smallest wave I ever saw, a sort of half-mast flicker,
Like a woman drying her nail varnish—
And then joined his august charge
Well out of sight of this unseemly rabble.

That was in 1959
Still long ago, and far away,
But at least I got into earshot.

*　　　*　　　*

Now COMES THE SEVENTH and last time
Of me and the man I never met;
Though this time I came closest to it
And, privately, I count it as my one and only score,
And it was only just the other day.
We have a friend
Who is a one-subject bore,
And the one subject is herself;
Over the years she has become
Sole Minister of her own Interior
And Life-Time President (unopposed)
Of the British Boring Board of Control.
She is a sculptress
(I am changing the role a little
To protect the guilty)

And, by one of those strange turns of fortune
Which make one feel the world is grotesquely, permanently unfair,
She was invited to a party at Buckingham Palace.
'Oh, it was so *dull*!' she told us,
Her eyes swivelling up to heaven
Like a pietistic Virgin Mary doll.
(How can it possibly be 'dull', to go to Buckingham Palace
For the first time?)
'But I did talk to Philip—' (the bloody impudence
Of that form of address!)
'And of course I asked him if he knew the work of Ariosto Vascovec;
'You know—the Pole who did that marvellous inert abstract thing
'We have out on the patio.
'Can you imagine?—he looked absolutely blank!
'Obviously he'd never heard of Vascovec,
'And I had to explain everything,
'And especially the attitude Vascovec took
'In that article he wrote for *Nuances*
'About my own Spatial Inruption experiment—
'Well, it's more of a *movement*, isn't it?—
'That everyone is talking about these days.
'Do you know, Philip wasn't in the least interested!
'In fact he didn't even pretend!
'All he did was nod now and again
'And then he suddenly started talking about boats!'

At that heartening, even joyful moment,
I felt that I had met the man at last,
And that long-ago-and-far-away
Was here and now.